The Poems of Sextus Propertius

The Poems of
Sextus Propertius

A Bilingual Edition

Translated with an Introduction by

J. P. McCULLOCH

University of California Press, Berkeley, Los Angeles, London

1972

The Latin text from the Loeb Classical Library Edition, with a
translation by H. E. Butler (Cambridge, Mass.: Harvard University
Press, 1939), by permission of Harvard University Press.

University of California Press
Berkeley and Los Angeles, California
University of California Press, Ltd.
London, England
Copyright © 1972 by:
The Regents of the University of California
ISBN: 0-520-01714-5
Library of Congress Catalog Card Number: 78-115490
Printed in the United States of America

874.01
Pro

Contents

Introduction

THE ALERT reader will quickly discover that in these poems Propertius did not write his autobiography; they contain too many opacities and contradictions to make sense as a personal history of the poet, at least as the kind of personal history that would satisfy the careful scholar. Unfortunately, facts about Propertius from other sources are scanty. There are, however, fragmentary bits of information found in the poems and elsewhere which everyone agrees are more likely to be true than otherwise.

Propertius was born about 50 B.C., probably in Assisi, although there is some learned contention on this point. He was young when his father died, and part of the family estate—it was an equestrian family—was confiscated in the land seizures of 40 B.C. Although he was obviously well educated, Propertius admits that he had no inclination to take up law, the usual career of a young man of his class and education. He may, however, have traveled abroad, thus enjoying a customary preoccupation of his peers.

For several years Propertius carried on an affair with "Cynthia" (whose real name was probably Hostia); an educated freedwoman and a courtesan, she possessed considerable ability. She had light hair and dark eyes, and was sexually attractive. The affair was not a harmonious one, and, as revealed by the final poem in Book III, Propertius and Cynthia parted in bitterness. In a later poem (IV.7) Propertius is either suggesting that a reconciliation took place before Cynthia died (not long after the separation), or is simply recalling earlier and happier memories once his love was dead. He may have married and fathered children after Cynthia died. He died fairly young, probably about the age of forty.

These details are, for the most part, unimportant, for the real Propertius lives in his works. Although Propertius did not write for the historian, the reader of his poems, even in the poorest translation, encounters brilliantly illuminated bits of a man's life and thoughts. Thus the poems, with allowances made for poetic license, convey a good deal of information about Propertius. What is revealed is his mind, a mind of considerable genius and peculiarity. He is a romantic; and, as Professor J. P. Sullivan has pointed out (in "Cynthia Prima Fuit: A Causerie," *Arion*, I [Autumn, 1962]), he may well have been an early example of a Freudian type:

> Freud describes this character-type, which is not neurotic but found among ordinary healthy people and even among people of exceptional qualities, in the following way. Such men require certain conditions before they fall in love—"the need of an injured party," husband, betrothed, or lover; it must be "love of a harlot," although this element may depend on anything from the faintest breath of scandal attaching to a flirtatious wife up to the open sexual immorality of a prostitute or a *grande amoureuse*. And this last, which suggests the possibility of her being unfaithful to him, is connected to the jealousy necessary for such lovers.

In my opinion Sullivan's view of this aspect of the poet's personality is correct, but the reader may judge for himself. Certainly it is true that Propertius inclined toward an involvement with women which was adventurous even by Roman standards. The first poem in Book I clearly reveals his feelings about marriageable women, and II.7 expresses his views on the prospect of respectable matrimony. Propertius is really "married" to Cynthia, and he would have it no other way. When rejected by his beloved courtesan, he resorts to boys and to a less fortunate class of prostitutes, but always he hopes for a reconciliation with his real love. When he declares he will have no more to do with bawds, it is merely *accismus*, a convention of the times.

The love poems and those dealing with death have the ring of strong conviction. Horace never looks at death in the alarmed and unphilosophical way Propertius does, for death in Propertius is a much more personal and fearful thing than in the customary rhetoric of Augustan Rome. Propertius dreads death; he lives with it in fascination. His obsession with death, second only to his obsession with Cynthia, is neither stoic nor in any way cowardly. "Romantic" is the word that again comes to mind:

> I am not afraid now
>   of the shadowy afterlife,
>   nor do I pine away
>   thinking of fate's due,
>   the ultimate bonefire;
> But I do fear
>   that your love's strength
>   will not survive until my funeral . . .

Propertius writes of more than love and death, though these concerns are at the center of his great poems. Pastoral fantasies, travelogues, friendships, and myths find a place; and above all, there is Rome. Unlike his contemporaries Horace and Tibullus, he was strictly a city poet. Rome, the imperial city, comes alive in the pages of Propertius. It is rather an odd place, as a quick glance at IV.8 will show.

Since Propertius did not admire everything about imperial Rome, he infused his ceremonial and patriotic poems with an irony difficult to mistake. Mistake, though, was the rule until Ezra Pound seized upon Propertius and actually read the Latin. Pound has been unjustly faulted for his lack of scholarship, but several generations of learned men before him might more justly be condemned for want of sensibility. If the critics who damned Pound's interpretation of Propertius would read a modern poet the way they read Propertius, they would universally be thought dense. Propertius was at least as great and subtle a poet as, say, T. S. Eliot. Propertian scholarship before Pound looked more at the word and the phrase than at the whole poem or the corpus of poems. Can any man now believe that Propertius meant to honor Augustus in IV.6, or to glorify conquest in III.4? Could not some of the dreadful poems in Book IV be mock-heroic? If so, they would be at least comprehensible, though scarcely less dreadful. Let those who wish go to the text, but in doing so they should keep in mind that the poet who wrote IV.10 also wrote IV.11. The best and most obviously sincere poems in Book IV were written for women.

Aside from the hypothesis of the poet's anti-imperialism (the alternative seems to me to be the poet's mental decay), it is undeniable that Propertius was an unwilling conscript as a court poet:

> But Callimachus has a narrow chest,
>   cannot rumble with enough majesty
>   for the godly songs,
> Nor can my diaphragm sustain

the rough verses of Caesar's Trojan lineage.

. . . .

To each his own tune . . .

Maecenas has been spoken of as Augustus' "minister of propaganda," and it is certain that he pressured Propertius, as he would have pressured any poet of merit in that period, to write patriotic, official verse. Propertius acquiesced, with the enthusiasm to be expected of a sly and beleaguered love poet, but I do not see that he ever bit the hand of his patron. Propertius, either prudently or as a friend of Maecenas, kept his sarcasm low-keyed and directed it at other targets. The poems that insist upon Maecenas' peaceable virtues may have their share of irony, but I doubt it. Propertius was certainly more cautious than Ovid, undoubtedly because his disagreements with the Emperor were based on principle, not on style and temperament.

Propertius was not the first Latin elegist. Catullus occasionally used the elegiac meter, and Gallus, whose poems are lost, may have made it the conventional medium for subjective love poems. Quintilian preferred the elegiac verse of Tibullus to that of Propertius, but fairly pointed out that some readers liked Propertius better. Propertius was writing in the middle of a tradition; yet one has to keep in mind the differences between poets in that tradition, most of all between Propertius and Tibullus and Ovid. Tibullus' pastoral settings and limpid style are another world; Ovid learned and borrowed much from Propertius, but a gulf separates them because Ovid did not take women seriously. This disparity of temper is far more important than any divergence in technique. There is no frivolity—and no contempt—in Propertius' attitude toward women.

The elegiac meter is Greek. The early Greek elegy was

[5]

occasionally a metric for love poetry, but the Alexandrian tradition in which Propertius took so much trouble to place himself was not a tradition of the subjective love poem, or scarcely of the love poem at all. That a poet should be a learned man, Propertius took from Callimachus—and also the idea that "a fat book is a lot of crap." The love elegy is Latin, and Propertius is its greatest master.

Anyone who would translate Propertius must justify doing so in the light of Pound's *Homage to Sextus Propertius*, itself a great English poem. Pound responded to the foolish criticism of his poem by denying, with his usual vehemence, that it was meant to be a translation of Propertius. Despite Pound's denial, however, *Homage to Sextus Propertius* is, by customary standards, a translation, a masterly and extraordinary translation. There is scarcely anything in it which does not have a clear origin in the Latin. What gives a translator the right to try again is not any defect in Pound's poem, but rather the purpose of the poet. Pound translated selectively and to his own ends, and he left a lot of excellent poetry in the original. Moreover, the structure of Propertius' poetry is unlike that of Pound's in *Homage*. The looseness and the digressiveness of the Latin, though usually not deemed virtues, in my opinion give the poems a rich and suggestive texture which is worth trying to reproduce in English. Pound strung his hard and brilliant fragments together in a way that produced a different quality, a richness and suggestiveness of another kind. It is important to remember that Pound never intended to translate into English a large portion of Pro pertius' Latin poetry.

My translation is not always faithful to the Latin text. I have added a few lines of my own, usually transitional, and have deleted perhaps a score of lines from the original. The omissions stem from the best of all reasons: I could not, in the context in which I found the lines, translate them into

English. In three or four instances mistakes I inadvertently made in translating seemed so much better than the correct renditions that I have kept them. Occasionally I have moved lines from one place to another. Those who object to the liberties I have taken should seek out more literal translations or, if they enjoy reading Latin poetry, should go to the original text of Propertius, which is provided in the book.

In arrangement, I have for the most part followed the Loeb edition. I have accepted the customary division of Propertius into four books, although I question the validity of arguments against division into five books. Yet to disturb tradition and mark out a new path would be to inconvenience the reader. I have departed from the Loeb text in using Arabic instead of Roman numerals for individual poems, and also in occasionally combining several poems under one numeral heading. For example, I have rendered as one poem, II.18, the three poems numbered II.xviii, II.xviiiA, and II.xviiiB in Loeb.

I am grateful to the National Translation Center for its generous grant and to the editors of *Arion* and *Delos*, who printed several of my translations of these poems, for their encouraging interest. The advice and criticism of James Hynd were most helpful, and without the assistance of Kay and Odin Toness and Sara Clark I would never have finished this translation.

The Poems of Sextus Propertius

BOOK I

1

The flame first arose
    with the gleam in her eye,
& I bent my head then,
    lowered a proud glance
    at Eros' insistence,
       & thus I learned.
& a hard passion taught me
       to abhor virgin girls,
    taught me also
       to live without benefit of discretion.
For a year now, this madness, unfaltering
  though the gods float hostile above me.
Yet he fled no hard labor,
    who captured Atalanta
    fleet-foot & flint-hearted though she was.
He wavered through Parthenian caverns,
      faced lank-haired beasts in the forests,
    defended her against the centaur Hylaeus
     & got his head cracked for it,
  & lay wounded on the cliffs,
but Milanion's devotion broke and won
     swift-footed loveliness.
Thus effort & devoted prayer
    may do some good, occasionally,
  but for me,
    Aphrodite is languid,

forgets her art
                & craft & former ways.
You magicians who delude with moon rays
         and consecrate witchwork at the magic cauldron,
      come change the way Cynthia's heart beats against me,
          turn her lips paler [1] than my own;
Then only will I credit your claim
            to dominion over river & star
      with Medea's arcane song.
And my friends, you are much too late,
           who would lift me up—
   but still, seek some way
           to take this coal from my heart.
I will undergo iron and fire with fortitude,
        but release this voice
           broken by desire,
that I may speak out against her.
Arrange my passage past all borders
          to the ocean's uttermost rim,
     where no woman may perceive the way.
Whosoever shares a secure and lasting love,
     stay here at home, if the gods
          hear your lifted invocation.
For me passion's taste is bitter in the night;
          solitary love never fails.
& I warn you, avoid the evil.
       Let each man cleave
         to a faithful woman, when
    and if decorous love has found its place.
& I promise you this,
      if you don't attend my words
         you will remember them in affliction.

[1] In Latin poetry, pale lips and cheeks customarily signified a dismayed lover.

2

Why go forth in the streets
　　with elegant coiffure, my love,
　　　　moving in subtle curves of Coan ² vestment,
　Orontean myrrh in your hair,
　　　　advertising peregrine adornments?
Why cover native grace
　　with commercial refinement,
　when your beauty is radiant on undecorated limbs?
No herbs can improve
　　so beautiful a figure,
　& naked Eros loves no contrived beauty.
Consider what fine colors
　　strike from the rude earth;
　wild ivy is the best ivy,
　& the most splendid arbutus
　　surges from backwoods caves,
　and wild streams glitter
　　in untutored streambeds.
Our Italic shores persuade us
　　with pebbles, their native jewels,
　and the birds sing without any instruction.

It was not Phoebe's cosmetics
　　that set a fire under Castor,
　nor was Pollux kindled with such refinements;
No jewelry raised ancient discord
　　between Idas and inflamed Apollo,
　nor was Hippodamia carried off in a strange chariot

²The island of Cos plays a large role in Propertius' poems. Its silks
and wines were symbolic of other riches, such as Philetas and his verse
and, by extension, elegiac verse in general, particularly that of Pro-
pertius.

due to the dazzle
of unnatural radiance.
These worthy beauties depended on no gemstones,
        and the glow of their faces
    was of surpassing excellence,
        better than Apelles' paintings,
and they burned for no multitude of lovers,
        and virtue was sufficient adornment to beauty.

I fear for good reason. . . .
        I would not be thought less of
            than those others. . . .
To be able to please one man
                is adornment enough
    when Phoebus presents you with song
    & Calliope grants you her Aonian lyre
    & your words please my ear uniquely;
All these virtues please Minerva,
            and Aphrodite also;
& by their grace
                you will always be to me
                    most charming;
For me you need no extravagances.

3

Like Ariadne languid on desert beach,
    Theseus' keel laid into the sea
        & departing,
Or like Andromeda sleeping close by the flint
    she was strung to so lately,
Or a maenad lying limp
        from her dance
            among riverine herbs;
So Cynthia's breast heaved in supple rest
        head cradled loosely in her hands
            when I came in drunk, stumbling
                with wine fumes,
        the glass run out
            & the flame trembling in the slave boy's hands.
But with desire unquenched
        I undertook soft approach,
            bent onto the couch
                burning with two fires;
        lewd Liber laid hold of me,
                and then Eros, one hard as the other.
Lightly I tried to embrace
            her sleeping form,
                kissed her covetously,
Yet I feared to wake
            my brawl-proven Cynthia,
                fearing her claws,
but like Argus gazed raptly,
        and I put my wreath in your hair,
            and as I bent over you
    a wealth of gifts poured down,
& it was my pleasure to brush your disordered hair
            & bestow secret fruit on your ungrateful sleep
                with hollowed hands;
And how often you drew in your breath

with rare movement,
and I was falsely fearful lest you feel
the unwanted weight of nightmare
or strange incubus,
Until the fluctuating shadows
running before the moon
through the window,
persistent moon,
lingering wheel of light
touched your eyes and opened them;
And then, an angry speech,
elbows propped up
on the soft couch,
"So you return,
strike home to our bed again,
but only after you were expelled
from some girl's door.
And where have you spent
this long night of mine
now that the stars grow faint?
Damn you,
may you lead the sort of night
that I am forced to,
you debauched drunkard.
I led sleep astray
weaving a rhythm
at the loom
& tiring of that
took to the lyre & sang
my abandonment and your lingering
with a strange lover,
until
soft winged sleep
darkened my cares
among tears."

4

Bassus, why do you praise
   so many young women,
      trying to turn me from my mistress?
Why not accept it? I will stretch out
      the remainder of my life
   quite well pleased with my thralldom.
Iterate, if you please, your praises
         of Antiope's figure,
     & the beauty of Spartan Hermione,
     & whatever lovely women
    adorned ancient generations;
for Cynthia's name will not be engraved beneath theirs;
   and lesser figures cannot compare with her;
  Not even the worst judge
    would be so odiously wrong
       as to dissent in this matter.
But corporeal beauty is the least of all reasons
      for the blaze of passion;
there are greater things
for which I would perish, die with pleasure;
   the native glow to her complexion,
      her lovely skills
  & ineffable delight under silent cloak.[3]
The more you would unbind our love,
      the tighter you pull the knot;
and your enticements
   will not go without retribution,
     she will learn of it
& she will be no silent enemy;

---

[3] "But corporeal beauty . . . cloak." In this passage Propertius, quite typically, assesses Cynthia's physical charms as both her least and greatest virtue.

[17]

she has an angry and busy tongue,
   & you will be held dear under no lintel henceforth
& your company will then be
       most unwelcome
         & forbidden to me.
Indeed at no altar will she fail to curse you
     squeezing hot tears from her eyes,
   however sacred the altar stone be;
   for no ruin enrages her more
     than the god departing, & love cloven;
       our love most especially.
And may she remain this way always;
    I ask it of heaven;
  and may I never find in her
     any cause for sorrow.

5

Exercise some prudence
   in your envy,
 & mute your troublesome cries;
 Leave us alone on our present course.
What is it you want,
  to know the fires of lunacy,
   to feel the worst of evils,
 & leave your tracks among hidden coals,
   & choke on a poisoned elixir?
She is not at all
 like your usual vagrant girls;
  adamant fury is her custom,
 & even if she abstains from cursing you
   at her altar,
 she will give you a thousand anxieties,
 & you will have no sleep,
   she will not take herself from your eyes.
She can shackle more turbulent spirits than yours,
  & you will beat frequent retreats to my door,
   & your virile oratory
   will fail with stammering,
& a trembling fear will shudder from your bitter tears;
  terror will transform your face,
 and whatever words you wish for will abandon you
   in the middle of your complaint;
and you will lose track of your whereabouts,
   & your very name.
 But thereby you will learn
  the weight of my chains
& what it is to walk away
  excluded from her house;
and you will no longer be so astonished

       that my face is pale
    & my body wasted.
Nor will your worthy ancestors come to the rescue,
   for love forgets to honor antique phantoms.
If you give her some small sign
       of indiscretion
  how quickly your once fine name
     will be common noise in her ears.
I will not be able to console you
   when you come looking for me,
      for there is no cure for my own wounds,
but you will share my discomfort in equality,
    & you may weep on my toga,
        if you return the favor.
Therefore give up your wish, Gallus,
    for when she brings you the answer to your prayer
    she will bring you more pain than you bargained for.

6

No fear deters me
　　　from cruising the sea with you, Tullus,
　no terror turns me from bending sail
　　　into salty Aegean wastes;
I would climb mountains in your company,
　　　penetrate Memnon's kingdom.
But Cynthia's words, her grave prayers
　　& her pale lips
　　　　enforce my lingering;
　　　her arms encircle my neck.
Her shrill voice,
　　　　a fire in the night,
　　cries that the gods have ceased to be;
and she refuses me,
　　　& counters my anger with menaces.
I cannot endure such complaining,
　　　　not for an hour.
To hell with any man who can love in apathy.
Is it really worth it,
　　to tour scholarly Athens,
　　　　or behold the riches of Asia?
Is it worth bringing down
　　　a clamor of revilement,
　　making her mar her face
　　　　with crazy fingers;
　　　is it worth her declarations
　　that she owes that wind kisses
　　　　which moves against me,
　and that there is no evil worse
　　　　than a man unfaithful?

You, Tullus, ought to try
    to rise to your uncle's glory,[4]
       and restore old laws among our forgotten allies.
You passed your youth without Amor,
    your loves being arms & the fatherland;
and may Eros not bring you
       into toil like mine,
      may he not enmesh you in such tearful affairs.
But allow me
   to remain in these prone circumstances
      that providence has decreed for me,
     & to abandon my soul
    to whatever wanton measures she might wish.
Many have ruined themselves freely,
      loving too long,
& may hell receive me still among that number.
I was not born to swordplay & glory;
   the Fates rule that I subtend Love
    as my exclusive service.
Whether you walk over
    yielding Ionia
      or where the liquor of Pactolus
       dampens Lydian earth;
  whether you go afoot by land
     or by sea with oars to your agreeable office,
If, then,
    at some future hour
    you think of me,
  you may be certain
  I live under this same bitter star.

---

[4] It is not clear what the glory of Tullus' uncle was. H. E. Butler (Loeb translation) makes him proconsul of Asia.

7

While you speak your appointed piece, Ponticus,
        the affair of Thebes;
    song of cold steel
            between brothers—
    inviting comparison, if no evil come of it,
        with ancient Homer, the master himself
(if only the fates go easy on your efforts)—
I meanwhile am always agitated
            patching up my affair,
        looking for some sign
        from my unbending mistress,
and I am bound over less to genius
            than to pain,
    & I sing the hard moments
        she gives my manhood,
    & to this measure
        I polish out my years;
but it's where my fame lies,
        & may my name go down forever
            with these songs.
Let them laud me only
        in having pleased
            the learned young lady
    & in having borne up
            under her unjust attacks.
Hereafter let lovers neglected
            read closely,
& do well in learning from my troubles.
And you also, Ponticus,
        should you be brought down by Eros
            from the homing true curve of his bow
(though may the gods' scroll

roll out no such doom for you)
then your distant ramparts
and your far-marching armies
will vanish in oblivion, from then on neglected;
And you will wish
to bind down more supple verses
without much luck,
love being insufficient
to lift up its own canticles;
and you will then take great notice,
& I will seem no mean versemaker then;
indeed you may have me at the head
of that whole not ungifted pack,
and I do not think
the young will stand mute
at my graveside,
but they will call me
the poet of their flame
who lies there.
Beware of hauteur, epic poet; despise no love songs;
Love coming late is dearly bought.

8

Are you undetainable by love
        & my disquiet, madwoman,
           or do you long for frosted Illyria?
& is it your heart's desire
      to sail under the first wind
             to join this superb gentleman,
          whoever he is?
Have you considered the passage,
        the wind's force
& the sea's rumble,
      the board bench to sleep on,
        the pain of the hoarfrost
          gnawing your pretty ankles;
And how will your lovely frailness
          serve you
     as strange snows drift down around you, Cynthia?
I pray that the season of ice be doubly prolonged
        & the Pleiades detain themselves
           below the horizon
& the seaman's tackle lie idle;
May your moorings
          stay knotted to their post
        by the water's edge in Tuscany.
And may no ill wind dissipate this prayer;
yet should that wind rise,
      may it carry your sails
        safely forward
           in the running sea
though I stand alone on an empty beach
        with pain in my heart—
look back on my clenched fist then,
       O woman of benumbed sensibilities.

You have lied to me, & you deserve no goodwill
    from this quarter,
  but still,
may the gods guard your ship
     & your oars beat with good fortune
   past the Ceraunian headland,
     & get you to Oricos safely.
As for me,
  no girl can entice me away.
    You are my life,
& I will remain at your lintel
    in bitter mourning,
nor will I leave off asking sailors
   your whereabouts;
You may go beyond Scythia, Cynthia,
    but you remain my love always.

$8a^5$

She remains here
    oath & presence
      & I have won;
Let the disgruntled go hang.
    She couldn't withstand
      my assiduous prayers;
  The covetous & envious
    must now forsake their joy,
      my Cynthia forsakes the new way.
I am yet her love,
    and for me,
      she loves this city also,
     & she says that without me
      no realm might delight her.
She chooses to lie with me
    in my narrow bed,
      and she would be mine alone,
       no matter what;
  even without the rich emoluments
    to be found in ancient kingdoms
    or gold in Elis
      to be got from horse racing.
Whatever fortune *he* might give,
      or promise to give,
    will come to nothing;
not even her respect for profit
      will remove her from the folds of my cloak.
Not by gold
did I twist her into this orbit,

---

[5] Although there is no break in the manuscript, I.8a is clearly a separate poem.

nor by Indian pearl,
    but with the offering of alluring song.
The Muses rule over love,
       & Phoebus is never far from love,
    & I rely on these gods
      in my affair
    & rare Cynthia is mine.
Now it is allowed me
       to lift my new bough
     to heavenly reaches;
She is mine by day,
   she is mine by night,
     no rival will break and steal
      a love so strongly bound;
& this present glory
     will be acknowledged
      until my white old age.

9

I told you your time would come, love-mocker,
   & now you are no longer at liberty
       to bestow fine words so freely,
& you lie supplicating and pliant in her hands.
    This new-bought concubine exercises now
      a queenly dominion.
The priestess-oracles of Zeus
     cannot speak with more authority
       than I can
  as to which girl
    will snare which bachelor.
I have some skill, some experience, in these matters;
     I have felt the ache,
       looked through the tear-shadowed eyes.
Would to god I was still a stiff & clumsy novice,
    my burden of love laid down;
  what comfort is your solemn anthem
      your lamentation at the lyre-raised walls
     of Thebes brought down?
Mimnermus is better than Homer
    in matters of the heart.
Soft love demands a polished tune,
   so go and put aside your somber books
     & sing the song she wants to hear.
The notes might be different
    if you lacked this abundance—
      why go thirsty in the flashing stream?
If you tremble now,
   what will you do
when passion's full fire consumes you?
    These are the first sparks only;
   you will burn

       & be left in ashes.
If you but knew, you would as soon
     face an Armenian tiger, or chain yourself
        to the wheel of hell,[6]
         as feel the blade of love in your loins,
           & lie unable to refuse her anything
             when she is angry.
A lover's itinerary is demanding,
         & Eros is not on your side.
Do not be taken in by her easy contentment;
       you must mount her with ever more vigor
           to keep her yours,
           and the gleam in your eye must be for her alone, now,
            and love allows no night not spent with her.
O Ponticus, abstain from the game
        of whispered seduction;
If your soul were oak or flint
      you might still be the loser,
     & your spirit is somewhat ethereal.
You failed to see
       Eros lurking in ambush,
         & now you are caught in his bone-cracking grip.
But admit it—
    & to speak of your passion
        may perhaps ease it.

[6] See IXION in glossary.

10

Gallus, I was with you
    when Eros first drew you among his delights
        as you reclined amid tears,
    a joyful sensual night;
    the mere remembrance pleases me,
      & I pray for you in its memory even now,
that night when your arms encircled her
        & I saw you linger, Gallus,
    and string out the silences
        between your words.
Voyeur of your dalliance,
      I could not leave you then, though the moon
        reddened in decline
    & dreams slid against my eyes,
        such was the fire in your whispers.
You trusted me then;
      let this be your reward for pleasure confided.
I have kept your pain hidden,
    but there is greater loyalty than that.
I can fuse broken loves,
    draw open her folding doors;
  I can heal new love wounds;
    the cure rides with my tune.
I have not walked in Cynthia's love for nothing;
    She has taught me what to do
      & what to beware of.
Don't quarrel with her
      in her sadness
and speak not too proudly
    nor too seldom.
If she cries for some favor
    neither scowl nor refuse it;

and when she speaks kindly
        make sure her words
         don't fall in a void.
Despise her, & she will stir with anger;
   Hurt her feelings, & she will never forget it.
But if your pride recedes,
      and you throw yourself under love's jurisdiction,
        then she will yield up joy to you.
Choose not your freedom
        & a desolate heart,
  and remain in delight with one woman.

11

You [7] idle at Baiae
    Eye the sea
        & the lagoon built by Hercules,[8]
& I spend my nights
    thinking of you
    although that fact may have escaped your notice.
Does your love recede with distance?
    Has some enemy of mine
        counterfeited the flame
            & taken you from my songs?
May you lie at ease
    in a bay-borne skiff
& may you swim leisurely
    in the small lagoon
    hand over hand
through low and yielding waves,
But may you not
    lie voluptuously
in the rustle of soft whisperings
    on the quiet sands.
The common stain of falseness
    often follows a girl on her own,
    she being unmindful of love's usual icons.
Not that I doubt you.
  I know your renowned reputation,
    but by the sea at Naples

[7] In this poem, as in others, Propertius moralizes about Cynthia, expressing a desire that she be chaste. Although his concern may be genuine, had she followed his advice and abandoned the life of a courtesan he would have had a good deal less to write about.

[8] Hercules' lagoon is the Lucrine Lake, said to have been formed when Hercules built a causeway at Baiae on the Bay of Naples.

Eros should be greatly feared.
Therefore pardon me
    if my books have wounded you,
charge it to my anxiety,
    Neither mother, home, nor kin
        holds me as you do,
You are my life and home,
        my continual delight,
    I have no other care,
    & when my friends run across me sad
        or find me joyful
    I may say you are the cause.
Amuse yourself no longer
    in a decadent resort
    whose waters drift lovers apart
    & whose beaches
        spawn accusations.

12

Why do you pretend
   I lack interest,
  O gossips & watchers of Rome;
     why level this accusation of apathy
   as the reason that our love hangs fire?
She lies as far from my bed as the Po
     lies from the river Don;[9]
She no longer coils around me
    as she used to in her love
      in bare-breasted embrace.
Her whispers only echo in my ear now,
      & have lost their sweetness—
        yet once I pleased her—
  in that time none loved as we did,
   none loved with such fidelity.
I fear some evil eye was jealous,
     some envious spirit undermined our love.
  I wonder
     what herbs
       from high mountain meadows
     were the divisive potion?
I am not now
    what I have been
    and wayfaring may change any girl,
  and the greatest love
    is a diaphanous thing
  in danger of disappearance.
And now for the first time
I know the length of the empty night;

[9] The Don, though not a literal translation, conveys the idea of great
distance.

the only voice is my own
    hanging somberly in darkness.
Any man
who has a girl present to cry out to
    can be thankful,
  even salt tears please Eros,
& if a flame dampened can be rebuilt elsewhere,
    Love finds servile pleasure
        in such altered ardor.
But I cannot break our covenant
    or love another,
  for Cynthia was my first love
      & will be my last.[10]

[10] Cynthia was obviously neither Propertius' first love nor his last, but, so far as is known, she was his greatest love.

13

I expect the usual thing, Gallus,
    your usual untempered glee
that my affairs lie in shambles,
      my love riven from me,
      leaving a lonely place in my life.
But I won't mimic your gibes;
  I wish you luck instead;
       may no girl cheat you.
But even while your notoriety spreads
  (for never lingering
       with the girls you ensnare),
     even now the blood leaves your face,
      even now late-coming love
      brings down ruin upon you, draws your feet
  to her gate, then needles bravado
      with indecision, & you sneak off in retreat;
This the retribution, Gallus, for your callousness;
  one girl will avenge all those others.
No more girls from the streets now;
     she will welcome no recruit to your bed.
  I know all this
    not from any oracle, or any loose tongue;
  Can you deny my witness,
  that I saw her grow weak
     hanging from your shoulder;
that I saw tears lace your arms entwined,
   & saw you stammer after words
     to bare your soul?
And that I also saw what I can't modestly write?
Such was your passion,
  struck against frenzy,
     that nothing might have broken that embrace;

an embrace not incomparable with Neptune's
    when his desires tightened around easy Tyro.
No comparable flame enkindled Hercules in heaven
    when he first felt connubial joy
    after the deadly ridge of Oeta.
One night like that one pales all past flames,
for the firebrand she sets under you
    burns pretty robustly.
And she won't let you recover your pride,
    nor will she let you be stolen away.
A fire now moves you, & there is no marvel in it,
    she being worthy of Zeus,
    like Leda, nearly, & more lovely than Leda's child.
Her resplendence surpasses
    the old-time Argive beauties,
  & her eloquence would bring her any god.
Since love has beaten you down,
    use defeat to your advantage;
no other vestibule merits your worthy attendance,
    my dear Gallus, and she may overlook your errors,
    since you are new to this sort of thing.
So let her be the exclusive measure
    the only hope of your heart's desire.

14

Granted you recline voluptuously
    drinking Lesbian wine
        from a fine embossed cup
           down by the Tiber,
      and wonder at the swift-measured oar beat
          of the boats
      and at the slowly towed barges,
  and though the forest emblazons the summit behind you
         like the Caucasus;
These attractions can't contend with love,
  which concedes nothing to riches.
For if she sleeps beside me
    & if we pass the day
        in the pleasures of the couch,
    then the very gold of Pactolus is mine,
      & the Red Sea's jewels.
Then kings must be second to me
      in my elation
(and may such joy endure
      until death reeves it off),
for with love adverse
    who can enjoy his money?
The rewards of wealth are of no account to me;
    if Aphrodite is cruel,
      she can wrack heroes
        & crack tougher hearts than mine.
Love will step past Arabian jeweled doorways
  & does not fear, my dear Tullus,
    to climb into the purple bed
& roll the unfortunate youth
    around in it in torment;

& then what good are colored weaves
of silken bed hangings?
And as for me
while joyous love is with me,
I won't waver in my disdain
for kingdoms & the gifts of kings.

15

I have feared your inconstancy, Cynthia,
    feared hardship from it,
but no such nefarious bad faith.
The turning of fortune puts me in pain,
      yet you pay no attention,
  offer nothing to allay my anguish.
And you sit here redoing your coiffure,
      after last night,
          idly prettying yourself,
admiring oriental pendants
      set against your breast,
  like a bride on her way to the wedding.
Now, Calypso wasn't thus "distraught"
    when her Ithacan set sail;
therefore her protracted weeping,
    a desolation of ocean around her,
      and she sat mournful, her hair let down,
    and damned the wide sea's injustice;
and she grieved for Odysseus,
    being unforgetful of the delights of the years past,
      though never after would she behold him.
And your distress
    is not like that Lemnian queen's
who remained without moving
  in the chamber Jason was riven from,
    consumed by love, hearing only the wind that took him,
    and she knew no love after.[11]
Exalted Evadne, glory of Argive virtue,
    went down to the flame of her husband's pyre—

---

[11] An allusion here to Alphesiboea, who killed her brothers after
they had murdered her husband Alcmaeon, has been omitted because it
seems out of place.

[41]

however no exemplary models
        could change your ways—
but your affairs might have been
            conducted more nobly.
Speak no more of it;
        your words renew lies, they anger the gods
        your neglect maligns.
But if chance brings you into evil circumstance
    you will regret the hard time you gave me.
        But that's hardly possible—the great waste of sea
        will first fall away, or the years run
        the other way, or love cease beating under my ribs.
Be what you want to, except another man's concubine.
        You should not degrade your shining eyes;
            for I believed your lies on their account,
                when you swore by them
        that if you lied you would put them out
                with your own hand. Can you lift up your eyes
        into the high sun
            with no tremor? For you know your own lewdness.
For whom now does your face grow livid, and the tears
    glitter in your eyes? Eyes I have gone to hell for.
Believe these words, lovers, and not a woman's flatterings.

16

That door,[12]
    formerly thrown open to conquering heroes,
    gateway famous as Tarpeian virtue,
    entryway before which gold-worked chariots used to park,
    that door often anointed by tearful captive supplication,
now groans under the nightly quarrels of drunkards,
    and resounds to the pulse of worthless fists.
No lack, now, of dirty wreaths for the columns,
      & one can always find a few torches discarded,
          signs for the excluded.
But no gate can defend her,
      my mistress,
    from nights of infamy;
          that gate now subject to obscene songs.
Nor does Cynthia renew her good name
      and abstain from evil more exuberant
        than the dissolute age demands.
That door will be brought under bitterer lamentation
      by my stretched out night watch;
    I will never let those doorposts stand in silence,
        no song of enchantment resounding.
"Janus crueler than my mistress
    why are you silent,
      the folding doors closed tight?
Why no admittance, love undisclosed,
    why no thought of giving in
      to the transit of my secret prayers?
Will no end be conceded to my misfortune,
    no end to evil dreams

---

[12] This poem is spoken by the door, an acceptable phenomenon in Latin, but for the English version I have had the poet speak instead.

on a tepid threshold?
The midnight sighs
as I lie there,
as do the declining constellations
& the air floating frost under the morning star.
Only Janus never laments men's pains,
he answers nothing,
on silent hinge.
If only my whisper would drift through a crack in the wall
and strike & turn my mistress;
then let her keep her heart armored,
I doubt if she could,
or keep tears from her eyes,
or keep her breathing even.
Now she lies straining against more fortunate arms
than mine;
my words move with nocturnal winds.
That gateway, foremost cause
of my misfortune,
is unbroken by my gifts;
Janus, you have never been wounded
by any words of mine;
none of these drunkards can say the same.
I deserve not to go hoarse with long complaint
and unquiet vigil
in Hecate's realm.
I have spun out tunes
with new verses
in your service;
I have planted kisses on your steps.
And I have often turned
before your dingy columns
& brought due offering
with secret hands."

[44]

Thus my speech
   to which I added the other outcries
      used by wretched lovers,
those clamors rising
  like the birds of sunrise.
And that door is damned forever
      by its vice-ridden mistress
      & the tears of the poet.

17[13]

I should never have left her
    to venture forth seaward
      for now I exhort the kingfishers
        of the desert seabeach,
and the port of Cassiope
      will not greet my ship on time,
& my prayers and vows fall on unwelcome coasts.
The winds cut into a scream
      in my ear;
    they rage as Cynthia used to;
shall fortune never bring calm breezes?
  Shall this thin-sanded beach cover my corpse?
O Cynthia,
    ameliorate your harsh complaints;
  there is retribution enough
      in the night & slanting shoals.
Can you sit dry-eyed and and hope for my death?
    For you will never hold my ashes to your breast.
God damn the man who first
    set canvas to ship's mast
  and first made a road of the reluctant ocean.
It was less an affliction to struggle
    with the caprice of my mistress,
 who is a rare woman, though hard of soul,
    than to stare at the dark outline
  of these coasts backed by unknown forests
    & lift invocation to Castor, patron of seafarers.
Had fate buried me before I left
and my gravestone stood a marker to our love,

---

[13] This poem and I.18 sound more like fantasies than like true accounts written in the circumstances described.

then she would have thrown the sacrificial locks
        on the funeral fire
    and laid my cinders to rest with roses
    and cried out my name in grief
            and prayed to Earth not to lie too heavy on me.
But now, let the comely daughters of Oceanus,
        daughters of Doris,
            release my white sails
        and lead me to a safe refuge,
            felicitous escort
                    of a choir of sea nymphs;
Let them do that
    if they have ever felt the wounds of love themselves.

18

A desert void
        & silence
                share my pain
    with the west wind drifting
        in the empty grove.
  Here may I sing
            my secret pain
                with no ear hearing;
        the silent cliff shall not betray me.
Where shall I pick up the thread,
        the beginning of your present disdain?
Why have you taken
        to dispensing grief?
Lately, you loved me,
        now I stand outcast;
I would have you think
            on the justice of it;
                what enchantment engenders this mutation?
Is it the shadow of suspicion,
        do you consider me unfaithful,
you of nimble opinions?
            If so
  you might contemplate returning
        for I swear that no fair foot but yours
            has trod on my threshold.
I owe you rancor
        for this ache in my heart
            but I would not affront you
        in my anger,
it would only inflame you
            to an orgy of self-righteousness
        and cause you to cry

and your bright eyes to swim
                with rolling tears;
Have I hung out too few signals
                of my desire?
Have I seemed too little sanguine,
                love unseen on my face?
The oak tree & the pine tree here
                sacred to Pan
        witness my love. They have heard the melody
        in the shadow of their leaves
            & Cynthia's name
                is engraved in bark.
        The number of cares your injustice spawns in my heart
                is a secret of your silent entryway;
    I am well adjusted
            to your overbearing pride
            your commands, etc.
    I endure them without complaint
            & I am rewarded now
                with these cold hills
            a rocky path
        & hard sleep,
        O godly fountain,
        & my solitary outcry
        accompanies
bright high-toned birds
                only
    but nevertheless
    they shall hear your name repeated
                Cynthia
    as shall the forest
            & the quiet rocks.

19

I am not afraid now
    of the shadowy afterlife,
  nor do I pine away
    thinking of fate's due,
      the ultimate bonefire;
But I do fear
  that your love's strength
    will not survive until my funeral;
this fear is deadlier
    than the march to the grave;
Eros has not brushed my eyes so lightly
  that love comes not into them;
    my dust will not settle
      unhindered by love, & forgetful.
The hero Protesilaus in dark hell
    was not unmindful of conjugal delight,
and burning to caress her, his joy, with ethereal hands,
his shade returned to his ancient home in Thessaly.
  And likewise, whatever becomes of me,
    my spirit will be yours always;
    great love cannot be confined
      by the sands of doom.
If that choros of beauties
    plundered from Troy by the Argives
    should come to be with me
I would yet prefer your greater charms
    to their loveliness.
And however long old age
might delay our union
  (and may Tellus grant you old age)
    your bones will be met with tears.
And may an equal love live in your heart

[50]

as my own cinders glow;
Then death will not come bitter to me
whatever place it finds me;
Yet I am apprehensive
that you will disdain my tomb,
some iniquitous love urge you therefrom,
compel you to dry your eyes;
the best girl can be bent
by such insistent incentive.
But while it is given us,
let us rejoice
in still-living love
although all time
is not long enough for it.

133657

20

This cautionary note, Gallus,
  out of continual affection
    (take care it doesn't drift
      as many things do
        from your mind)
that ill fortune not descend
      on your careless affair.
Your young man, the flame of your desire,
    is as pretty as Hylas, at least as glorious.
Whether you walk streams sacred & shadowed
               in Umbrian undergrowth
  or the Anio cools your ankles
    or you promenade whatever prodigious coast
      or by whatever water meanders friendly,
Always watch out
  for enrapturing girl-spirits,
    nymphs hungry with desire—the Italian kind are as erotic
                  as any—
  so that you will not go desolate, lovelorn
among cliffs and cold lakes, as Hercules did,
    distraught on the hidden banks
      of the wild Ascanius.

The story has it
    that Argus once set his prow for Phasis,
      a long sea ride from the dockyard at Pagasa,
and, his ship past the Hellespont, he glided under the cliff face
    at Mysia to mooring,
    where all hands rested by calm seaboard,
    heroes bedding the soft sand with leaves.
& Hercules' young friend went inland, sent looking for water,
  & Zetes & Calais floated in desire behind him,

[52]

sons of the north wind,
Calais then over him, airy fingers, then Zetes;
trapped under their wings, his lips nuzzled
by fleeting breezes,
from below, he, Hylas, beat them off.
And the winds abandoned that pursuit,
& he became the hamadryads' windfall,
at Pege's well, down from the mountain,
liquid nymph haunt. There
wild apples hung under trees
visited by no man,
& lilies gleamed in ponceau fields.
In his fairy meadow Hylas plucked up flowers,
& then, leaning unwarned over entrancing water,
loitering to the lure
of his own image,
he cupped his hand, leaning on one arm
& his beauty's gay dazzle
struck with wonder
the burning dryad choros;
& they nudged him softly down,
dragged him down wellward;
Then the choked cry,
wrapped with water.
And Hercules called his name,
but silent air answered
from the steening.

The moral of that story, Gallus,
is keep an eye on him
your boy Hylas;
Never entrust a comely young man
to the tender mercies
of these prowling young women.

[53]

"You, soldier,[14]
    scrambling from our common ruin,
        sword cuts from Tuscany on you,
            eyes swollen,
                eyes turned on my groan;
    I was with you—
        but bring joy to your parents;
            keep yourself alive,
    don't bring your sister to tears
        knowing how I died;
    how Gallus got through Caesar's swords
        to be cut down
            by some unknown hand.
Leave,
    keep the secret
        of my mountain-strewn bones."

---

[14] In this poem the dying Gallus, possibly a relative of Propertius, addresses a comrade in the army of Lucius Antonius, defeated by Octavian in the Perusian War of 41 B.C.

22

You ask me, Tullus,
   in the name of our friendship
what is my lineage
and where my home is.
If you know the graves of this country
   around Perusia,
   a place so deadly to the fatherland
      in civil war,
Etruscan dust so painful to me,
      where my friend's bones lie unburied—
I was begotten there
   where Umbria borders
     the rich and fruitful plain below.

BOOK II

1

You would know the source
     of these many engravings, these words of love,
   this book of supple words,
      words from the lips softly.
Neither Apollo nor Calliope
  sings in my ear,
but Cynthia's genius presides
     & shapes my songs.
If you would have her walk glittering
       clothed in Coan tunic
   this whole volume will be Coan-clothed.
If her hair falls in her eyes,
  I say her hair is splendid
    & she walks exalted
    & delights in my praises;
Or if her ivory fingers
   strike a song through the lyre
   I display suitable wonder
   at her artful touch on the strings;
Or if she directs her entreating eyes downward,
   & with flung-away tunic
     wrestles naked with me
 then our struggles will be
    a reborn Iliad;
Her delicate words and deeds
    flesh a great epic.

[57]

Maecenas, if the fates had appointed me
  to inspire armed heroes,
I would not sing of Titans,
   nor of mountain laid on mountain
    by skybound giants,
nor of ancient Thebes,
   nor the Trojan ramparts
    in majestic Homer's song,
Nor Xerxes' command that the seas merge,
  nor old Remus's kingdom
    nor the pride of great Carthage,
nor how Marius saved the day for us
   against the German menace;
But I would speak instead of Caesar's affairs,
  I would intone Caesar's wars,
    & after that I would sing Maecenas.
And when I would raise the song of Mutina & Philippi,
   graveyards of our citizens,
    & the clash of ships off Sicily,
   or the plundered hearth fires of the ancient Etruscans,
   or of Ptolemaic Pharos seized,
  as much as I strummed an Egyptian air
   & sang of Caesar dressed in mourning,
   conqueror of seven rivers & of kings
   brought chained in gold,
   & the triumphant bowsprits of Actium
   carried up the Via Sacra,
my muse would have your name woven in that tapestry,
 Maecenas, loyal in arms, loyal in peacetime,
   & Caesar's comrade.
But Callimachus has a narrow chest,
 cannot rumble with enough majesty
   for the godly songs,[1]

[1] The phrase "godly songs" replaces the Latin reference to one of Jupiter's quarrels.

[58]

Nor can my diaphragm sustain
   the rough verses of Caesar's Trojan lineage.
Sailors spin tales of high winds,
    plowmen likewise discuss oxen,
      soldiers old wounds, & sheepherders their flocks;
& as for me
   I speak of coiling combat
      on a narrow couch.
To each his own tune, let each man
    polish out his day
     in the exercise of his proper skills.

—and if I remember correctly, she vigorously condemns
    other nimble girls,
  and because of Helen hates the whole Iliad.

It is one glory to die for love,
    another to enjoy the fruits of it;
   May this singular love's benefits
     be my great joy.
Even if I taste Phaedra's murderous potion,
   or if I die by Circe's herbs,
     or even if the fire under a brass witch cauldron
   warms a spell against me,
     even so,
      the woman has ripped away my senses,
  & they will remove me from her house
only at my funeral.
There are medicines for pain,
  and of pains
  only love loves no artful alleviation.
Machaon cured Philoctetes of his snakebit shin,
  & Chiron brought light to the eyes of Phoenix,
  & Asclepius the god

[59]

restored extinguished Androgeus to his father's
fireside,
& Telephus was cured by the same lance point
that bit him;
But if a man can remove this grievous love
from my heart
that same man can hand an apple to Tantalus
& dip water out of Danaïan urns, lighten
the liquid burden on delicate necks,
& that same man can unloose Prometheus from his cliff,
& beat off the vultures feeding at his belly.
Therefore,
when the fates demand back my life
& I become a name chiseled briefly in marble,
Then, Maecenas, glory & hope of our youth,
& my hope & glory also,
if by some chance your travels lead past my sepulchre,
halt your British war chariot with its carved yokes,
& read, as your tears break
the grave silence,

BROUGHT HERE BY ENDURING LOVE

BOOK II

2[2]

I was free, & had planned to live single
  & sleep in my bed alone,
 but this peaceful life was cheated by love—
  Why is a mortal woman so inhumanly beautiful?
Zeus, I can understand your secret loves
    in the old days.
Her hair is honey-colored
 her hands long and slender,
Statuesque, she moves like a goddess,
  like Pallas Athena before her altars
  breast concealed by the aegis.
Moreover, she is no less spendid
  than that demigoddess
   stolen from the marriage feast,
lovely prize of the centaurs;
 or the virgin Brimo
 who lay with Mercury by a sacred stream.
Indeed the immortals should concede,
  even those who pulled off their tunics
   for judgment on Mount Ida;
Let old age never change her beauty
  even if she should live as long
   as the prophetess of Cumae.

[2] W. B. Yeats has translated a fragment of this poem.

3

You, Propertius, bragging yourself invincible,
        have now tumbled into her pit,
    your proud spirit captured,
            trussed to your own desire.
Every month some new alarm,
        and now another book of disgraces.
A fish might come out & stroll on the sand,
        or a boar take to the sea,
if I were able to pass the night
    in the propriety of study.
Love may be put aside
            for a little time,
    but not cured.
It is not her fine ivory beauty
            that seizes me
    (although no lily compares with her,
        & her complexion is like rose petals
            floating in milk,
    like snow & Spanish cinnabar)
nor is it her hair
    flowing light over her neck,
        nor her bright eyes
            which sparkle in my soul,
    nor the Arab silks she walks lit by;
I am not so frivolous as that;
But with the cups thrown down
            she dances like lovely Ariadne
            leading the bacchanalian choros,
and when she strikes up a tune
        with Aeolian plectrum,
her lyre equals a goddess's, a muse by her fountain;
    Her graven verses rival those

of antique Corinna,
    & if she reckons her songs as fine
       as Erinna's were,
             can she be far wrong?
Candent Amor sneezed a bright omen [3]
      at your birth, Cynthia;
  the gods assembled your virtues,
   don't think you got them from your mother.
Such gifts are somewhat inhuman;
    ten months are insufficient
       to bring them to light.
Born the greatest glory
      of Roman womanhood,
  you are most likely, of our local beauties,
    to be thrown into bed
      by a god.
You will not frequent
  human beds exclusively.
  Helen returns to earth again,
 should I wonder if our young men kindle?
Troy, you would have gone down
     in more splendor for Cynthia—
once I wondered why war gathered
      below Trojan breastworks,
  why Europe came to Asia
with sword & spear
   in the cause of a woman,
but I see now why Menelaus demanded,
    why Paris refused to comply.
A woman's loveliness
     was a worthy reason for Achilles' downfall
    & Priam's gamble with his kingdom.

[3] Sneezing was considered a good omen.

[63]

If some artist
 would outdo the ancient masters,
  let my mistress be his model,
   & inspire his brush;
His work would burn Aurora in the sunrise
  & Hesperus at sundown
   with the fire of envy.
And should I break loose from her,
  may I fall in love elsewhere,
  & thus expire in sharper pain.
The bull first balks at his yoke
  but then accustoms his strength to the plow,
and a young man loves first
  with struggling emotion;
 but he learns love's poise in time,
 learns to bear love's bondage,
 as Melampus wrapped in dirty chains,
   chains of a cow thief, learned to endure,
his peculation being for love, not gain,
  for beauty,
  a beauty soon a bride
     in Amythaon's hall.

4

Often, often,
  you must first complain
      of her own delictions,
Often you must ask
  & often go with favor denied,
 and often gnaw your fingernails
     without good cause,
and too often hear your own feet moving
      pacing out anger & doubt . . .
My hair reeked of unguents,
     but to no effect,
  & my slow walk was a measure of vanity;
In this affair
  no herb-blade potion, no witchery by night,
    no grasses burnt by Perimede's hand
      have any strength,
for here causes are indiscernible,
     no stroke flashes in the light of day,
 it is a dark road these evils ride on.
The stricken man
  needs no physician, and no soft bed,
 it is not the season, nor a cold wind
     molesting him—
He walks forth—and then surprised friends
    discover him suddenly cut down.
    Whatever love is, it walks invisible
     & unforeseen.
But for what lying oracle
     am I not a prize catch?
And what old woman has not heard
     my turning dreams ten times?

Those who will love women
        are no friends of mine,
           let my friends take their pleasures in boys
for thereby you come down the flume
          in a safe hull;
small waves on a small beach
        float no man to ruin;
one word deflects his anger,
       whereas she
  will scarcely be satisfied with your blood.

5

Rumor idles through Rome, Cynthia,
 with the word of your whoring;
Had I deserved this, I might have expected it,
  but you will grieve in your turn, my love,
I will leave this place,
  slip out seaward
    with the first good wind;
I daresay one
 from the world's deceitful girls
  will rejoice in being
    the beacon of my song,
    & will neither use me so badly,
      nor dance on my feelings,
      & will notch her sharp words only for you, Cynthia.
Too late, then, your eye-glitter of tears,
  for black shadows hover
    over the long day of our love.
Now is the time
  to walk apart
  while the rill of anger runs,
for I know my present discomfort
    is a forecast of love's return.
My god, the waves of the sea
  aren't as variable
    under a fresh north breeze
as lovers are, wavering with soft words after anger,
  and storm clouds change less quickly
    with the precarious wind out of Africa.
Twist free from your unjust yoke
while you can, Propertius;
  the first night is the hardest,
    after which love's pain

begins to abate a little.
But may the mild rule of great Juno
spare you from real harm, my love;
may you come through unsinged
by the fires in your heart.
The anger of the horned bull
is not the only anger;
there are softer replies to injustice.
I would not rip the clothes from your deceiving beauty,
nor will I break through the door now shut
or lay hold of your pulled-back hair in anger,
nor would I trace the marks of my knuckles on you;
I leave that to louts undeserving
of ivy wreaths in their hair.
But I may pen a verse or two,
& they are hard to erase,
"Cynthia of radiant looks & light words,"
and although you dismiss your murmuring detractors
in contempt
perhaps my art will bring a paleness into your face at last,
perhaps a song will return you the pain.

6

The chamber of Lais
            wasn't comparably manned
                & all Greece lay prostrate
before that sliding door;
    And Thais knew no such crowd,
        Thais in whom
                the men of Athens took their pleasure,
Nor Phryne, whose profits might have raised new walls
                for blasted Thebes.
There are too many
                of these pretended kin of yours
                    gleaning these familial kisses;
    and these ephebe portraits injure my eyes,
            & the names going with them resound
                with the pain of jealousy in my ears;
Cradled boys alarm me, & your mother's kisses are wounds,
        and when some woman, some sister,
                passes the night with you,
my fear suspects a man under the tunic.
This damned jealousy, this burning flaw,
    has opened great wars, so history has it;
It laid proud Troy in dust;
    the same bitter madness goaded the centaurs
                        to war at wedding feast,[4] grinding chalice
                                        underfoot.

And closer to home, Romulus,
    suckled with crude bitch-milk
left the Sabine rape as his example to posterity,
    & now Eros dares any crime in Rome.

[4] The reference is to the abduction of Ischomache by centaurs at her
wedding feast.

Blessed are Alcestis & Penelope,
   & any woman loyal to a man's gatepost.
Why all the shrines to chastity,
     if any girl will walk where she wishes,
       if any bride may choose her occupation?
And these painted spectacles on our Roman walls
     are not eyed by our young ladies
         to no purpose;
no innocence resides in the gaze, or in the things beheld;
 folly and discord follow silent delight
    wrought by the painter's hand,
& may painters groan in hell for it.
  In old Rome
    no such discordant pleasures
     lit the beholding eye.
Not without reason
   has the spider veiled the holy places,
    Not without reason do the blades of grass grow long
      & wild in sanctuaries of abandoned gods.
And what may guardians prevent, if the girl is unwilling
         to be prevented?
No sour watchman may protect such a vestibule.
  But good faith is its own chaperone, Cynthia.
& as for me
   there will be no wife,
     no seductive young woman
      but Cynthia,
   my wife & mistress always.

7

Hers was a true delight,
    when that law was repealed;[5]
      that edict we wept over,
        our tears extended, the decree divisive.
But a love such as ours cannot be riven by any god,
      not Zeus himself.
"Ah, but Caesar is powerful."
    But his strength is in war,
        the scepter of conquest means nothing in love.
I would sooner lose my head
      to the executioner
than abandon this flame at a bride's will,
    or pass by your shut door,
      a married man
with a damp eye, your lintel forsaken.
What dreams would my flute sing to you then,
    flute sadder than funeral tuba?
My blood will cede no soldiers,
      but if I might follow your one true camp,
      even Castor's great horse
would not be a suitable mounting.
For only in love, indeed,
     did my name deserve to be chained to glory,
       glory borne beyond Caucasian snows.
You alone please me, Cynthia,
 let me be your singular pleasure also,
and your love will mean more to me
      than the title "father" ever could.

---

[5] A law requiring Roman knights, a group including Propertius, to marry had evidently been passed and then repealed. Propertius could not of course marry Cynthia because of her lower social status.

8[6]

You will not have it, friend,
   that the tears melt from my eyes,
     when love out of time past
      is stolen from my arms?
Love spawns the bitterest hatreds;
   I would be a milder enemy
     if he wished merely to cut my throat.
How can I behold her
  against other arms;
    Cynthia lately mine,
     called mine no longer?
The turning of all things
   curves love awry;
  You must stand victor or loser
    in the circle of love's wheel.
Great lords & tyrants bite the dust;
   High Troy & Thebes
     have been thrown down.
What gifts I gave, & what great songs I spun;
   but this brazen girl never spoke,
     never said "I love you."
Have I casually borne
   too many years
    a woman without probity
     and her household?
Have you ever thought me a free man, Cynthia?
   Will your high words ever fail at my ear?
Propertius, will you expire in the best part of your manhood?
Is there no precedent?

---

[6] In the Loeb edition II.8 has been rendered as two poems, but it seems to me to be one poem, as in the manuscript. The break after line 44 indicates the omission of lines.

[72]

Didn't Haemon join his bones
    with miserable Antigone's,
        his own knife under his ribs?
He could not go home without her.
Pass away then, Propertius,
    & let her rejoice
    that I leave men's company.
Let her censure my shade,
    & chatter at my ghost,
  & dance over the funeral coals;
        let her tread on my bones.
But you deserve to go with me,
    gore staining the iron.
Such inglorious departure would dishonor my name—
    but it would be an equitable settlement.

. . . .

Yet empty-hearted Achilles, his prize girl taken,
        stopped work & carried his sword into hiding,
        saw the flight,
            the Achaeans flowing back by sea's edge,
            saw the Dorian tents afire,
        the torch of Hector gleaming among them,
    saw Patroclus' formless corpse
        abraded by blood & sand
        fallen with hair outspread—
all on account of
        a girl's figure.
This the fury
of broken love's pain.
    With his plunder back,
            then came Achilles' revenge—
                somewhat late;

And he hauled great Hector
          after Haemonian horses.
Any astonishment is, then, unwarranted,
    that love is my proper conqueror,
        for I have neither the mother
           nor the arms
    that Achilles had.

9

I used to be
    where he is now
        but with chance
and in due season
        she will reject him also,
        and burn for another more.
Penelope lived inviolate
    through twenty years,
        a woman worthy of
                hotblood princely attention;
    She put them off by craft and skill
        each night loosening & undoing
            her day's weaving
    never expecting to see Ulysses
& growing old in her own house.
            And Briseis
clutching Achilles' corpse
    raked her white face with her nails,
        she, a captive,
mixed tears with his blood,
    Achilles laid out in the yellow shallows
            of the river,
    blackening her hair in mourning
            with ashes
and with her small frame
    bore Achilles' large-boned body.
At that time neither his mother, nor Peleus,
            nor his bereft Deidamia
was at his side,
    but yet Greece rejoiced at her trueborn offspring,
        & war did not extinguish decency.
But you, you

cannot lie unoccupied in your bed
a single night,
& cannot endure a single day alone, you shameless whore,
and indeed you & your lover laugh
as you sprawl in your cups,
& jeer and make jokes at my expense.
And this man you want is the very one
who first jilted & abandoned you;
May the gods make him your permanent affliction.
Is this the acknowledgment of my vows
& prayers
when death hovered close by your head
and your friends stood grieving around your couch?
Where was this lover then?
And what if I had been soldiering in the East,
or if my ship had ridden at mooring
in the Western Ocean?
You lie and dissemble well,
that being a thing all women learn.
The shoals of the Syrtes do not shift in a storm
as quickly
as a woman's love pact is broken in anger,
no matter how trivial the cause,
nor do the leaves fly in the winter wind
with such abandon.
But I see that this intent of yours
pleases you; I yield to it.
May Eros riddle me completely;
the blood is on your hands,
and great honor shall it bring you.
The stars and morning frost,
and the door you once left open,
all bear witness
that I never loved anything in this life

[76]

more than you.
    And it remains so, despite everything;
I will take no other mistress to my bed,
      & I will part company with Aphrodite,
      & if I have drawn out my years
        a steadfast and godly man
may the gods then grant
    that your bedmate
      become a stone in mid passion.

. . . .

As the Theban kings fought
    despite their own mother,[7]
so would I with him, despite Cynthia,
providing I could divine beforehand
      a favorable outcome.

[7] The brothers Eteocles and Polynices killed each other despite the pleas of their mother, Jocasta.

10

The time comes
   for a new dance on the mountain,
      a new rite on Helicon;
The time comes
    to chant horsemen under the hill,
       and I will now sing of battle,
           & squads of heroes, & Caesar's Roman camp;
And if my strength fails,
    still, a laudable essay
 To try the great song
           brings its own commendation.
In a man's early years, his tune is a love tune;
    let age sing of swordplay;
   War will be my canticle
      when Cynthia's beauty
     is well inscribed in my books.
I would now wear
    a graven frown
      & learn a new lute,
    my spirit rising from the low song
     taking strength out of heaven,
       for the work needs a booming voice.
Now the Euphrates rolls
    unguarded by Parthians,
     & Persia grieves to have cut down the Crassi;
India kneels before Caesar,
        & virgin Arabia trembles in her tent;
For Caesar's hand will soon menace
the rims of the wide earth,
    & I will follow along
      tall among camp poets;
    may fate reserve me that honor.

[78]

But when we cannot reach
          a great statue's pinnacle
     we lay our wreaths
               at the foot;
and so now, without means
          to lift up a crown of song
     I put my myrrh in the fire
               with the simple ceremony of poverty,
for my verses are not yet baptized
                    in the fountain of Hesiod,
          but their tune still flows
     from the bright stream holy
               to Aphrodite.

11

Your song must wait
    on a new singer
    or else you will be suitably unrenowned;
Let him praise you
    who would lay down his seed
                 without fruit.
The truth is,
    though you will hardly believe it,
        that these gifts of yours
           will be borne off with you
               on your couch
  on that bleak day to come,
  & no traveler
      passing by
        will see your white bones
    and know & compliment
        the shining mind
that once graced them with wisdom.

12

Would your wonder
        not prove him dextrous,
            that artist who first painted Eros puerile?
He first
        drew out the truth
        that love lives at the expense of judgment,
    and that great goods
            may be run through
                for a fickle girl's love;
And it was not without reason,
        fitting the god out
            with inconstant wings
    to move lightly in the heart;
        And we are broken in the surge,
            and the bright air moves
                in no sure direction.
It was not without reason,
        the barbed shafts depicted in hand,
            The Cretan quiver nestled beneath the shoulder,
        seeing how he strikes,
            & strikes before we safely see the menace;
        and with that wound comes madness.
The young god sticks yet to his youth
            & his bolts stick in my heart,
                but his wing feathers are ruined,
                no wingbeat leaving my heart;
                    his wars break through my blood.
But what delight is there
        to rage in my bones?
A prouder god
    would bring his sword
        into other hearts—

better to stain a virgin youth;
     for you lay your whip
          on a thin shadow,
          not on the man I was.
And if you bring me
          to absolute ruin,
          who then will lift up your song?
This light Muse within me,
               is your greatest glory, Eros,
          and after me what melody
               will celebrate her face,
     who will sing her hands,
          & what canticle
               will light the sloe eyes,
     & set forth the slow footfall,
          of Cynthia, my beloved?

13

Like the bright arrows
        driven home in a multitude
          by Tuscan bowmen,
      the flaming missiles of Eros stitch my heart;
Eros orders me
   to walk under the oriflamme
          of the slender Muses
       & live in Hesiod's sacred grove;
Not so I might sing wild creatures
         down mountain valleys in Thrace,
       or float my lyrics among the oaks of Helicon;
But so I might astonish a girl,
       take her with my song.
Thereat I should be more famous
    with my art
      than Linus, lyre teacher of Orpheus.
I admire more than her beauty,
     nor is it enough
   for a woman to be of a pure & proud descent.
Let it be my joy to have chanted my verses
      reclining with a brilliant girl
  & for my meters to have found esteem
      in her hearing.
These things fulfilled,
    the public in its wordy confusion
      no longer concerns me
For I will be content with Love for a judge.
   If by chance
  she is peaceful
   and pleased at my poems
   I disdain then
    the hostility of the gods.

13*a*

Whenever, therefore,
  Death shrouds the faint light in my eye,
    proceed thus with the funeral:
Set forth, Cynthia, with no long retinue,
  walk without ostentation
    & without effigies;
let no sounding tuba
    fan a complaint
        in the void of my doom;
lay me on no ivory-foot couch,
    lay the corpse on no golden bier,
    set out no row of censers smoking;
Let only a short procession be strung out;
        a plebeian burial.
And in that solemn train
        three books will be sufficient wealth
            borne down to the queen of hell,
    and you will follow after,
        wounds on naked breast,
  no weariness muting my name on your lips,
    and you will seal my cold lips then
        with an ultimate kiss,
  and then bestow the onyx chest
        with its Syrian treasure;
& when I am cinders,
    by the flame set under me,
    lay the ashes in burnt clay,
    build no great sepulcher,
        & plant laurel on the grave,
        that the shade cover the extinction
        of the fire;
and inscribe this verse:

[84]

BOOK II

And the glory of my tomb
    will be no less known
        than Achilles' blood-stained mound.
And Cynthia, when you arrive at the end of things, remember
  come down this same path
    in death
    to this stone by my memory
& meanwhile,
      don't despise this grave;
  the earth remains alive to some little of the truth.
Would that one of the triple Fates
    had murdered me in my cradle;
  for why is the spirit kept
    only for the wavering moment?
In three generations of mortal men
  no man saw Nestor's winding-sheet,
    but if some Trojan archer
  from Trojan ramparts
    had brought short the far-strung doom
      of his old age
    he would never have seen the interment of his son,
& he would never have cried
  "Death, death, why do you loiter more,
    you come too late."
Yet lamentation for a friend gone
is not uncommon;
Love is the everlasting due
    of those who have now passed by.
Witness Adonis, in splendor stricken by the boar,
  in the high ridges of Idalia,
    a pretty youth laid out

[85]

in the mountain marsh,
and there
      came the great goddess Aphrodite,
         hair floating out in mourning;
But with neither effect nor reason
      will you call back the silent shadow, Cynthia,
      and bones are mute.

14

No joy equal to mine
   was Agamemnon's
      at fallen Troy's fruits,
& no such delight
          was sea-wandering Ulysses'
        beached in his well-loved Ithaca,
Nor was Electra [8] so pleased
  as she embraced the urn in tears,
    her brother thriving,
Nor Ariadne, seeing Theseus safe
        out of the threaded maze.
My ecstasies exceeded all theirs
      in the aura of our night's conjunction;
   such nights are reserved for gods;
     my immortality thus now assured.

Formerly when I went to her
   a shambling beggar
she would abuse me after;
   worse than a dry spring,
     she would say.
Now, though, her iniquitous pride subsides,
  & she no longer toys with my feelings,
    but god how I wish I had known;
     the secret of no help to me now.
I am a burned-out shell,
    beyond help,
and the path was well lit,
     & I was blind,

[8] In Sophocles' *Electra*, Orestes, Electra's brother, came home disguised and carrying an urn supposedly containing his own ashes.

[87]

but no man sees well
    an erotic beam in his eye.
But then, this magic:
    return her disdain,
      and she will come in the morning
        though she turned you out
  the previous night.
And others came, & shouted, & rattled her door,
    but my supple mistress reclined in my arms,
a greater conquest
    than Parthia plundered.
She is my captured gold, queen, & victory chariot.
I will nail my gift to your column, Aphrodite;
      under my name, the carved verse:

    THE POET LAYS THESE GARMENTS
      AT YOUR ALTAR, GODDESS,
    FOR A WHOLE NIGHT, SHE TOOK ME IN

Now my boat comes to shore, O light of my eyes,
    a full ship, shall it break in the shallows?
If you change now, Cynthia,
    through any fault of mine,
      may the gods strike me down,
May I be struck down
    in your very chamber.

15

Ah, delightful night,
    radiant with joys
        couched in whispers;
Our hot whisperings of love
          burned under the lamp
          and how we rolled & struggled
when the lamp was darkened,
   & how we wrestled,
        her breasts bared one moment,
         the next putting me off with closed tunic.
And she nuzzled my eyes
    with her soft lips
     & reproached me for lying there calmly.
We exchanged embraces,
        coiling, uncoiling,
         entwining arms first one way, then another,
   and our kisses lingered in abundance.
No pleasure comes from blind twisting about;
      It mars lovemaking;
      the eyes should light our caresses.
Paris himself was brought to distraction
  at the sight of Helen naked
     coming from the chamber of Menelaus;
Endymion was naked when he inflamed the heart
      of Luna the moon, they say,
    and she came to lie with him,
      the goddess being nude also.
But if you will lie abed obstinately clothed
you will have your tunic torn off
      in my fist,
& further provocation, on your part,
    will earn you livid arms

to display to your mother.
Aging breasts do not yet
    keep you from bedplay;
only women who have borne children
    and are shamed by it
      need be thus abstinent.
Let us satisfy our eyes with love
    while Fate allows it;
The long night comes
    for which the day will not return.
Let us lock in an embrace
    that no day will come to sunder;
      Let the coupled doves of Aphrodite
      be our example.
To want the fire of passion to die
    is wrong,
    for true love has no fixed measure.
The earth will sooner delude the farmer
    with a false bloom of spring
& sooner will the sun whip the black horses of night
    across the sky
and river water run backward
      and the abyss be parched
    and fish swim thirsty
Than I would love any but Cynthia;
    I will live faithful to her
      & hers I will die.
As long as she yields such nights to me
    a single year is a long life,
      with many nights I would be immortal, even
      with one evening a god.
If all men conducted their lives after my example
    & lay down heavy with wine
    there would be no brutal death by ship or sword,

our bones would not turn in the sea off Actium
nor would Rome suffer triumphs over her own
       & ache with mourning.
Certainly our descendants can say
      that our chalice wounded no god.[9]
Do not abstain from life's fruits just now
        with the light yet with you,
   give me all the kisses you can
      and that will still be too few;
  and just as drying-out garlands shed their leaves—
you see them floating
        strewn here and there in the wine cups—
so now lovers with high hopes
  may find the morning
      closing out their fate.

[9] This odd passage for such a poem—"If all men . . . wounded no
god"—says much about the poet and about the times in which he lived.

16

Your newly come Illyrian,
    your praetorian treasure,
    is of some concern to me as well;
I cannot applaud his escaping
        rock-shoaled Ceraunia.
Ah, Neptune, if you had heard my prayer
        what riches you would have had.
Now, the laden board & the banquet, without me;
    Now, her door is swung wide, in my absence.
But Cynthia,
    I trust your native quickness
        won't overlook opportunity,
an opportune harvest, or perhaps a shearing.
        Then, his substance yours,
        invite him to hoist his threadbare sails for home.
Cynthia attends
        no bundle of rods,
    & she cares for no accolade,
but she loves her boyfriends' togas
        or the fat wallets therein.
And from me, she wants Indian gemstones
    & demands gifts shipped from Phoenicia,
        demands them constantly.
I wish no man in Rome was rich,
I wish Caesar's palace was straw,
    & no woman up for sale;
    and then a woman's hair might grow white
        in one house.
And Cynthia
        would not
        lie down elsewhere then
    seven nights on end

polished limbs stretched out for so foul a man.
And I haven't wronged you
    (you must grant that);
it is, rather, that lovely girls
        will run lightly through a multitude.
And this barbarian, a coal in his loins,
    paces before your gate,
& suddenly he reigns in my place.
O Aphrodite, aid me,
    may his constant lust dismember him.
Can any man buy her,
    enjoy bartered love?
Then by god she will be undone.
    Remember how bitter were Eriphyle's gifts,
        and how Creüsa burned in her bridal gown.
Can't my wounds be healed by tears
        or will my pain bed down
            with your vices always?
Some days have passed now,
        in which I have had no heart for the theater,
            or the games; and I rise up from a full table.
My shame, this great chagrin,
        may it cure me of folly.
But perhaps love has no sense of honor,
    perhaps lovers are shameless
& heedless of ridicule.
Witness Antonius, who lately filled the sea
        with damned soldiers,
    their cries hollow in the wave troughs;
        ill-founded love leading him on,
    turning his keels to the earth's rim,
        a refugee.
(And it is Caesar's glory & virtue
        that he conquered & laid away the gauntlet.)

But may I see all your praetor's riches,
      his robes, his emeralds, his golden chrysolite,
sucked off by a shrieking wind;
    May they turn into dust, or dissolve into water.
Zeus is ungentle with perjury in love;
    he is not deaf to prayer.
    You have heard the thunder splitting heaven,
    seen the lightning in the house of Aether.
These are no threats from the Pleiades,
      from rain-bringing Orion.
The god of Olympus has his signs of displeasure,
      & he once shed tears at a woman's guile.
Lying girls do not escape forever.
    You might remember the possibility of retribution
      & shed your Sidonian tunic [10]
    when the south wind blackens the sky.

[10] "Sidonian tunic." I.e., ill-gotten gains.

17

To lie, to break the promise of a night's love,
   is to stain your hands with your lover's blood.
I am the singer of these songs; how many times I have filled
   the bitter night with silence,
       an exile from your chamber.
May your heart beat less coldly
     seeing Tantalus with a dry mouth
        by an abundance of water
          falling away, enticing his thirst,
Seeing Sisyphus at his fantastic task,
    laboring behind the rolling boulder on the mountainside,
and seeing that a lover's road is harder,
    a fact the wise should know.
I once bore men's envy, but now
   the price of admission is a week's abstinence.
O I would get some satisfaction, my faithless Cynthia,
   leaping off a cliff, or taking fine-ground poison
       in my hands
now that we can no longer meet in the cross-paths of Hecate
      under the dry moon, & lie in repose,
   & I cannot whisper through the chinks in your door.
Ah, but for all these things, despite them all,
   I would not change you,
for the time will come when your tears will betoken
      some feeling for my faithfulness.

18[11]

Assiduous complaining
   spawns retribution;
     A woman often breaks on a man's silence;
If you have seen anything, build no quarrel on it;
   If you have been hurt
     deny the pain.

What if my hair should whiten
   & age web my countenance?
Aurora didn't disdain old Tithonus [12]
   in her eastern palace,
  she frequently embraced him hotly
    before she left with her horses,
  & as she lay limbs laced with his
    she complained of the cycling days
  as the sun came
& she decried Olympian justice as she mounted her chariot,
   and did quotidian duty in the world unwillingly.
Tithonus living was a compensation
    for her lost Memnon,
& it was the joy and pride
   of dawn's excellent deity
  to sleep with an old man
    & kiss his white hair.
But you would hate me even if I were a stripling youth,
  though you will be
    a withered hag
in the light of future sunrises soon enough.

[11] This elegy, with unusually abrupt transitions, is presented as three separate poems in the Loeb edition.
[12] See Ovid's *Amores* for a quite different version.

Indeed the custom of Eros
to bring grief to those
whom he has treated well before
comforts me somewhat.

But you
even now you recklessly emulate
rouge-cheeked British girls,
you entice men to pleasure
with the gleam of foreign cosmetic.
The tinge of Belgian lipstick
on a Roman girl
is an odious thing;
the greatest beauty is always as nature made it.
Let evil overtake the girl
who deceives with dyed hair,
save a place for her in hell.
You can appear more truly beautiful to me
by appearing more often.
What of a girl who smears her face
with blue shadowing?
Can an azure face be lovely?

Since you have neither brother
nor son
I should assume their duties;
Always be fastidious
in the custodianship
of your chamber
& do not go seductively veiled
& ornamented.
You might avoid indiscretion,
for rumor walks by land & sea
& I will believe
rumors of your infamy.

[97]

19

You take your leave from Rome,
    though it is no wish of mine;
I am pleased only
            that it's a lonely country
            where you will be without me.
No seductions in those virgin fields,
        no flatterers drawing you from upright chastity,
        no commotion before your windows,
a sound sleep, with no acrid speeches
                on the other side of your door.
You will live without company
                & look out on singular mountains;
No amusements will divert you from rectitude;
        country temples [13] are not consecrated
            to your libertine rites.
You will see there
        only the drawn-out furrow with a bull at the end of it
                & the collapse of grape leaves
                    before sickle swing;
You will bear thin myrrh
                to shrines little visited,
                offer a small goat to a wild altar's fire,
& dance bare-legged in desert places.
    May no man intrude on this.
And I
        will turn to the hunt, delight in Diana,
    lift up vows in her worship,
                and lay Aphrodite
                    to one side,

[13] Lovers often met in temples.

[98]

& set snares
　　　　for the untamed foot,
　　　　　　offer horns to the pine tree,
　　yell behind ravening dogs—
　　　　　　but forgoing the lion chase, of course,
　　　　　　& pursuit of the boar;
I am better suited to confront instead
　　　　　the subtle hare,
　　　　　　& nail birds with reed arrows from a tight bow,
　　where water veils the groves with light
　　　　　among shining herds in Umbria.[14]
But remember, whatever you do there,
　　　　　I will join you
　　before Lucifer lights the morning
　　　　　　too many times more.
Keep to the aforesaid things,
　　　　　and no empty forest
or winding creeks feeding through moss on long ridges
　　　　　　will keep your name from my lips;
I would not wrong you in your absence,
　　　　　　or be wronged.

---

[14] These two lines, although suggested by the Latin, are not a strict
translation.

20

It eludes me why
  the hot tears mark your face
like Briseis bereft of Achilles
        & why you cry more bitterly
        than unhappy Andromache.
My god, you rave and beseech heaven
    to rectify my supposed unfaithfulness,
    & complain that I no longer love you.
              Why?
Why is it? The nightingale mourns with no such racket
            among the leaves in Attica,
    nor is haughty Niobe guilty
      of letting slide so many tears
          down the mountain,
        despite those 12 tombs.
Even if I were stashed away
        in Danaë's treasure donjon
      & my arms shackled with brass,
    yet for your benefit, my dear, I would sunder brass
          & break out of the iron tower.
I don't give a damn
      what others say of you
& I adjure you
        return the favor
    and doubt not my fidelity.
I swear to you by the sacred bones
        of my father & mother
—& if I deceive you, may their spirits exact a hard death—
that I will be yours until that final darkness;
    we will be carried off together.
If neither the luster of your name held me
        nor the glory of your looks

then I might yet be bound by your delicate ways.
    The full moon has risen in the night seven times
      since the lounging street-corner gossipers
      began their whispers of you & me,
  and in that time
      I have often been welcomed under your lintel
        & shown the pleasures of your bed.
I bought not one night with gold or gifts;
    whatever I have been with you
has been through your passion
      & I give thanks for it.
Many desired you, & you sought only me—
    can I forget such fire
        & such favors?
If it happens, may the foul Furies seize me;
    may I be condemned by a bleak judge to hell,
& gnawed by wandering buzzards,
      & may I labor without end
  on the hill under that slippery boulder.
Send me no more begging tablets;
    I will be as faithful at the last as at the beginning
& in this I am forever vindicated;
    Alone among lovers
I do not undertake love quickly, or rashly end it.

21

May Aphrodite devise
　　　as many evils for Panthus
　　　as he invented lies about me;
You must admit
　　　I fortune-tell as well as Dodona's oracle,
for your pretty lover has got himself a bride.
　　　Are so many nights passed away & lost?
Is your honor unruffled?
　　　　　Notice: he sings in freedom
　　　　　and you lie alone; you were taken in
　　　　　　too easily.
And you are now a topic of their conversation,
　　　& it is his sneering declaration
　　　　　that you came to his house
　　　　　against his will.
May I be damned absolutely
　　　if he wants anything at all
　　　　　but the renown of having had you;
　　　No small glory for this bridegroom.
Thus strange Jason once cheated
　　　　　that girl from Colchis,
　　ejected her from her house,
　　　　　Creüsa then installed therein;
And Calypso was deceived by a boy from Ithaca,
　　　& she later beheld her lover
　　　　　stretch out his sails.
You young women who offer too quickly,
　　　with only a whisper at the ear,
　　　　　learn, now deserted, not to say yes too lightly;
But already, Cynthia, you have begun
　　　looking for another;
　　　one who might stand more firmly.

Lunatic girl,
     caution can be learned in one easy lesson.
But for all that,
    I am yours, my love,
      in good health or in sickness,
       in whatever place,
        or whatever the nature of the times.

22

Once
    many girls pleased me equally
        & you know, Demophoön, that a good many evils
           came of it.
No crossroads bordello escapes my probings;
    I explore not in vain,
        & too much theater has ruined me;
Some provocative girl
    standing with her radiant arms outstretched
                            inviting
    her lips rounding out
        the rhythms of her songs,
And even then my glittering eyes
        search out my own undoing,
    & light on some gleaming attraction,
        some girl sitting with uncovered breast
        with an Indian jeweled clasp in her hair
        & a lock of hair down over her eyes,
And if she refuses me
    with a hard look
        cold sweat trickles down my forehead.
You ask, Demophoön, why I am so tender
    to one & all.
Love has no reply to such a question.
Why do Cybele's cultists lacerate their arms
    with sacred cutlery
        & slash themselves
      to the twisting cadences of the Trojan fife?
Nature fashions each man a vice
    & Fortune ordains continual love as mine.
Even if Thamyras' fate walk behind me
I would never be blind to beauty,

my envious friend,
   & if you think me thin, & feeble in the joints,
      you are wrong.
Serving Aphrodite is never too much work
    but the question is allowable.
For often a girl's proving lasts the night
       & I retain the power of my ministry until dawn.
Jupiter laid the northern constellations to rest
        two nights on end for Alcmene
   & the heavens were two evenings without their king;
     But he did not return to the thunderbolt
      languid from his labors;
        love is always renewable.
When Achilles rose from Briseis' embrace
     & went out, did the Trojans panic any the less
       in the face of Thessalian lance point?
And when ferocious Hector walked forth
      from Andromache's chamber
     did not Agamemnon's fleet have good cause for fear?
Either man could bring down walls
      and splinter ships,
   & in love I am
      as Achilles was, or lusty Hector.
Consider how the sun & the moon serve the sky,
   & two hawsers keep a ship better
      & twins are best for a worried mother;
Even so one girl is too few for me;
    if one will not have me
     another will receive me
     & lie hot with me
       with eager strength.
If one girl is angry
     with my ministrations
      she should know there are others waiting.

22a

You need not enter my door
  if your heart hardens against me,
    but come to me
        if you love me yet.
But why waste words?
    To be left waiting for one's love
        is a pain that penetrates the soul
    as none other,
    & how the victim's breath
        wracks him in his bed;
He refuses to believe she won't come
    & he fatigues the servant boy
        with that question
        with the unchanging answer,
    & sends him to verify
        the ill turn feared.

23

Quondam disdainer of the common way
       & paths of the vulgar unlettered,
Propertius now inclines
     to go with the multitude,
    to partake of the public tank;
That water is sweet to me now.
Should any freeman enrich
       his lady's slave boy
      that he might have words from her, in writing?
And be always inquiring
    whether her feet tread the Campus,
      and where on the Campus,
and "where is she now, in the shadow
      of which portico is she now?"
Then, after labors eloquent as Hercules'
     to get a letter:
"Have you no gift for me?"
Then it becomes your pleasure
   to return the knit-browed stare
      of some sour chaperone,
   & often then your captivation leads you
   to lie in secret
    in some dirty hovel,
a hell of a price
      for one night in a year.

But one may turn elsewhere;
there is that girl
    who strolls in liberty
      with her cape thrown back
    and no cloak of fear—
  is she not more

to your liking,
she whose slippers polish the path
in her promenade
on the Via Sacra?
No hesitation
when you ask her to come,
no delay,
and she is more demure in asking
what your astringent father has given you
(that gentleman who cries out so much
at your expenses).
Nor will she demand your instant departure
saying she is afraid
saying her husband returns from the country,
returns this very day.
Let these girls from Persia & Syria
be my delight;
I want no more of this furtive modesty
in my lady's chamber.
You have this choice only; love or your liberty
since no man may both love
and stay free.

24

"And you will say this,
      with your book gotten notorious,
    & your Cynthia inspected in the Forum?" [15]

Now, such words
      would break sweat onto any man's forehead,
    whether from embarrassed honor, or a wish
        that certain affairs remain unspoken.
But if Cynthia's breast moved close
      in her pleasures again,
  I would not be called Rome's chief prodigal,
      & have an infamous reputation
  making its way through the streets;
and however much I burned
      with misdirected lust,
I could at least manage
      to dissimulate in the matter.
But let no man be amazed
    that I look for cheaper girls
for they display a seemlier moderation
        in backstabbing.
    Does my reason seem fickle?
And as for Cynthia, at one moment
    she demands a fine fan
      of peacock feathers,
with the next she would cool her fingers
       with jewels; and she will risk my anger
      wheedling for ivory dice
  & whatever gaud glitters along the Via Sacra.
I will be damned

---

[15] In the rest of this poem, Propertius defends himself against this anonymous reproach.

if the expense bothers me,
but it is the shame,
   being an anecdote
   in the career
      of this treacherous woman.

24*a*

Was it your will, from the first,
    that I delight in *this*? [16]
Doesn't your face burn, my inconstant lovely Cynthia,
    when we consume one night in love
& with the next you declare me
    a burden to your bed?
You would go through my songs & extol them,
    & now does your light love
        drift off so quickly?
Let this other gentleman compete
    in talent or skill, & in so doing learn
to confine his desires to one house.
Of if you are amenable, try him, give him
    some Herculean test, [17]
or have him choke down whatever you would have him drink,
    seawater after shipwreck, or poison,
& abstain from no misery in your service
    (I rather wish your whispers demanded
    equal efforts from me),
  and then your bold friend might pale a little,
    who now slides into good fortune,
    swollen & boasting.
It will not last a year with him,
    but Sibyl's eons would not divert me,
  nor Herculean workouts,
    nor the black day at the end of things.
You will collect my bones, saying,

[16] Propertius is referring to one of Cynthia's many infidelities, which were probably more numerous than his own.

[17] The "Herculean tests" are specified in the original, but it is hardly necessary to reproduce them in English translation, where they would sound very strange.

"Ah, *you* were faithful, and never betrayed me,
though ordinary blood ran in your grandfather's veins,
    & you had no money."
Neither pain nor wound could change me;
    Your great loveliness is no burden,
        though I stagger under it.
Perhaps some few have perished for your figure,
       but I imagine more have victimized you,
    after certain examples;
for Theseus prized Ariadne—as far as Naxos,
   & Demophoön cherished Phyllis, for a time,
& Jason laid up safe in his hold
     deserted his enchantress finally.

But then it is a troublesome girl
     who will fit herself out for a crowd.
Do not gauge me against rich men, or the wellborn,
     for they would not come at the last
     to gather up your ashes—
as I would.
But I would prefer a prior departure,
      you sending me off
   with bare breasts
  & hair loose in lamentation.

25

My grief, my lovely sweetheart,
    a pretty pass we've come to
        when fate forbids invitation,
But I will make your splendor
       most notorious,
    with your pardon, Calvus, and your leave, Catullus.
The old legionary sleeps
        with laid-aside sword,
      & an old ox will no longer plow;
The rotting ship lies on deserted beach,
      & the ancient scarred shield stops dust
        on the temple wall;
But years will never desolate my passion,
    not Tithonus' age and not Nestor's.
Cruel Perillus, slave to a hard king,
     had it better roasting in his own bronzework;
   and I would even prefer
      hardening at the look of the Gorgon
    or to suffer under the fowls of the Caucasus;
But I stand firm.
  The water eats away the blade
     and dissolves flint,
But no love that persists
    & bears undeserved insult
     is worn down by the lintel it waits under.
The lover supplicates when scorned
    & admits wrong when himself wronged;
      always returns with reluctant foot.[18]
But you, you puffed-up fool,
    while your affair prospers remember

[18] Up to this point Cynthia is being addressed; from here on it is her lover who is addressed.

women waver considerably, no woman is permanent.
Does any man give thanks
    while the storm hisses on sea-foam,
      when splintered keels float on lee shores?
Who demands the prize in mid race
    before the wheel grinds over the goal?
The hot winds of love
  drift and whip
    from unexpected quarters,
and love tripped up late is ruinous.
  While she yet esteems you
    confine your delight in a silent heart
  for lavish praises
    undercut love in unknown ways.
Enviable possessions are usually transient;
    Remember that while she still wants you.
If Cynthia were a girl pleased by ancient fashion
  then I would be where you are;
    I am defeated by current style.
But these times haven't changed my nature;
  Let each furbish his own path.
You who want too much
  will suffer pain
    like a needle stitching the eye.
You see an enticing white glamour
  or dark radiance;
  Either seizes and inflames;
Likewise the plebeian girl
  and the girl
    vermilion-cloaked;
  both wound the soul;
One woman is enough
  to bring nightmares out of the dark;
One woman is tribulation enough.

26

In that night, my love,
    I dreamed a broken keel,
    your tired arms splashing
        in Ionian spindrift,
    and heard your duplicity confessed,
yet you couldn't raise up your head,
    long hair heavy in the sea,
        like Helle turned
            by billows shining purple,
that girl once mounted softly
        on a golden ram.
I feared
    you might become a name
        on the sea's list,
    another loss mourned by seamen
        gliding in those waters.
Ah, what prayers I lifted then,
  To Neptune, to the Gemini, & to Leucothoë—now a deity;
And hands awash in the sea-swirl,
    you cried up my name,
        as if you would soon slide under.
And if Glaucus had seen your eyes,
        you would now be a sea nymph,
        to the raucous envy
        of the Nereides.
But a dolphin came under you,
        came to your rescue,
        the same who saved Arion from the sea-grip,
    lyre & all.
But I,
    in the meantime, had dropped
        from the high cliff,
    when panic broke the dream.

26a

Let consternation reign through Rome,
    that I captivate so great a beauty,
    let the news of her enslavement astonish them.
No "rise up from my bed, poet," from her,
    not for a Persian king [19]
        or a golden river; [20]
When my song enchants her
    she avows disdain
        for wealthy men.
And no girl honors the measured verse
    with rites so sacred;
Faith and steadfastness in love
    are worth a good deal,
    and the bearer of great gifts
        may expect a great return.
If she considers carving through the long sea,
    I will stay fast by her side,
    and the wind will slide us
        through the same waves;
    we will lie on the same beach
        shadowed by the same leaves;
We will drink from one well,
        lie together
            on a shipboard plank,
& I will stand against savage easterlies,
    endure cold cutting from the south
        slatting the sails,
and endure the storms that bruised Ulysses,
and jostled the Greek ships aground in Euboea,
        and the winds that broke through

---

[19] Cambyses is named as the Persian king in the original Latin.
[20] The literal translation of the Latin would be "rivers of Croesus."

the two cliffs [21]
when the dove lit on the Argo
to lead the way into the unknown sea.
I fear nothing,
if she remains the light of my eye.
If the god of lightning enkindles our bark
then the waves will wash us naked
onto the same coast;
or let the seas suck me under
if the land may shield her.
But Neptune isn't hostile to Eros,
being his great brother's equal
in amorous disposition;
Amymone will testify to that
who in Argos knew the strength of godly embrace
to break a dry season,
when the trident struck in the swamp,
& the god paid off his promise,
a flow from a golden spring.
And Oreithyia, reft by Boreas from her home,
insisted he wasn't so bad, her plunderer, the north wind's god,
who rumbles in mountain & high ocean.
Have faith, Scylla will weaken for us, & Charybdis,
who drives her riptides endlessly in a waste of ocean.
No blackness will cut off the starlight;
Auriga [22] will glint clear
above bright Orion.
And should I give up my life,
my body entwined with yours,
I would prefer
such a departure
to any other.

[21] The two cliffs are the Symplegades, two rocks at the entrance to
the Black Sea which dashed against each other to crush whatever passed
between them.
[22] The Latin has Haedus, or the Kid, which is part of the constella-
tion Auriga.

27

In the clear skies of the night
  men seek to know
      which star gleams auspiciously,
      which shines evilly,
& they demand to know when and through what chance
  Death will come upon them.
We may run down Parthians by land
    or British pirates by northern sea;
Each course is fraught with blind menace
  and men fear for their lives in battle,
    for Mars bears a two-edged sword;
  Men fear fire and ruin at home
    and the poisoned cup at banquet;
And only lovers may expect death
          without the chill of fear;
Neither sword edge nor the cutting north wind
nor the sight of the ship of hell
    with dark canvas
        from the reeds of the river Styx
need cause lovers to tremble,
    indeed even after the funeral fire
      a woman's anguished cry
may call up her lover,
    a shaded vision
        from the darkness.

28

Zeus save her, I pray you,
    Do not stain godly hands
        with such evil,
           the death of so beautiful a woman.
Now burnt wisps of air move
      in a dry season;
   now the earth glows arid
      under the glimmering Dog of the night sky;
But no fire of heaven brings this fever,
      rather her own neglect,[23]
        her disesteem for deity
          at the root of it,
   as in the disasters of other lovely girls
        in times past;
Now wind & sea drown out her invocations.
      Has comparison wounded Dione,
         goddess envious of all competing beauty,
    or did you neglect Hera's shrine?
        Or slight the splendor of Athena's looks?
A sharp & audacious tongue
      is the frequent gift of pulchritude,
   and your words & loveliness
      work to your injury.
Death yawns close and dangerous,
    but an easier day may rise
      from this extremity.
The Nile was the water trough
    of the horned goddess Io
in her early years

[23] This line and the preceding one, together with some others, indicate that the poem was written after Cynthia had safely recovered from her fever.

but her fortune has improved.
   And Ino once strayed through the world,
      but now mariners implore the blessing
of that lady transformed, the sea nymph Leucothoë;
and Andromeda was put out in chains as food
     for the creatures of ocean,
     but renowned Perseus made her his bride;
And Callisto once
      rooted through Arcadia as a bear,
   whereas her stars
     now stake out the sea-lanes
      for night-filled sails.
If ill fortune carries you
      to the rites of the pyre,
then go and exchange stories with Semele
    of the perils of glamour and good looks,
and you will take the foremost place
    even among Homeric heroines,
& there will be no votes cast against you.
Prepare yourself as best you can,
    meet calamity with dignity
    though destiny strikes you hard;
and God & your funeral day
    may both be held off,
    and Hera herself may grant a stay,
for the pain of a comely girl's death
    is a knife even in her cold heart.
The magic-twisted rhombos [24]
falls silent, sings no longer;
  the altar flame drifts out,
    the laurel lies smoking,
& the moon now declines to descend from heaven,

[24] A rhombos is a bull-roarer.

and in the night
      from a dark bird,
a bleak tune
      hovering,
          a prophetic note.
But we will float together
      under the sails of the raft
on the indigo lake of hell.
    Pity us both, I pray, not one of us.
If she lives, then I may live also;
      should she fall, then I too will die.
I consecrate these words with a song,
      & I will dedicate these words

    ALL-POWERFUL ZEUS
    CHOSE TO SAVE HER

& she will sacrifice
      & bow before the altar
   & give thanks for deliverance
      from extended peril.

28a

Persephone, may your mildness continue,
Death, abstain from more cruelty,
 for your throne
 raises its shadow
 over too many thousands of lovely women;
Let this one remain here,
  aboveground,
it is not asking too much.
 You have carried off Iope
 & Tyro glows pale in your realm;
Europa is with you,
 & the dam of Minotaur,
and all those comely ladies of Achaea
 & of Troy the long-standing,
   the overthrown kingdom of old Priam
    & Phoebus Apollo;
And the ancient beauties of Rome
  are all gone among shadows,
   smoke in the consuming fire.
Beauty is not long-lived,
  nor is fortune,
mortality awaits both.
But Cynthia, since you have come through this great peril,
 O light in my eyes,
 sacrifice to the Moon,
 reward the Moon with a dance & light a watch fire
   for your vigil;
Ten nights for the Nile goddess also,
   do it on my behalf.

BOOK II

29

In the evening late [25]
    ambling drunk
        without her, the flame of my soul
      & no hand of a servant to guide me;
  a stripling gang came from the dark,
      and fear shadowed my eyes
    seeing the torch glitter on the barbs
          of the arrows;
   and they came bringing chains
    & they came nude,
  and one lewder than the rest cried:
"Ah, the notorious poet, consigned to our tender mercies
    by the fury of his girlfriend. Grab him."
Then they put a rope around my neck,
    & I was thrown down among them,
    & when they were through
    one of them declared:
  "Don't think we aren't on a worthy errand;
    your mistress waited several long hours
      for an undeserving lover, a fool out
        sniffing around other doors.
But when she takes off her Phoenician gown
    & moves her heavy eyes
      you will breathe an odor sweeter
      than herbs of Arabia,
    an odor that is love's own work. Notice
We come to the house according to our orders."
  And thus with this escort
I returned to my mistress

---

[25] The original reads *hesterna*, "last night," but I have changed the phrasing to make it accord with the ending of the poem. Usually, as in the Loeb translation, II.29 is given as two poems, the second starting with line 32, "And the dawn had come."

        once again.
"You should learn to pass the night at home."
And the dawn had come,
    & I wondered if *she* had kept a chaste couch
        & indeed she lay in bed alone.
And I was dazzled;
        she had never been more splendid,
            not even when she went before Vesta
                emblazoned in purple
                    to narrate her dreams
            so neither of us should come to harm.
She shone in the radiant splendor of nakedness,
    & as she awoke she cried:
        "What? A spy
            with the sunrise?
Do you think I am like you? I am not so nimble.
        One lover is plenty,
            except I would rather have
                a better one than you.
However, you may notice that
    there are no traces of lovemaking in the bed,
        no signs of rolling about in the sheets
            or of two having slept here.
Note that my body doesn't heave with my breathing—
        you know well enough what the signs
                of infidelity are."
Having said this
she kept me off
    with her right arm
as I tried to kiss her
        & then she rushed off
            in her loose sandals.
Since then there have been no pleasant nights:
    my reward

[124]

30

as watchman of her fidelity.
What hardness of soul
      rules these preparations
            for a sea voyage
      to shore dunes past the Hellespont?
Where will your madness take you?
      There is no sanctuary
            from what you run from;
Pursue exile into Russia,
            you can't outrun Eros the god,
                  not even with the aerial wingbeat
                        of Pegasus saddled,
                  not even if Perseus lent you his shoes,
                  not even shot through broken winds
                        by wing-footed sandals.
The high Mercuric road
            will get you nowhere.
Love stretches yet over you,
            indeed over all lovers,
      & bends heavy on once free necks.
And the god keeps
            a sharp-eyed watch,
      & once he has seized you
            he allows you no proud glances
                  from then on.
But if you commit some peccadillo
            your prayers can head off his anger—
                  if they are prompt.
Let hidebound ancient men decry love's banquet;
            their ears are filled
with antique words;
      let us, by this measure,
            burnish the present path, my love.

In this place
    let the bone flute ring
        which Minerva slid into the Maeander
        for swelling her cheeks.[26]
Shall I be disgraced, that I live
        contending peaceably with one woman?
If any crime is involved,
        it is crime at love's command,
        let no man reprove me.
Let it be your delight, Cynthia,
        to hold me softly
            in rain-struck declivities
        on moss-backed ridges;
and there, you might see the Sisters [27] lingering
        in the high cliffs
            where they sing the secret affairs
                sweet to Zeus in the old days;
        how Semele was consumed in his fire,
            how Io's love brought ruin down,
                how finally the god came
                in strange plumage to Troy [28]—
no human stands who could resist those wings,
        so why am I
        alone the accused defendant
                in the common crime?
Let it not disturb you,
that those ladies look respectable;
        Even that choros knows

---

[26] Several lines of the Latin following this line are unintelligible in the context and have not been translated.

[27] The Muses.

[28] Possibly a reference to Ganymede, who was beloved and carried off by Zeus in the guise of an eagle.

what love is like,
      if one [29] from among them truly lay
            on the rocks of Bistonia
            squeezed by her apparent boyfriend.
And when they put you
      at the front
            of the dance,
      Bacchus behind
            with his bright lance,
   only then will I endure
      the sacred corymb
            dangling at my ears;
Without you
      what is my genius?

[29] Calliope, with whom lay Apollo, disguised as her lover Oeagrus.

31

You demand to know
         why I come to you late?
Well, today I stopped for the grand opening
         of Apollo's magnificent portico,
built by munificent Caesar;
     a lot of Punic columns spaced out,
             statuary between pillars, a plethora of Danaïdes.
Inside, the temple
built of bright marble
(what god doesn't like marble?),
& at the two gables ran solar chariots,
     and the doors are worked in fine Libyan elephant tusk;
one depicts the fall of the Gauls,
         kicked off Parnassus,
the other displays Niobe's death;
And round the altar stood Myron's oxen,
         four cattle animated by the signature
             of the sculptor's art.
And in the shrine stood Apollo himself, lord of Delphi,
     in a long robe, between mother & sister,
         & in an attitude of song—
     he seemed prettier in marble than otherwise
             lips open to the silent lyre's tune.
(That's why I am late in coming to you.)

32

Sin alights in the eye
   of your beholder;
     desire resides
   in the eye's gleam;
You walk undesired
      only when you walk unseen.
Why do you seek out the quavering oracle
       at Praeneste, O Cynthia?
Why do you make for the walls of Telegonus,
   and drive your fancy chariot
      to Herculean Tibur,
& roll through the Appian Way to Lanuvium?
Better to walk here
     in your idleness,
but I cannot trust you
     when the crowd sees you go
      with enkindled pitch-pine
       light in the glade
   in Hecate's ritual.
You shy away, now,
    from the muck of Pompey's colonnade;
     you steer clear of Rome's coffled plane trees,
      & the stream threading lightly
     from silent Maro
  through the city in a whisper of spirits
      into the Triton's mouth.
But you go astray in this madness;
     you run from my eyes, not from Rome,
   and you think you will trip me up;
but your nets are laid badly,
    your scheme is transparent.
& I know you will feel

the ruin of your reputation
    as much as you ought to;
It is nothing to me, personally,
      that loose tongues abuse you,
      that no good is spoken of you in all Rome.
One cannot, after all, trust gossip,
      eternal enemy of loveliness;
    and after all, you have not been caught
      poisoning anyone,
    the sun has brought no such crime to light;
    and if you consume the long night
      in dalliance
      once in a while,
that small wickedness leaves me unwounded.
Helen betrayed father & country
    in her amorous mutability,
      & was brought back alive, no writ condemning her;
And Aphrodite herself
    was borne down by Mars's violent love
      & she is no less
      a respectable luminary on Olympus;
and Paris once laid a goddess [30] among sheep
      in full view of Ida's whole population,
    hamadryads saw it, & sileni,
      & the father of that dance; [31]
and you, Naiad, you gathered the fruit,
    catching it as it fell,
      in a hollow place on the mountain.
And after that swarm of disgraces
    can anyone ask "Why is she rich?"
      or "Who was the donor" & "Is his money respectable?"
Rome's cup spills over

---

[30] Oenone, nymph of Mount Ida.   [31] Pan.

if in these days
    one girl abstains from the fashion.
Lesbia enjoyed these pleasures before Cynthia,
  & the second can no more be blamed than the first.
The man who cries out for the lean virtues of old Rome
      cries out that he is a newcomer here.
You could no more dry the streaming sea
   or take down the high stars
     than enforce virginity in Rome.
That was once the custom, in Saturn's reign
    before Deucalion's waters rolled through the world;
But after the flood receded, tell me
    who kept a chaste bed,
what goddess was content with one god only?
& don't forget Minos' gleaming queen
   with that bull,
  & Zeus, entering the brass donjon,
      nor could Danaë deny him.
If you would follow illustrious examples,
  the exemplary Greeks, the exemplary Romans,
  live in liberty then, with my understanding.

33

Now the cycling rites return;
   for ten nights now
     Cynthia has let the night bleed out
to mysteries engendered
       in the heat of the Nile.
The sacrament sent
    from the Lady of Egypt
     to the daughters of Rome
is most odious,
   inflicting hard abstinence
      on longing lovers.
You were always a bitter goddess, Io.
For your secret nights with Zeus
     you felt the dust
     of the world's roadways;
Hera crowned you with horns
   & you lost your girlish voice
     & the oak foliage wounded your mouth
and in your stall
   you shifted bitter leaves in your jaws.
Have you become disdainful
  now that you've become a proper deity?
Do Egypt's dark children
     please you no longer,
      must you come to distant Rome?
Does it please you
     for girls to sleep alone?
Watch out, wild goddess,
you may find the horns all anew,
  your ritual driven from these hills.
Nilotic cults are alien to the Tiber.
  And you, Cynthia, you enjoy my distress too much.

But come, after these starlit exemptions,
      let us triple our efforts.
But you notice my words
      only to smile at them.
Icarian oxen turn the stars slowly
      on their northern axle;
Phlegmatic, you continue to drink
      undaunted
        at midnight.
Doesn't your arm tire
    of throwing the anklebones?
God damn the man
    who first made wine from the grape
      & ruined good water with it.
The peasants of Attica
      who did in Icarius
        for making them drunk
were not altogether wrong,
   for the wine scent is bitter.
      Eurytion the centaur, & Polyphemus also,
would testify to that.
  Wine imperils glamour
     & gets the better of manhood,
& a woman in the heat of wine
    may forget her proper lover.

But . . . I speak too harshly,
  I don't mean it.
Bacchus cannot change you,
     so imbibe and look lovely;
the fruit of the vine
     becomes you.
Your trailing laurel hangs over the cup
     & my music

[133]

lifts your soft voice.
Let the wine drench the table
and foam from your golden chalice;
no woman withdraws
to her chamber alone
with pleasure;
Love always compels
a certain desire
for a certain one . . .
And the fires burn hotter
with absence;
It is too long abundance
that retards the flame.

34

Would any man
        entrust beauty he loves
                to the care of Cupid?
Through such naïveté
        was my mistress nearly removed
                from my affections.
The words proceed from experience;
        no friend is reliable in love
                and rarely will a man not try
        to obtain what beauty he sees.
Eros sets kinsmen apart,
        sets one friend apart from another,
                brings men out of agreement into conflict.
Menelaus made his guest welcome,
                collected his pay as a cuckold,
        & Medea followed a stranger out of Colchis.
Now Lynceus, would you lay hands on Cynthia?
        Would shame not palsy your grip?
Good thing she's a girl fixed in her affections,[32]
        but if she weren't, could you live in such turpitude?
Strike out my life with steel or poison,
                take your choice,
        but desist from chasing this one girl.
May you be my lifelong friend,
        master of all my affairs,
        excluding affairs of the bedchamber;
I want no man (or god, for that matter) as a rival;
                My own light shadow raises suspicion,
                and I endure fear & trembling

[32] This line should dispel the long-held scholarly notion that Propertius lacked humor.

when there is no cause discernible
    but my own fool's passion.
But you broached those words
    while drunk,
  which is forgivable,
    for wine sets words awry,
but your mask of austerity will never fool me,
    for you know as well as the next man
    what a fine thing love is.
Now that you have at last lost your mind
    with this desire
  I delight only in your new allegiance
    to my lovelier deities.
What good do your Platonic platitudes
    do you now, and those weighty expositions
    of the nature of things?
What hope lies
    in your tuneful Greek plectrum?
Your ancient masters wrote no love manuals;
    better to attend the Muse of Philetas,
    & hearken to the dreams
    of modest Callimachus.
If you put to verse again
    how the course of the Aetolian river-god
    was broken,
& how the eddying Maeander loses itself
    in its own convolutions,
  or how Adrastus' horse Arion
pronounced the obsequies
    at the bleak burial of Archemorus,
It won't help you, having no bearing
    on your present situation,
nor will retelling how Amphiaraus' chariot
    fell into that hole,

or the story of Zeus's striking Capaneus to cinders.
Leave lofty noises to Aeschylus
    & quit unraveling your talent with the choros;
instead cut your verses on a narrower lathe
    & come sing in your own fire.
Homer was not immune to your ailment, nor Antimachus,
    for beauty sneers at godly greatness.
But no bull plows without apprenticeship
        on a noose,
    nor can you undergo grim love just yet;
        but let my song be your beginning.
No girl asks reasons
    for the way of the world
        or the course of the moon,
    or if a judge sits enthroned
        beyond the waters of hell,
    or if it is a god crackles the lightning.
Consider my condition: a small fortune,
        no generals among my forebears;
    yet I reign at the table
in the company of young women,
this being the product of those skills
        you take so lightly.
Though a man wounded
    (Eros' true aim has struck me down)
I have enough strength
    to relax among old wreaths.
I leave to Vergil such fields
    as Actium's coast watched over by the sun
        & that big fleet of Caesar's—
Vergil, who lifts up the Trojan sword again
    & recasts walls on the Lavinian coast.
Make way, you Roman writers, & you Greek writers,
    for the Iliad lies forgotten

& a greater work sees the light of day.
But Vergil, you also sing
    beneath the shadowing pines of Galaesus,
    & your reed flute polishes Daphnis' tune
        & the tune of ten apples
            & an unweaned goat given
    to break a girl's resistance.[33]
And if Vergil tires of his oatstalk,
        the libertine dryads will still celebrate his name
            which can bring enchantment
            to the adages of Hesiod.
Speak of what field the wheat will stand in,
    what ridge the grape will fatten on;
You sing like Apollo ruling the turtle shell
        & the result will not go unnoticed
            or unthanked by your readers,
whatever their feelings
about my kind of poetry.[34]
Varro as well took up amorous verse,
            with weightier matters done,
        Varro being the great flame of Leucadia;
and love was wanton Catullus' tune,
            thus Lesbia is more renowned than Helen;
and love gave Calvus voice
        when he sang Quintilia's threnody;
and the late love-wounded Gallus spoke
        to the same measures;
And now
        if the gods let it be
        Propertius lifts up
    his exaltation of Cynthia
        among the great songs.

[33] At this point I have omitted a tiresome list of Vergilian stories.
[34] Two lines of the Latin, which compare Vergil and the poetaster
Anser, have been omitted here.

BOOK III

1

Eidolon of Callimachus, & holy Philetas,
   I ask your sufferance,
    let me tread in your wood;
I come down, the first votary
       from the crystal fountain
    to weave Italian mysteries
       among the Greek dances.
Lift your voice, under what cliff
    did you thread your song?
What beat did you move to,
   what waters cleared your lips?
Let no one detain
   Apollo among weapons;
      let polished blades of verse be honed
     with the fine-grained pumice.
These songs will lift me up
    to a more exalted altitude;
my Muse rides victorious
      with flowered horses,
& the torches of Eros
      burn in my chariot;
a turmoil of dabblers in verse
      coming after.
Why do you give your horses their head
      in such useless contention?
No wide road ascends the mountain
    of the Muses.
Many will add honor to Roman annals;
     and some tout Bactra in Persia
as a fit imperial cornerpost;

But my pages bring
by undefiled path
a book down from Parnassus
that you may read in peace.
Pegasides, crown your poet with a delicate wreath,
no hard diadem will do.
My good name
now trod down
will flower on my grave.
Dust fertilizes our reputation;
our lips round out
the names of the dead
with greater reverence.
Who would know of the citadel
brought down by the timber horse,
or of Hector befouled beneath the axle
hauled three times around Troy's wall?
Priam's illustrious sons [1] would not be known
in their own lands;
There would be little known of Ilion
twice seized at the will
of the Greek numen.
Homer himself, who recounted the ruin,
has seen his work grow
with running time.
I foresee that Rome will praise me
after the fire;
my tombstone
will not be disdained.
Apollo
who hears my vows
will see to it.

[1] The names of Priam's illustrious sons, given in the Latin, are omitted
here, as is also an obscure allusion to Achilles.

2

Let us meanwhile
   return to the ring of song,
       let its usual pleasure touch her.
Orpheus allured feral beasts
       with the Thracian lyre
         and bewitched the rivers;
The singing lute strung mountain rocks
   into a Theban wall [2]
and Polyphemus' song
   wheeled about the foam-speckled horses
        of the sea-goddess Galatea
beneath the fires of Aetna.
Should we then stand amazed
      that a crowd of maidens cherish our words,
   we who are favored by Apollo
       & beloved of Bacchus?
My dwelling is simple,
   its roof without gold,
      without ivory vaults;
no black-marbled colonnade graces the porch,
   I have no fields of fruit trees
     nor fountains watered
        by the Marcian aqueduct.
But I go
   a companion of the Muses,
   my verses are favored by those who read,
    & Calliope does not tire
      of my dancing tune;
My book celebrates
   a fortunate woman,

[2] See AMPHION in glossary.

My songs will be a monument to her beauty,
    for neither the rich pyramids
       lifted high beneath the stars
   nor Zeus's great sanctuary
          on the mountain of heaven
          nor the golden crypt of Mausolus
is spared death's final ravages.
   Fire and rain erode their greatness
     & they will be ruined & broken in,
But the name of genius is hewn
        in timeless glory,
the grace of genius eludes destruction.

3

In the mountain's soft shadow
     I stretched recumbent by springwater,
        Pegasus' spring on Helicon,
   thinking I would versify a tale
     of Alba's kings & royal works,
       thinking I had it in me,
& I set my lips to the great fountain
     where Ennius formerly drank,
    father Ennius, who sang the Curii,
      and the javelins of their adversaries;
who sang of the kingly plunder
     in the craft of Aemilius;
    who sang of Fabius Cunctator
      victorious,
   and sinister misfortune at Cannae,
    & of the gods hearing pious rogations
      & the Lares driving Hannibal
        from the sacred places;
and of the cry of the goose [3]
     so propitious for Rome.

But Apollo watched from the trees
     before a cave
   leaning on his golden cithara
    & said:
"Lunatic, who asked you to muddy
     the fountain?
Your glory lies elsewhere,
  so roll your small wheels
    on softer terrain.

---

[3] The outcry of geese in front of Jove's temple warned the Romans of an attack by the Gauls.

Your book will be the lonely reading
   of a nervous girl awaiting her lover
  & will be put down at his arrival.
Propertius, why do your tunes
  revolve in wrong orbits?
Your skiff is fast and light,
   let your oars flash close to shore;
  avoid the trackless sea."
So spoke Phoebus Apollo, & with ivory plectrum
  he pointed out a footpath
    moss-grown on the forest floor
 and a sea-green cave
   studded with chrysoprase,
  tambourines hanging from the walls,
   from soft stone concavities.
& the mysteries of the Muses
    floated among the rocks,
   & a clay idol of father Silenus stood there,
   & there were reed panpipes,
    & Cytherean pigeons crowded their red beaks
    into the Hippocrene cistern
  & the nine delicate-fingered deities
   were about their work,
  winding ivy on the staff,
   measuring song to the lyre,
   lacing roses into wreaths,
whereupon Calliope, the fiery beauty,
touched me, & spoke:
"Be content to follow the path
   of the bright swan always;
  shun the road of the rattling cavalry,
   shiver no airs with brass-throated war note;
Keep the stain of war from the leaves of Helicon.
 The standards of Marius

stand without your help,
        & you need not celebrate
            Teutonic wars reddening the dismal Rhine,
                clotting its waters with corpses.
            You will sing instead
                of the lover in laurel
                    waiting before his truelove's lintel,
            you will sing the passwords
                    of drunken night flights,
and through your artful incantations
                    guarded girls may be sung loose
                        from their suspicious proprietors."
So said the goddess,
        & she then baptized my lips
                from the fountain of Philetas.

4

The Führer [4] considers
  invading the opulent East;
  slitting the jewelly waters
    of the Arabian Sea
      with his fleet,
the loot to be considerable,
        and the farthest earth will bear Rome's heel.
Tiber and Euphrates will both run beneath
      our bundle of sticks,[5]
& the Parthian trophies will shake under Zeus's artillery.
  Slide war-toughened prows into the sea
      & unfurl the canvas,
    conduct armed horses to their usual service
      and I will sing to your good luck.
Go and expiate
    the dishonor of that disaster of Crassus;
      Do well
      for our annals;
May father Mars & the fateful fires of holy Vesta
  grant
    that before my days run to a close
      I may see chariots returning,
          axles groaning with plunder,
and hear the cheers of the crowd
        as the horses pick through the throng.
And I will watch the procession,
      Cynthia's lap for a pillow,

---

4 Propertius' phrase *deus Caesar* was not yet usual in Augustan poetry.
In order to convey the nature of this piece and to clarify Propertius'
attitude toward Augustus, I have been crude where the original was
subtle, thus taking liberties with this not very good poem.
  5 The fasces, Roman symbol of authority.

    & read out the list of cities seized,
        gaze at the javelins
of the vanquished cavalry,
      the bows of the trousered barbarians,
        and their captured chieftains
           sitting close by their stacked weapons,
all led by Caesar.
Let Venus aid her progeny; [6]
      Aeneas has yet his great descendants
      and the spoils of war go to those
        who labor to win them.
I am content to applaud on the Via Sacra.

[6] Venus' progeny are the Roman people, particularly the Julian line, of which Augustus was an adopted member. There is, however, a possible reference to Propertius himself as Venus' great poet.

5[7]

Love being a peaceable god
 we lovers venerate peace,
   & I struggle only with my mistress.
My soul doesn't ache for secret gold
   & attendant misfortunes,
  I don't slake my thirst
   from jeweled chalices,
and the fat Campania isn't burdened with my oxen,
   & I wield no shovel in Corinth
  looking for buried bronzes.
Primeval earth & contriving Prometheus
  were a ruinous combination;
and men were made
   with bodies more excellent than minds:
  Prometheus forgot the soul
   in his art:
that should have been shining perfection,
  flawless & true before all else.
Now we are wind-tossed on wide oceans;
  we go looking for trouble,
   and are always restocking our armories.
But treasure to the slough of Acheron?
    Most unlikely. You will ride
   the ship of hell, fool,
  with no shirt on your back.
The victor will come with the vanquished,
  Marius with Jugurtha; rich Croesus
   no less a shadow than the beggar Irus.
But the death most preferable comes
  after we have tasted the fruits of life;

[7] Nothing else in Propertius' work is quite like this unusual poem, which should be read together with III.4.

And it is my delight to have worshiped Helicon
      from the beginning
         as a youth,
    and to have joined the Muses' dance.
Let it be my everlasting pleasure
       to lace my soul with wine
         spring roses wreathing my head;
and when the heaviness of years
      puts an end to love
        and white age dusts my black hair
    then vouchsafe certain pleasures;
To learn the nature of things,
     & what god governs this world;
       To understand mysteries;
         the waxing & waning of the moon,
      how the horns of the moon come
   to round out the month,
       where the winds come from
         whistling in the high seas;
    what the fluting east wind seeks for;
the source of the clouds' everlasting mists; I would know
if a day will come
      to bring down the towers of the world;
   let it be my pleasure
      to learn why the red arc in the sky
        feeds on the rainwaters,
       why the earth moves under Mount Pindus;
   why the sun's bright ring mourns
       with horses enshrouded in black;
& why Boötes delays in rolling the oxen & wagon;
   why the Pleiad choros meets
      with close-set fires in the sky;
  why deep oceans don't overrun their rims;
   and why the year fills with the four seasons.

Whether underground such things exist
    as the rule of gods,
      and if there are giants in torment there;
   whether black snakes twist Tisiphone's face;
        whether the Furies torture Alcmaeon
        & hungry Phineus.
If they exist there, the wheel, the sliding boulder,
          and thirst in the running stream;
   If triple-headed Cerberus guards the mouth of hell,
        & if Tityos is bound to his 9 acres;
Or if these stories brought down to us
    are mere fiction
   and there is nothing to fear
    after the final fire.
This is the remainder of my life,
    that which awaits me.
And you, pleased so much by war,
      bring back the standards of Crassus.

6

Tell me, Lygdamus,
    what you have observed
        of your mistress and mine.
And without lies,
    and your yoke might thereby be lifted.
You wouldn't buoy my spirits
        with empty gladness,
    you wouldn't deceive me,
        bringing back news you suspect I would like to believe?
No envoy should come
    bearing empty words,
      and a slave should be truthful
    if only out of fear.
Now, begin at the beginning,
    if you remember anything;
      I will take it all in with eager, doubtful ears.[8]
You saw her cry, thus, with unkempt hair,
    a great quantity of water spilling from her eyes, Lygdamus?
& you beheld
    a mirror thrown down on the couch,
        & the jewels no longer adorning
      her lovely fingers;
Did a sad gown drape her delicate shoulder,
    did her jewel box lie closed
        at the couch-foot?
And you say the house was dreary? and the maids
    sad at the loom, Cynthia not gone
      from among them?
Did she dry her eyes with the wool,
    & bring up my complaints in a shrill voice,

---

[8] The reading "eager, doubtful ears" is a plausible translation of the Latin, given the context.

"Is this his promised reward for me—
        the promise you witnessed, Lygdamus?
     & Lygdamus, a slave who lies is in trouble.
Can he abandon me,
     leave me miserable for no good reason,
     & now keep housed the sort of woman
        I prefer not to speak of?
He delights that I shrivel up in my bed
        without company.
If it would please him, let him dance at my funeral.
It is by no talent
        the bitch has beaten me,
  but by love-philters, by potions;
he is brought to her by the rhombos
        circling on its string,
and by awful swollen bramble toads,
    and the bones she has cut out of snakes,
      and screech owl plumes got from low-lying tombs,
and the wool riband wound
        around his effigy.
But unless my dreams sing portending nothing,
     his pain will be late, but sufficient
        at my feet.
The spider will foully web
    his empty bed,
     and in their nights together
       may Aphrodite herself lie elsewhere."

If these lamentations
came from a true soul,
       Lygdamus,
        then run the path back
     and by my mandate report
    that I may have been angry

in my tears, but never false,
  that I am turned in a similar fire,
and that for a week and a half I have lain *completely* pure.
If, by some chance,
    you bring about a joyful reunion, then—
        insofar as I can help—
  you will be a free man, Lygdamus.

7

Hot pursuit of gain
etches worry into the brow,
    leads down a steep road
        to a premature end;
wealth the seed of our rising inquietude,
        feeder of vice. In that service
my friend Paetus set linen to wind, toward Alexandria
      in the usual treasure hunt,
      and was buried in the surge of the windy sea;
The fortune he sailed for
      left him bereft of youth and life,
and he floats in a distant gulf
    nibbled on by curious fish,
and his mother can't bury him with the proper ritual
    or plant his corpse among kinsmen.
Now the seabirds float over his bones,
      his tomb the liquid Carpathian.
His life was a trifling plunder
      for the sea's doyens. Why,
      Neptune, did you fracture that keel?
And other good men sank in the sea
      with that hollow ship
    as well.
And he pled his youth,
      pled a bereaved mother,
    bootless cries in the choking sea,
      for the waves have no attentive gods.
His ship was moored fast to the rocks
      but the night storm struck
the hawsers through
    and swept ship and crew away.
Gods, give his body back, at least, to dry land;

His life is lost in silent sea-depths.
Let him lie sand-drifted
   and when a seafarer sails by his grave
      let him say that brave men
         might well fear death by water.
Go build curved keels,
      weave the sails of death;
   men's hands have wrought such ruin at sea.
Earth being too small a tomb
we add the ocean,
   by artifice we lengthen
      the evil path of fortune.
Can an anchor hold a man
      whose household gods cannot?
What shall a man merit
      whose homeland is too small?
What he builds is at the wind's mercy,
   for rarely does a hull get old and rot,
   and you can't count on a safe harbor.
Cruel Nature put the sea
      at the disposal of avarice and ambition
         usually unrealized.
A wild coast testifies to Agamemnon's grief,
    where the pain of Argynnus
       brands the waters below the mountain.
For a drowned youth
      the Greek ships did not weigh anchor;
      Iphigenia killed for the delay.
And rocks broke the triumphant fleet,
      Greece thus shipwrecked and sea-ravaged.
A few at a time Ulysses mourned them, his friends,
   his wit worthless against the ocean waves.
Had Paetus contented himself
   with cultivating his fields

and his patrimony,
    he would still enjoy the boisterous banquet
        in the warmth of his hearth-gods,
           a pauper, but a dry one.
Poverty would then be a minor complaint.
He was not cut out for for the scream of sea squalls,
      and his hands were burnt by the rope;
The marbled bedchamber & well-pillowed terebinth couch
      were more his style.
But the running sea
   tore his nails at the last;
A hard night saw him drifting by ship's timber;
      many evils convened that he might perish.
He wept and cried out,
     black brine closing around him:
"Aegean gods, water rulers,
   Lords of the wind and waves washing over me,
     where have my best years gone?
Did I sail these narrows
     crime staining my hands?
I am driven against cliffs,
   I am struck with the trident.
Let the surf float me up
     on an Italian beach
       that my mother may bury me."
The churning water took him then,
     the last words and days for him.
Nereus' hundred daughters, born of the sea,
     might have helped him,
   and Thetis, who knew a mother's grief once.
And as for me,
   the north wind shall never ravel my sails,
      and I will remain here where I belong
      at the portals of my mistress.

[156]

8

It was a most delightful melee
    we enjoyed last night under lantern light
when with choked cries of rage
    & multiple maledictions
    & reeling in the heat of wine
you shoved over the table
        and flung the glassware at my head.
Come on,
  go after my hair with gusto
    & lunge at my face with your pretty claws,
swear to burn out my eyes with a close-held flame
    & rip the toga from my shoulders;
For it proves a true fire of love.
No woman free of Eros' hammerlock
     cries out in such manner.
She who rails with an angry tongue
   does so groveling at Aphrodite's feet.
And she plays hard to get,
    hiding in a swarm of chaperones;
  or else she dances drunk in the street
   to the bacchanalian dithyrambs;
    & black phobic nightmares come to her each night.
A girl's portrait
     decorating a tablet
   is an apparition moving her to misery.
It takes no diviner
   to detect true love in this turmoil;
If it can't be fired to anger, love has no fidelity.
    Let my enemies
enjoy maidens of cold disposition.
Notice the marks of her teeth in my neck;
  let bruises tender evidence

that I have enjoyed her company;
I wish for contention in love, to hear cries
        & to see tears, whether mine or yours,
but I abhor secret words in your eyes
     & silent signals sent with your fingers.
I hate those heaving sighs in the night
    that never break through sleep;
I should always wish to have a woman of spirit.
The flame was sweeter to Paris
    after he broke through Greek swords
      to bring its fiery pleasure
       to Helen, Tyndareus' daughter.
While the Greeks gained victory
    & as rocklike Hector savagely withstood assault
      Paris fought the greater war
rolling & struggling with his mistress.
I will always contend either with you
      or for you, with my competition,
& I ask for no peace.

. . . .

Dance for joy, that no woman is as beautiful as you are; [9]
  you would grieve if one were,
    but still, it is suitable for you to be proud.
But to him, snare setter
  who would capture the pleasures
of our bed,
May his father-in-law
    last a century,
& his mother-in-law
     come to live with him.
If he has tasted the fruit
  of the fire

[9] These final sixteen lines are usually treated as a separate poem.

in a stolen night,
     it was through her craving
        to offend me;
She did not love him.

9

My lord Maecenas,
   come down from Tuscan kingly blood,
the groove of your fortune is clear enough,
so why, why would you have me engrave
          songs in the sea,
    & bend a thin mast with overspread sails?
It is most inglorious
      to take up a heavy pack
         only to break beneath it
and then run for cover;
No man is suitable for all things,
   the flame is not brought down
         from every hill.

. . . .

Some whip their teams for the prize at Olympia
   & some are born with the glory of speed afoot;
Some men are sown for peace
   & some men are raised for the armed camp;
the seed grows by its particular nature.
But Maecenas, having received the precepts
     that govern your life,
        I will go past your example.
Your glorious axes could fall in the Forum,
      your law handed down there;
You could, if you wished,
     beat down the pikes
        of the quarrel-prone Medians
         & nail enough trophies to your walls
          that they would creak with the weight.
Though great Caesar gives you the power
      to do what you will,
        and wealth insinuates its way

                    into your coffers
                        at all seasons,
you still keep back, and live in shadows,
                    without ostentation;
you draw in the overstretched sails.
But believe me when I say
your name will equal Camillus' in men's judgment;
        and your name will be on men's lips,
    and your footfall will be heard in glory
                    close behind Caesar;
Good faith will be your true monument.
I, however, will not cut through distended waves
        in a boat under full sail;
I remain in the backwash.
    I will not spill out again the tearful story
        of the towers of Cadmus incinerated by father Zeus,[10]
        or of 7 battles equally disastrous.
Nor will I again recount
        the story of the Scaean gate & Pergama,
                Apollo's rampart,
nor the return of the Danaän ships for the tenth spring,
            when the Greeks plowed under Neptune's walls,
            after that Palladian stratagem with the timber horse.
It is rather my joy
    to have won a place among the books of Callimachus
        & to have sung
        to Philetas' Doric measures.
Let my scribbling
        set a fire
            under young men and under young women;

---

[10] The Latin here may refer to the destruction of the walls of Thebes
by the Epigoni, as W. A. Camps has it, or to the incineration of Semele
and the palace of Cadmus when Zeus appeared to her in full glory. I
have chosen the latter interpretation.

Let *them* cry my deification,
     & bear sacrifice to my altar.
But,[11]
         with you as my general,
           I will sing Jupiter's artillery,
        and the giants menacing heaven;
     and I will sing the 2 kings fattened
         at the teats of the forest wolf.
I will lay out the warp of walls shored up
         at Remus' killing,
     & I will weave bulls through the high Roman hills;
My genius will inflate itself
       at the drop of a word.
I will attend your chariots
        singing hallelujahs
      from one rim of the world to the other;
I will sing how the Parthians dropped their lances
      in astute retreat;
   & the camps on the Nile broken through
        by Roman iron,
     & Antony done in by his own hand.
Merely
    grasp the reins
        of the new course undertaken,
    and give me an auspicious banner
   as my wheels roll forth;
This is your laudable concession, Maecenas,
    and it is your due
     that men should call me
       one of your company.

[11] I have translated the excesses of the final section of the poem as sarcasm, and if the tribute to Maecenas at the beginning is honest, as I believe it is, then this treatment is tenable by assuming that the final section is a protest against what Maecenas would have the poet write, not a complaint about Maecenas himself.

10

In the red-lit dawn
  I beheld with wonder
    Muses at the couch-foot,
And the omen they brought
  of a most special birthday
    echoed in the morning;
So let it be
  a day without clouds
    and the sky without winds,
a day in which the waves slide gently
    onto dry beaches,
  and one in which
    I see no grieving
      in the day's light.
Let marble Niobe suppress
  that glissade of tears
and the complaints of the kingfisher fall
    silent on sea dune
    and Itys' mother have respite from wailing.
May my dearest mistress
    so auspiciously descended
  rise up now and supplicate
    the prayer-demanding gods,
and first dispel the night's sleep
    with clear water
    and arrange that shining hair,
And next, Cynthia, put on those silks
  that so captivated Propertius,
    caught his eye,
& make sure your hair
  doesn't lack for flowers
    and entreat the gods that the beauty

which is your strength
    be everlasting.
May you always be
    sovereign queen of my affections.
When you have burned incense
    before the crowned altars
    and the flame has glittered
through the whole house
    with sanctification,
Let there then be consideration of a banquet
    where the light will run out until morning
    among the wine cups.
Anoint yourself with saffron & myrrh from onyx cask
    & let us dance to the shinbone flute
    until the hoarse tune fails;
Indulge yourself
    in light words
    & may the cheer of the feast
    keep off unwelcome sleep
& the nearby roads ring with reveling.
    Let there be dice thrown
    the rattling bones determining
    who will be flogged by Eros' wing feathers
and after the wine is consumed
    and the exact hour comes
when Aphrodite prepares
    the sacred ministrations
    Let us fulfill the year's rite
    in our bed
    & thus complete the commemoration.

11

Will you be amazed
    that a woman can twist my life,
        bend virility to her desire?
Your mocking lacks decency;
    no shame lies in lacking means
      to shatter the yoke,
        to fracture the chain.
It is not a matter of cowardice.
There is no better forecast of a fatal sea
    than a sailor's intuition;
  the bite of the blade teaches soldiers fear,
    and I sing a new tune, now,
      my youth gone,
and you might well walk fearfully
    after my example.
Enchanting Medea set fiery bulls into action
under a steel yoke,
    & planted the clash of iron
      in the sword-bearing earth,
  closed the great jaws
    of the guardian reptile
      so the golden wool might go to Aeson's house.
And the fierce queen of Amazons [12]
    rattled arrows among the Greek ships
    from horseback;
& she conquered her conqueror,
    with the radiance of loveliness laid bare,
      splendor under golden armor.
And Hercules, who raised the pillars
    of a world pacified,
took down a day's worth of weaving

[12] The queen of the Amazons was Penthesilea, slain by Achilles at Troy.

                    in Omphale's service—such was the glory
                        of her beauty, she who was once lacquered
                            by Gygaean lakewater.
Semiramis, mistress of Babylon,
            erected ramparts,
                    brick upon brick,
ample for two chariots passing
            neither axletree clipping the other;
She ran the Euphrates among her towers
            & ruled above Bactra's genuflections.
And there is the example of gods
        and the example of heroes.
                    Zeus himself
                    is disgraced in his own house.
And remember the affair of that woman
        who lately tainted our swords with shame,
            who took her salacious leave
even among servants. Whose fee,
        from her foul suitor,
                    was the battlements of Rome
                    & a senate under her dominion.
The dust of Alexandria spawns artifice,
            Egypt's bloody crimes stain Memphis,
                where the sand absorbed Pompey's triple conquests.
No coming day will blot out this infamy;
            better, Pompey, had you died,
                    ill that time in Naples,
            or bent your head to your father-in-law.
Slattern queen, the stain of Ptolemy on her,
            queen of whores under the skies of Egypt
she would have Anubis bay at Jupiter,
            drown out the bugle with the jingle of sistrum,
& slide past the Roman prow
                    with a poled barge,

                    [166]

& unfurl the mosquito net as her canopy
   on the Capitoline,
hand down law among Marian monuments & arms.
And Rome, ruling the world from 7 hills,
   cringed at a woman's power.
What good would it be
   that we crumpled the axes of arrogant Tarquin
   only to now endure a queen?
But she retreated to her twisting Nile in fear,
  and her wrists knew our chains;
Rome saw her arms under the hollow teeth
   of sacred snakes,
  & by secret arteries
   her limbs drew in dreams.
"Why did you cower, O Rome?" she said, "for one of your
   citizens was a man."
Her voice thus, from the wine fumes.

11a[13]

But now, unshaken Rome,
  pray for a long day for Augustus.
Curtius went into the cleft,
      founding his monument thereby,
& Decius broke battles from horseback,
  & Horatio's footpath still testifies to that bridge cutting.
The gods threw these walls up,
      & while Caesar retains his health
          Rome need fear nothing from heaven.
Where now are Scipio's warships, or Camillus' standards,
      or Mithridates', lately seized by Pompey's fist,
& where is Hannibal's loot, & the trophies
          of Syphax beaten?
And Pyrrhus' glitter is ground in the dirt underfoot.
Apollo will bring to mind again
      the sharp edge of armies broken,
  & the one day of war that did so much;
and the sailor must now be mindful of Caesar,
              in port or outward bound;
even the sea
      being his domain.

---

[13] This poem is usually considered part of III.11. The original text is confused, but I follow H. E. Butler's transpositions and continue from *Curtius expletis* with a new poem in order to save III.11 from complete disintegration.

12

Postumus, can you leave her, tears in her face,
                              Galla your wife,
        & follow the soldier's trade,
                    behind Caesar's flags?
What good is Parthian plunder,
              your wife's prayerful cry unheeded?
If the law allows it,
        let them all be damned equally,
              who go abroad looking for gold,
    along with any man who prefers
            the arms of the camp
                to those awaiting him in his bed,
You must be unhinged,
          to drink from distant rivers
              at day's end,
      helmet for a bucket, mantle thrown over your arm,
      while she, meanwhile,
      will toss in her bed with each hollow rumor,
      afraid your manly valor
        will bring you to a bitter end;
afraid the Median arrows will sing
                  at your riddled death,
  or that you will fall by iron
    at the hand of some cataphract
          on a gold-trimmed horse;
afraid you will be brought back in a jar,
              something to cry over;
              and that is how they bring them home.
You are several times blessed, Postumus,
        in such a chaste bride;
      your custom is somewhat unworthy of her.
Think what she might do here, unshackled from respectable
                                        fear,

her husband gone, with all Rome
instructing her in dissipation.
But you have nothing to worry about,
her bed will never be for sale;
and she won't dwell on your harshness.
And when fate remits you safe & sound
Galla will embrace you
with no crime to blush for.
And Postumus will seem
to a wondering audience
another Ulysses—at least in his choice of wives.
Ulysses, after all,
was undamaged by his delay, a 10-year campaign
from Ismara to Gibraltar, overcoming all obstacles:
Circe's alluring cunning, the Cyclops' den, the binding lotus
weed,
the waters rumbling from Scylla to Charybdis & back
again,
incautious hunger, tearful Calypso's chamber,
a long cold swim, the black hall of noiseless
shadows,
the siren's sea
got past with deaf men at the rowing bench;
and he renovated an ancient bow
to the ruin of a number of suitors;
at which point his vagrancy ended—
and he came home safe, & not in vain,
for his wife retained
her honor
& his.
But Aelia Galla,
if necessary,
would surpass that record
of marathon chastity.

13

Women's desires endear the night,
   Rome's ruined fortune being Aphrodite's doing;
This rioting luxuriance
                  cedes these evils.
Gold out of India,
         nautilus from the eastern seas,
               purple from Tyre,
Bedouin cinnamon brought camelback
                  out of Arabia;
  These are weapons in the wars of love,
    And they seduce chaste girls
         shut up in their rooms,
  even those girls disdainful as Penelope.
  Matrons walk abroad
           wearing the goods of spendthrifts
           & linger before our eyes
              with the booty of harlotry.
There is no reverence, no reluctance in asking or giving,
    or if there is
          the delay is removed at a price.

Oriental burials display more honor
          when the red dawn lights the husband's pyre
           & the bier receives the last torch;
Then the commotion of wives with outspread hair begins,
    wives devoted enough to struggle with one another
         to follow their husbands
and escape the disgrace of widowhood,
    burning lip and breast against the dead.
Here, adultery only;
no woman in Rome sleeps with
    Evadne's fidelity

or Penelope's constancy.
It was better in the old days
    when our peaceful riches lay
            in crop & orchard.
Our forebears shook down apples
    & gave them as offerings,
        & fat baskets dark with blackberries,
    picked violets & lilies, offered grapes
        & glossy-feathered birds.
With these small seductions
            girls surrendered kisses to their lovers
                in secluded declivities and groves,
    a deerskin the only blanket over them,
        and the tall grass would make a bed,
                pine trees spreading slow shadows on the
                    ground around them.
Nor did pain attend the sight of godly nakedness.
The horned lead ram himself
            would restore the fat sheep
        to the deserted court
            of the great god of the forest.
And the gods of the fields
        spoke soft words to men
            before their hearths
and the god Pan was patron
        of hunters
of rabbit and bird
        under the cliff.
But now the forest altars are abandoned,
    gold blinding men to duty.
Money erodes faith;
        the law itself is bought
            & justice lucre-bound,
    no law but the grasping hand

[172]

& impiety.
Seared entrance posts witness the sacrilege of Brennus,
    Gaul who would have plundered
        the oracle at Delphi;
Lightning glittered and the laurel-topped mountain shook
    and Gallic spears were buried
        in a winter storm.
The foul murder of Polydorus by his faithless kinsman
    was due to the lure of gold.
And so that the gold-glint might be seen
    on her smooth-muscled neck,
        Eriphyle betrayed her husband
who was taken by the earth, he and his horses both.
    Rome is crushed by luxury;
        goods overwhelm her.
But no one believes it, having only my word for it.
The Trojans believed Cassandra less
    when she foretold ruin,
        saw alone
what Paris brought them,
  the armed horse
        inside the walls
            by treachery.
But her madness served its purpose,
    and her unbelieved words
        lent final credence
          to the gods.

14[14]

O Sparta of outlandish laws, outlandish custom,
    how I envy your virginal gymnasia,
  where naked girls enjoy the fun,
      the wrestling,
        retrieve stray balls, run
          to the song of hoopstick & hoop.
Girls stand dust-drifted
      at the race's end goal
   & in Sparta a girl may join the pancration
        giving & receiving her share,
          glove tight on delighted fist.
She wheels in a circle
      against the weight of the discus
        & a maiden may be seen
          running her father's dogs
in the long mountains of Taygetus
      her hair gleaming with hoarfrost.
        The Spartan girl
dances her horse in the ring
      & buckles a sword to a white thigh
        & hides her hair in hollow bronze,
          stripped to the waist like a warlike Amazon
        bathing in the Thermodon,
   or like Helen taking arms
      with bare torso
        & shameless complexion
among her brothers,[15] the god Castor the horseman
    & Pollux the boxer.
The law of Lacedaemon forbids

[14] This poem is an interesting sexual fantasy.
[15] Propertius seems to have invented this tale about Helen.

lovers to go separate ways
and you may be seen in the crossroads
     with your girlfriend,
        nor is any young woman
kept shackled up and guarded,
     nor need any man fear the vengeance
     of some sour cuckold.
You need no go-between
   & you don't have to cool your heels
     in the anteroom.
No crimson tunic deceives the inquiring glance
   & no woman relies on scented hair.
But in Rome
  women walk surrounded by custodians,
     the way narrow,
       not a finger insertable,
& you cannot find out
     how you should look, or what you should say;
      the lover travels an unlit path.
O Rome, if you would replicate
   the Spartan customs
   & take up their style of wrestling
you would be much the dearer to me.

15

These words
> that no storm break
>> over this love,
That I not lie
> awake nightly without you—
When I veiled my boyhood modesty
> with the robe of manhood [16]
>> & was set loose on amorous paths,
It was Lycinna tinged my soul
> those first nights,
>> oiled that roughness.
And it was free.
But it has been three years,
> & since then maybe ten words
>> have passed between us.
Your love buries my past;
> no woman since
>> has sweetened her chain
>>> around my neck.[17]

· ·

Now cruel Dirce swore to it
> that Antiope had lain with Lycus,
>> & this "crime" so aroused Queen Dirce
> that she had Antiope's lovely hair singed,
>> and she clawed her cheeks,
> and freighted her unjustly
>> with excessive labor at the loom,
and gave her a floor tile for a pillow
> and a black sty to live in,
and mocked hunger with water.

[16] The *toga virilis*.
[17] Some verses are missing in the Latin after this line.

Zeus, would you allow such a thing,
  wrist-cracking chains
   for this young woman of yours,
    no aid in her bind?
But Antiope, with her own body's strength,
  cracked manacles from her hands,
   then ran timidly to Cithaeron, mountain stronghold,
    night all around her, a sharp bed in thin hoarfrost,
   fear at her elbow, with the noise of vagrant streams
(she feared her mistress following).
And she came then to her sons,
  but Zethus was not much upset
   at his mother's misfortune,
& Amphion turned merely lachrymose.
But as silence settles after the east wind
   whirls against south wind,
 and the sound of the sand grows thin
   on silent beaches,
 so her knees slid to earth;
  & filial piety returns before bent knees.
(The old man that guarded these godly sons
  was worthy of Zeus their father.)
And as dutiful squires
  of their mother's honor
   they dutifully avenged her,
strapping Dirce beneath a bull
  for a bloody death through the fields;
This for the glory of their mother;
 and Amphion sang
  a paean of victory
   against the cliffs.
 But excuse my digression,
Cynthia,
 and excuse Lycinna

who has done you no wrong,
even though it is painful for you
to suppress your anger.
Let no talk stir
of you and me;
I hope I may love you
until the last fire
settles in its ashes.

16

With midnight, my mistress's letter
    declaring I should come,
        forgoing delay, to Tibur
where doubled turrets float
      over white rock cliffs
         and the waters of Anio fall
   in spreading pools.
With her mandate, indecision.
   In the night's veil
audacious hands might lay hold of my arms,
   but if I should delay, not come as she asks,
      her tears would be more fearful
than thieves cloaked in the dark.
     I sinned once before
     & paid a year's penance, repelled from her bed,
and those sharp and ready claws of hers
       are something to consider.
But no man would injure a lover,
     lovers being sacred;
Lovers can walk the road of the robber's nest,
     Sciron's road, and even the sands of Scythia
       molested by no man,
no man would wish to be so much a barbarian.
The moon glows over the road
  & the stars light the ruts therein
    & Eros the god himself
  flames ahead with a blazing torch;
Even the wide-slung jaws
      of the mad dogs of the highway
are turned aside.
For lovers the road is safe at late hours—
   there is no profit in scattering their blood

and Aphrodite protects them.
But—
  should my undoing come
     & she perform the proper rites
     my death might be atoned for;
the price is worth it.
  She will bring incense to the fire
     & adorn my sepulcher with a crown of flowers.
She will bow in a vigil
     hard by my tomb.
May the gods grant that she not bury these bones
    in a tumultuous place
      near the congregation of the road;
    in such places are the tombs of lovers defiled.
Bury me in remote ground
    in the shadow of a leafy tree,
    or on a wild beach
      under a sand heap.
I do not want
    my name found in the common highway.

17

My rogation to Bacchus, before his altar:
  Give me peace, & an auspicious wind
      fattening my sails.
Your wine heals pain
  & you can overcome violent Love's
      present disdain;
For lovers are united by Bacchus
      & also released from love,
    and for his part,
        the god is not himself a novice,
        this attested to by Ariadne in the heavens
carried there by his lynxes.
O drown this pain in my soul,
    for only wine or death
      will numb the torment,
a slow fire locked in my bones.
A sober night is always agony
    for lonely lovers,
      hope and fear alternately shearing their souls,
but if Bacchus brings sleep to my bones
        through his gift,
          the hot flush of wine,
      then I will plant vines;
    cleat rows of vines to the hills
      & by vigilance assure
      that they are not ravaged by wild beasts.
If I may fill my vat with wine-dark must
      & tint my ankles with the new grape's dye,
then I will live my allotted years
      in the god's abundance,
    & I will be known as the poet of his virtues,
& I will proclaim his creation
        by the zigzag flame of Zeus,

& sing how his dancers conquered the soldiers of India,
>How Lycurgus went mad to no purpose
>>with the new-brought drink,
>How the 3 troops of maenads reveled
>>in the doing-in of Pentheus,
>& how the Tyrrhenian sailors turned into curved dolphins
>>& slid overboard
>>>into the sea
>>>>from the vine-knotted ship,
>How his streams ran sweet through Naxos,
>>streams from which the people there
>>>drank his liquor.
And, with his white neck bent
>>for the slackened ivy clusters,
>>>the god's hair will be wreathed
>>>>with a Lydian turban,
his smooth neck smeared
>>with scented olive,
>>>loose robe brushing naked feet.
Dircean Thebes will beat the quiet timbrels,
>and goat-footed satyrs will play the reed pipe,
>>the cymbals will beat out the harsh Idaean dance
>close by great Cybele,
>>>turret-crowned goddess.
Before the temple
>>with the wine bowl
>the high priest will decant the wine
>>in a gold goblet
>>>over the offering.
I will repeat these things,
>sing of them
>not abjectly
>but with Pindaric cadence,
only free me from these iron chains
>& break through my mind's turmoil with sleep.

[182]

18

Where the sea is closed out
   from the shadows of hell,
   breakers playing on the warm pools
            at Baiae,
Where Misenus, Trojan trumpet player, lies sand-buried,
      & Hercules' causeway booms in the ocean,
      & where the cymbals rang for the Theban god
   when he went auspiciously searching
            through mortal cities;
That place is now hateful,
            stained with black crime.
Baiae, what inimical god
   has stood forth in your waters?
   Here Marcellus sank [18]
         to darker waves in Avernus;
his spirit moves vaguely
         among those pools.
What good did his bloodline
      or his highly placed mother do him,
      or his esteem at Caesar's fireplace?
Or the curtains floating
         over the crowds at the theater,
      & all the fine things his mother got him?
His sun has set
   in his 20th year;
his fortune swung on a short tether.
But go now,
   revive your spirit,
& pretend to the old triumphs,

---

[18] Marcellus died suddenly at Baiae; the imagery suggests drowning, although he is not known to have died from that cause. He may have been poisoned.

when the whole theater stood in applause;
Outfit yourself with gold again,
    & let the great games glitter again with jewels;
        for you will bring all this to the fire,
   & all men come to the fire,
        great lords equally
          with the wretched of the earth.
Terror lingers on the road,
     but every man's heel
        will rub that path.
All must come beg
    to the tune of the triple howl
       of the hound of Erebus;
All men must embark in the common boat,
    a grim & ancient man for oarsman.
Though a man look for security
        in iron & brass
      Death will yet take him by the hair
       & reave him from his hole.
Nireus went unexempted by splendid looks;
    Achilles went
       despite his muscle;
and no stream-borne gold saved Croesus.
But Charon, O pilot of pious ghosts,
    carry his spirit as men took his corpse;
Let his soul float on the sidereal ribbon
    far from the haunts of humans, where Caesar went,
& Claudius, who ruled the ground of Sicily.

19

You review our sins, declare man's soul is lust,
   but listen, when the flame breaks through a woman,
when you sunder the shackles of modesty,
      there is no measure to your frenzy.
A blaze in a wheat field might sooner be put out,
     or streams slide into their springs
    or the bleak shoals of the Syrtes allow refuge
    or the wild Malean coast welcome sailors,
than anyone hold you back in your desire
    or break the thrust of your unmastered passion.
Pasiphaë is my witness, who
      galled by the Minoan bull's disdain
         wore fir-wood horns that she might have him;
    & Tyro, glowing for Enipeus, wishing to lie
     with the watery god;
and Myrrha, changed to a leafy myrtle
    because she burned for her father.
Why should I have to speak of Medea, killer of children
      in her desire?
  Or of Clytemnestra, who darkened a kingdom
        with her crime,
   or of Scylla, who sold herself for
   a well-built Cretan—
Scylla whose razor to her father's hair
     cut down his realm;
       this was the dowry she promised Minos;
     such was the stealthy love
      that opened the king's gates;
And her reward
was to be dragged in the sea
    from the stern
      of the leaving ship.

Even so
   Minos deserves to be judge of the dead
      for he was a conqueror
      fair in his victory.
And you unmarried girls,
   may your pitch-pine wedding torches
      burn more auspiciously
   & with more moderation.

20[19]

Do you really think
    he gives a damn
        for your lovely figure?
You yourself saw
    how he abandoned your bed,
        a flint-souled man loving gold before beauty,
    & setting his sails accordingly.
But could all Africa be worth such a clamor?
And you,
   lacking good sense,
        keep rearranging his hollow words
        & and his empty oaths.
But now, perhaps,
another heart beats time
        against his own.
However,
   Your beauty is still potent,
     your Palladian talents are yet in order,
      and the great light of your learned forebear [20]
        shines in your eyes.
With a faithful lover
    your fortune will be sufficient,
    & there is a key to that treasure
       in my bedroom,
  if I may suggest it.

. . . .

The first night arrives.
    give us sufficient time

[19] It is possible that III.20 is really two poems, the second beginning with line 26. In any event I believe that the woman referred to is Cynthia, although W. A. Camps, on very slight evidence, argues otherwise.

[20] Cynthia (Hostia) probably claimed descent from the poet Hostius.

        in this great night;
Luna, let this first night
       be couched in your lingering
            splendor
and you, Phoebus, prolonging the downpour
       of the summer fires,
        shorten the road of your loitering flame.
But first the covenant must be made,
       the rules inscribed,
        the law written, in our new affair.
And Eros himself, with his own seal,
       binds fast the pact;
        the twisted sidereal diadem is witness.
Ah, how many hours
     must this discourse turn through
     before the goddess Aphrodite
       spurs us into lovely arms.
When the bed is not bound
     by true agreement
     then no avenging gods walk in the wakeful night,
     and violent desire
       will break the chain it forged;
But may initial good omens
     run continuous
       through a true love.
Therefore, whoever breaks
      our sacred contract,
      bound at the altar,
     whoever pollutes our mingled love
with outside embellishment,
Let all the pains known to love
     (& customary in it)
       then be his;
Let his privacy disappear

in the gossipy streets of Rome;
May that beloved window be
closed to him all night
despite all weeping.
Let him love forever
but be forever destitute
of love's fruition.

21

To break this hard passion
  I must make the great journey,
    Take the long road
      to erudite Athens,
And perhaps the flame
      constantly arising
      as I gaze at her raptly
        will then subside.
The fire feeds on itself and grows;
      I have tried all the patent medicines,
        but desire stays lodged in my heart,
  Eros oppresses me.
Her invitations are now few, refusals frequent,
    & when she condescends to lie with me
      she sleeps on the far edge of the bed,
        in her clothes.
One remedy remains: to leave,
      to shift my ground.
The road that removes me from her sight
      may remove her from my heart.
Come now, my fellow wayfarers,
      pull the ship into the sea,
    draw lots for oar duty,
    draw the auspicious sail to mast top
        & weigh anchor
  when the overslung sky
      favors the course of mariners
        on the glassy sea.
Farewell my friends,
    and farewell to the proud walls of Rome,
    & good-bye my beloved
      for what you were to me.

I will now be floated through rumbling breakers
> to the tune of my prayers to the sea-roaring gods
> through the Ionian Sea to the calm port of Lechaeum,
& the sails will be hauled down
> the small ship's mast.
From there, where the Corinthian isthmus
> cleaves the two seas,
I will foot the remainder of the road
> to Piraeus
> & I will mount the ramp of Theseus,
> slanting through the long walls up to Athens.
In Plato's school and Epicurus' garden
> I may begin to enlarge my wisdom
> & reap learned Menander's fruit,
& I will undertake rhetoric, the sword of Demosthenes.
> Of course I will take in the great paintings
> & please my eyes with the bronzework & the ivory.
Either the interval of years, or the long seas rolling between
> us,
> shall erase the scar in my heart;
If I die, it will be fate's work, not Aphrodite's,
> & I will not die in dishonor.

22

Has unheated Cyzicus
          agreed with you, Tullus,
     over these multiplying years;
     are you pleased with the sea's stir
          in the Propontis,
     and Cybele's beauty carved
               in the ivory tusk there,[21]
          and the road of the reaving god's horses,
               Pluto's road?
However much Helle's towers delight you
     may my hope for your return
               yet move you.
Should travel bring you
          to the sight of Atlas
          under the weight of all heaven,
          or the snaky Gorgon's corpse,
               or Geryon's stalls,
     or the scars in the powder of Libya
               where Hercules and Antaeus fought,
          or to the Hesperidean choros;
Should your oarsmen plash you past
               Colchian Phasis, & your ship's boards
          follow those of the Argo
               whose strange pine-form prow
          floated between cliffs under the flight of the dove;
Though you look out on the rim of Ortygia
     & the mouth of the Cäyster
     & the 7 flumes of the Nile at the delta;
What are all these marvels

[21] At Cyzicus there was a statue of Cybele made of hippopotamus teeth.

before the miracle of Rome?
What riches the earth bears, nature placed here.
      Our warlike rectitude
       is a glory without shame,
for we stand over the world
          with iron & piety; conquest tempered by justice.
Here we have the Anio streaming beside Tibur,
  & the Clitumnus running down out of Umbria;
and the Marcian aqueduct will probably last forever;
     & here is a fine lake below Albanus,
    & Lake Nemi floats under a cloud of leaves;
    & wholesome water flows from that godly spring,
         water trough of Pollux' horse.
Here glide no horned serpents, no scaly bellies here,
    no angry prodigies churn in our pools,
   no Andromedan chains rattle for maternal sin,
nor does Apollo turn his light from our banquets,[22]
    here no son is consumed in a far-off mother's fire,[23]
in Rome no pack of bacchantes
      ever howled under Pentheus' tree,
no Danaän fleet ever set loose from here
     after such dear sacrifice,[24]
nor has Juno the strength
     to bend horns onto a whore's head
    or demean loveliness with bovinity.[25]
Nor do we here record stories
    of sinister trees bent

---

[22] When Atreus killed Thyestes' children and served their flesh to Thyestes at a feast, the sun turned away its light in horror and left the world in darkness.

[23] Meleager's mother burned a piece of wood on which his life depended.

[24] The sacrifice of Iphigenia.

[25] See Io in glossary.

to wrench men asunder,[26]
Or Greek ships welcomed onto cliff rock,[27]
keel timbers curved to their ruin.
Here, Tullus,
   is where you came into the light,
  here is your most lovely home;
  In Rome there are honors
    to be won
    worthy of your ancestors,
    worthy citizens awaiting your eloquence;
Here an expectation of grandsons,
    & the well-earned love
    of a future bride.

[26] Sinis was a robber on the isthmus of Corinth who tied his victims to two trees bent toward each other; when the trees rebounded to normal position the victim was torn apart.
[27] See NAUPLIUS in glossary.

23

So it seems
    that my writing tablets
        which taught me so much
have come to ruin
        along with some pretty good verses
            written thereon.
My stylus has worn those tablets down
        with much use,
            & they bore certain verities
even if uncertified
        by wax & signet.
And they could soothe my girlfriends
        even when I wasn't around
            with eloquent verbiage;
They were not precious by gold affixed,
        being made of ordinary boxwood
        & old wax;
Nevertheless, I could always trust them;
        they were always worthy
        of the good things they won.
Sometimes they bore these words,
        returned to me:
"Certainly I am angry,
    seeing that you were most leisurely yesterday
        about coming;
    Perhaps she is more beautiful?
      Or were you strewing lies
        concerning my character?"
Or another time:
    "You will come today,
        & we will lie alone in idleness;

Eros prepares the night's festivities."
These words, & whatever else a quick & verbal girl
  might invent in her desires,
    when she devises the hour
  with alluring guile.
Ah, but now some covetous merchant
  inscribes his accounts in them,
  puts them in his monstrous files.
Any man bringing them back
  will have gold for his trouble;
  who would keep firewood
 when he could have
    a fistful of coins?
Boy, stir yourself & put this notice
    on some pillar
  & write that your master
    inhabits the Esquiline.

24

You worship a faltering flame,
 your beauty is illusion, woman,
 my eyes have made you vain.
Love praised you excessively, Cynthia,
 & now my face burns
  that my verses glorified your loveliness.
I often sang
  your manifold attractions
   so well put together;
Love considered it true beauty,
 not merc appearance.
I often rhapsodized on the radiance of your looks,
 an excellent counterfeit
  of the pale red light
of the morning star;
 but it was the glow of artifice,
   sheen of paint and cosmetic.
My father's friends couldn't turn me away from you,
  & no witch in Thessaly
   could have drowned my desire
in the whole salt ocean.
This I acknowledge without compulsion forced
  by iron or fire,
   as a man swamped in trouble's running sea.
I was seized by Aphrodite
  & I burned in her crucible;
 She locked my arms, bound them
   in the small of my back.
But as with a garlanded ship
anchored safely in port
 seething riptides & Syrtes' shoals crossed,
  so now I am safe

having found my wits
   with my wounds healing up.
O Right Reason,
    if there is such a goddess,
     I dedicate myself to your shrine
since Father Jupiter stood silent in heaven
      when I lifted my prayers
        for his ears.

Derision & laughter
  at my expense,
      jokes
    on the part
    of whoever would cackle at your banquets;
And I was reasonably faithful,
        your slave for half a decade.
But you will fling down your tears
    & bite your nails
      at loyalty departed
when I leave you;
and I am not moved by tears,
        it was by their artful flow
        I was gotten to this state—
you never wept, except in ambush.
  My eyes will trickle also
      as I swerve onto a new path,
but injury breaks my sorrow—
  you never tolerated any padding for my chains.
Therefore I say good-bye
    to your doors still tearstained at my words,
      the doors I never broke
        with my fist in anger.
May your hidden years oppress you,
    May the coming years line your face,
      years when your passion
will consist only in hating your own white hair.
  Ah, will your mirror applaud
      your withered features
    or will any man?
Can you endure rejection,

scorn coming the other way?
Perhaps, shriveled with time
 you will repent what you have done.
You might consider it possible,
 for it has happened before
 to others.
 I sing only a curse now.

BOOK IV

1

This present view, friend, where proud Rome rises
   was grass and high ground prior to Aeneas,
and the Palatine, sacred to Phoebus of ships
    pastured Evander's fugitive herd,
   & our present golden shrines
   come from clay gods.
In the old days no opprobrium lay
    in living in a rude house,
   & the god of the Tarpeian hill
    coughed from an empty cliff,
   & the Tiber was a trough for no cows,
& where steps ascend to Remus's temple
   a hearth was once boundary
     of the brotherly kingdom.
The senate, gleaming from its hill
   & now full of lordly togas
    once held fur-clad men with rustic hearts.
A crooked horn gathered the antique citizens
    in wordy assembly,
   & a hundred men in a meadow made a quorum.
No sinuous curtains then swung
    over the concave theater,
nor did the stage smell of saffron on feast days.
  No one went whoring
   after foreign gods, and the crowds trembled in suspense
    at their ancestor's rites.
Kindled hay lit the yearly feast of the Pales in those days,

(that rite now revived with the spilling of horse blood)
& impoverished Vesta took pleasure
in wreaths on her asses,
   while lean cattle pulled modest ikons;
Crosspaths were purified
     with the blood of fat pigs
      & peasants offered sheepguts to the tune of reed pipe;
& hide-clad plowmen laid about with rough whips,
   for the rites of Lupercus were in no way restrained.
Those rude soldiers didn't glitter in armor,
   but mixed it up naked,
      with burnt stakes for spears.
The riches of Tatius were a wealth of sheep.
And from all this came the 3 tribes of Rome,
   & the shining team of Romulus.
But our Romans now bear but the name,
   & are embarrassed at having in them
     the blood of the wolf's nursling.
O Troy, the gods exiled from your fireplaces
     were well sent here; the birds were auspicious
     for the landing of your ships;
the fir-wood horse had left us undamaged then,
   at the time when the old man clung to his son's neck,
   and no flame burnt Aeneas' godly shoulders.
Then came the great-souled Decii, & the axes of Brutus,
   & Dione herself bore Caesar's arms,
victorious arms out of the fire of Troy.
   This blessed earth received your gods, Julus,
     & shaking Sibyl, from the tripod,
      ordered Remus to sacrifice on this ground;
& the steady song of Troy's oracle
     to old Priam
has been borne out latterly.
   She warned them, saying:

[202]

"Wheel round your horses, Greeks, your conquest is ill-
         favored;
 Ilium will live, & Zeus will raise arms out of these ashes."
And what great walls
   have come down from the martial wolf,
   best guardian of our affairs.
May I honor these walls with a great song,
  but my voice rings weak;
    yet however thin the stream from my heart
    may it be in Rome's service.
Let Ennius wreathe his verse with a rough crown,
   but extend me your ivy, Bacchus,
  that my books may bring honor to Umbria,
  that Umbria may father Rome's Callimachus.
Assisi's citadel will rise out of the valley
   with greater glory
   as a consequence of my genius.
O Rome, favor me, this surge of oratory is on your behalf.
Citizens, give me a favoring sign; let the bird sing
   a good augury for my undertaking.
& I will sing the fall of Troy, & the raising up of Rome,
  & I will sing tombs in the earth
     & in the far-running sea
& I will sing of sacred days, & the ancient names of places—
  all this must be the goal of my sweating horses.
. . . .

"Misguided poet, where are you going,
   to speak of Fate without foreknowledge?
Your threaded work comes from no well-omened distaff.
   Lamentation will go with your singing, your own
      lamentation.
For Apollo turns away from you;
  you will wring a song from an unwilling lyre
    to your own disadvantage.

[203]

I will bring you the truth, or I am a most ignorant oracle,
  a prophet who cannot read the signs of the brass wheel.
I, Horos, am begotten of Archytas
      of the race of Orops of Babylon.
Conon was ancestor of our house
  & I have not fallen off from my kinsmen,
      the gods witness it,
truth comes foremost in my book.
    Nowadays the gods are made to have a price;
      Zeus is fallen for gold;
and they sell the signs gotten
      from the slanting wheel of the night sky
  & the lucky star of Zeus and the hard light of Mars,
    even the deadly light of Saturn
      will they turn to a profit;
    they explicate the moving stars of Pisces for a price,
     & the windy constellation Leo,
    & Capricorn washed in the waters of sunset.

"I foretold it when Arria bore twin boys
  (given weapons despite God's veto)
    that they would never bring their javelins home
to their ancestral gods,
  and two grave mounds now give credence to that prophecy.
  Lupercus fell by his horse with his face bloodied,
     & Gallus was cut down
    before the bloody hook of his eagle standard;
  two funerals from motherly avarice.
My predictions unwelcome, but fell out true.
And when Lucina dragged out Cinara's pains,
  delayed the burden of her womb,
  I said 'let her pray to Juno' & by god she delivered;
    the gift owing to my arcane knowledge.
"Such knowledge is not unrolled to Ammon in his sandy cave,

nor got from entrails spread out for the gods
    nor from the flight of birds,
      nor from shadows drifting up from magic pools;
Truth is unwound from the ribbon of the sky,
    in the path of the stars,
Truth lies in the 5 zones of heaven
        exclusively.
In the way of exemplary instances,
     recall Calchas to mind,
    who loosed ships that might better
      have stayed moored to their rocks;
he stained the iron
     with the blood of Agamemnon's child
& that blood stained Greek sails;
     nor yet did the Danaäns return.
But restrain your grief, O smoking Troy,
  look back at Attica's bays.
Nauplius raised up his avenging fire
     under the night sky
  & the spoil-heavy Greek ships
     went down with their booty,
& no more can Ajax rape & carry off Troy's oracle;
  Minerva would not let her be torn from her robe.
But enough of old stories.
I turn to your stars now; attend to that dismal tale.
  In old Umbria you were born
    to an honorable family,
Umbria where the fog from Mevania
    strikes the hollow plain with dew,
  where Lake Umbria warms with the summer,
& where the towers of Assisi
    rise above the hilltops—
ramparts to be glorious with your song?
    Do I go wrong in my story, or do I

touch your homeland?
And you had not spent your youth yet
    when you carried your father's cinders,
   & circumstances drove you to thinner Lares.
And whereas once a plenitude of oxen turned your land,
   Caesar's measuring pole [1] removed those tended fields.
But when you took off the gold amulet [2]
    and assumed the toga of freedom
before your mother's gods, at that time Apollo taught you
        some tunes
    & forbade you to rave from the Forum.
To mold & hammer the elegiac song
   is your appointed job—a treacherous undertaking—
but that is your camp.
   And with your example a flock of tunesmiths will come
            following after.
And you will endure hard combat under the arms of
         Aphrodite;
  You will be a strong contender with Eros;
But whatever victories your wars procure you,
      one girl will elude you.
And you will not break her hook, not by courage
    or by fighting the barbed shaft in your soul.
Whether you will close out the light from your eyes at night
   will be her decision,
    and you will weep at her orders.
A thousand spying guardians before her door
   could not help you,
    a small cleft will suffice.
Now whether your ship labors in a heavy sea

---

[1] "Caesar's measuring pole" refers to land confiscations after the Perusian War.
[2] The gold amulet was worn by sons of noble families.

[206]

or you walk unarmed among sword-bearers,
or the earth tremble and draw open
beware above all the 8-footed Crab
of the zodiac." [3]

[3] The Crab of the zodiac is an allusion to Cynthia's greed, since those born under the Crab were thought greedy.

2

The words of the god Vertumnus:

Multiform, but of one substance,
   I preach my own changes;
      let no man wonder at them.
A Tuscan god, I arose in Tuscan morning,
      but I forsook those fire hearths
         in the wars,
& I am unrepentant over my leaving.
It is this crowd delights me,
     no fane with ivory
        here before the Forum.
Tiberian water flowed here once,
     & oars pulsed in the shallows.
But the river yielded
      to the river's children, & they found a god
        in the river turning,
           called me Vertumnus.
And the new fruit of the cycling year is mine,
      for you know the change in things;
the grapes swell purple for me,
        for me the wheat spike ripens;
       they bring here sweet cherry offerings,
       canicular blackberries, red-gleaming autumn plums;
       here, the payment of fruit grafters,
      wreathed fruit in vow payment,
      when the pear trunk surrenders apples.
I pray Rumor's silence.
Other mutations go with my name; hear it & believe.
   I know all forms
       & will ornament any shape you will have me take.
In a Coan cape, a pretty girl;

in a toga, none would gainsay my virility.
Give me a sickle & headband twisted from grass,
          & you will call me a mower, swear it by oath.
I once bore arms & in arms won honor
     but with head-balanced basket I became again a reaper.
I am all sobriety in the courtroom,
   but with the wreath set for drinking
           you will giggle at my wine-drunk stumble.
Crown me with a miter & I will counterfeit Bacchus;
I am Apollo with the plectrum,
    a hunter with the snare;
with the reed I am the fowler's god;
I am a charioteer, a mounted acrobat.
With a cane pole I pull forth fish
   & I will go into the world
     with a long tunic, an elegant huckster.
I know how to lean on the herdsman's bent stick,
   & carry roses & asafetida in the dust.
And gardens are my great glory,
   thus the gifts before me, cucumbers, gourds, cabbages,
      these my insignia.
Nor does any flower stand open
      that will not grow languid handsomely
brought from the field to my wreath.
My name came from manifold forms;
    the shapes of the Latin tongue
      became my shapes.
And Rome has rewarded my homeland,
    turned a pathway into Tuscany Street;
This gift after Lucumo bruised the Sabines.
   I saw ranks turned & spears thrown down,
    & the rear side of their armor.

I have been

a whittled maple post, in ancient times,
    a poor god in a pleasing town,
but may earth spare Mamurius,
    graver of bronze, who poured another shape
for Vertumnus, one work with many honors.
But may the god who begot the rest
    keep this toga'd crowd
  before my feet
    throughout all time.

3

Arethusa sends this message
    to her husband Lycotas—
        if you may be called mine,
  being so much absent—
If some words are unclear,
    my tears render them so;
    should the letters seem ill-formed
        and uncertain,
    it is my right hand
        trembling in weakness.
Bactra beneath the rising sun
    beholds once more your presence,
and you are familiar to the Neuric army
        & their mailed horses,
    and to the icebound Getae, & Britain of the painted cars,
  and to the burning waves
    of multicolored India under the morning star.
Is this the marital faith
  pledged with the night's kisses
      when I was an awkward girl
& gave you my embrace, arms conquered by your wishes?
On my wedding night the torchlight flared ill-omened;
    a black flame from some torn-down funeral fire;
I was sprinkled from a pool of hell,
    nor was riband set right in my hair;
    no god floated with my veil.
I have hung offerings from all the gates,
    I weave now your fourth war cloak,
and O I hope oblivion was that man's fate
  who first raised a palisade
  hewn from harmless trees,
& contrived the shrill-boned war fife.

Better he to sit at one end of a rope
    than Ocnus obliquely feeding
      the small ass always.
Tell me, my husband,
  does the cuirass chafe your shoulders,
    & the weight of the javelin
blister your peaceable hands?
I would hope for these injuries
    & not the work of some girl's teeth;
    such neck wounds would hurt me also,
      leave me in tears.
They say your face gets thin;
    I hope your pallor
  is from wishing for me.
When the ashen night
    spreads over me at sundown,
I kiss left-behind weapons,
  and the bedcovers
    will not stay put on the bed,
& the birds before dawn are late to sing.
In the winter night I labor at the loom,
  purple wool for the life of the garrison,
  Tyrian cloth for the life of the sword;
I teach myself where the Araxes flows,
    that river you must conquer,
and inquire as to the mileage of Parthian horses
    between water holes;
& I study the world as laid out on the maps,
  the location of high Dahan,
    which land hardens with frost,
    which crumbles with heat;
I know which wind will drive your sails toward Italy.
And here

one sister comforts me
    in my distraction,
and a pale nurse swears falsely
    that it is winter keeps you.
How I envy Hippolyte! Bare-breasted she wore the sword
    & curled her soft hair
      beneath cruel battle crown;
I wish only that Rome
    let women march with the legions,
and I would go to war with you
    as faithfully as your pack;
  no ridge in Scythia would stop me,
  even when God steels deep water
    in ice and cutting cold.
Love is a strong god always,
  strongest in a true husband's wife;
    It is Aphrodite breathes on this flame,
    that it might live.
What good to me is shining purple,
    & bright crystal in hand?
All things fall silent now,
    & are without hearing,
and only with the rare kalends
    does the regular girl uncloset the Lares.
The small dog's whine pleases me,
    my only bedmate now;
I cover the shrines with flowers
    & enshroud the crossroads
    with sacred branches,
and Sabine herbs crackle
    in the ancient altar fire.
And if the owl note sounds
    from a nearby roof beam

or the low-burning lamp needs a wine offering,
   then it is time that this year's lambs
      go the the altar;
   time then that junior priests gird themselves,
      & warm themselves for new lucre.
Be not too proud, I pray,
   with Bactra beneath you,
     yours the fine linen reft
from their perfumed captains
   after the lead shot from the unwound sling
      is strewn on the bàttlefield,
& after the cunning bow shots
   have rung from the turning horses.
But in any case, when you have tamed
     Parthia's nurslings
may the headless spear [4] reward your chariot,
   and may you keep our bed covenant unbroken;
     May these circumstances attend your return.
I will at that time
   carry your war gear
     & offerings
   to the Capene gate
& inscribe beneath them:

FOR HIS SAFE RETURN

FROM A FAITHFUL WIFE

[4] The headless spear was a kind of medal for meritorious service.

4

These words lifted up
   over the stained tomb,
     the sacred trees of Tarpeia,
       the taken gates of ancient Jupiter.
Tatius ringed this mountain, planted a palisade
        of maple posts
         & raised his own tents behind dirt ramparts.
What was Rome then, when Cures' hornblower
    broke his long notes
       on godly cliffs hard by;
         when Sabines racked their spears in the Forum
           where Rome now hands down law to empire?
Hills were Rome's towers
    and the armored horse drank
    at a thin spring
       where the Senate sits now.
And in that place
    a fruitful grove
    secret in an ivied cleft
       where the trees sounded against native springs,
branch & reed pipe, Sylvanian home,
     the sheep went to the music
       to a shadowed well,
& Tarpeia, clay jar on her head,
   came down
     to bring water for Vesta;
& there she caught sight of that king, Tatius,
        on maneuver in a sandy plain,
      damasked iron raised over gold crests.
And struck by the regal countenance
   & kingly armor

she let the jar fall forgotten
  from strained hands.
Ah, Vesta, is one doom sufficient
  for a priestess oblate to another flame?
And Tarpeia swore, in more than one night,
  that the clear moon rose
   with evil meaning,
 & again, & again, she went down to the stream
   to tinge her hair therein;
 and came often before alluring nymphs,
  blades of silver lilies in her hands;
 this that her king receive no wound from Romulus.
Mornings she ascended the great hill
  overcast with early smoke,
  & came home evenings arms scarred by the thorn.
And on her citadel she lamented wounds
   no god might cure:
"O God, if only I sat before
   the fires of his garrison,
   before the main tent,
    Sabine swords gleaming in my eyes.
If only I lay captive,
  & as a prisoner saw his face.
I bid you good-bye, high hills, & also Rome
   crowning those hills,
  good-bye to Vesta,
   who will redden at my disgrace.
That stallion he rides, whose mane he smooths,
   will lay my desires to rest among his tents.
Who will stand in amazement
  that Scylla clipped her father's hair;
 what wonder that a sister betrayed
  the Minotaur's hideous horns,
 revealing the twisted way with loom thread unstrung?

I will bring shame to the beauties of Italy
    but I was not cut out
      to tend this virgin flame.
   Let that man who is astonished forgive me;
       my tears run down the altar.
The word passes
  that tomorrow they sanctify the city.
   Take, then, the dew-struck back
       of the brambled ridge, a slick trail,
      & treacherous, hiding quiet watery pitfalls.
O if I knew the chants of magic's goddess
  my words would serve your splendor
     with deeds.
You deserve
  the lordly toga, not that man of no mother
   who sucked the wolf-bitch teat.
Shall I then not be your queen, & bear children
   in your inner court?
  I bring a suitable dowry,
   I bring you Rome betrayed.
If I shall not be your wife, rape me then
   & requite in turn your own ruined women.
But I can break the cutting edge
   of armies set afoot.
I can bring brides to the covenant
   with my marriage robe;
Hymenaeus, lift up your measures;
   trumpeter, put away that wild music.
Lend belief to it, believe it, when I ornament your bed
   I will gentle your sword.
Now the fourth horn sings coming light,
   & the stars glide down seaward,
    I will search for sleep,
     search for you in dreams,

may your visage come lovely to my eyes."
Thus she spoke, relinquished to an uncertain dream,
   without foreknowledge of what furies lay in wait.
Vesta, holy guard of the Trojan coals,
     fanned the fire in her bones,
         augmented sin;
   & Tarpeia rose and rushed down
   like an Amazon by roaring Thermodon
     robe torn & breast laid bare.
And now in the city,
     ancient festival, ancestral Parilia,
     celebration of the early walls—
       a yearly banquet, feast of herdsmen,
    engorgements & games, drunken throngs dancing
        dirty-footed among piles of burning straw.
And the decree of Romulus came then:
abandon the guard posts,
     put down the trumpet.
Thus she reckoned the time come,
     & made fast the pact,
       herself part of the bargain.
Now her king, the slick hill ascended, the guard gone to the
                        feast,
    fell on the watchdogs, iron to the windpipe.
And all the city slept but Jupiter, the god wakeful over
                  retribution;
    the fatherland handed over thus,
     the trust of the gate broken;
    for she sought the bridal veil.
And the king (who at that point
     abjured treason)
   invited her to a royal couch
   & ordered her broken under shields.

This for the dowry,
    and from her the hill is named,
  her night watch thus rewarded with injustice.[5]

[5] I have not rendered well in English the ambiguity in the final line
of this occasionally touching poem.

5[6]

May brambles rise from the earth
    to cover your slattern tomb;
  may your ghost float dry,
  thirst being your hell.
    May a triple-throated hungry howl out of Erebus
      haunt your rotten bones.
This witch, she could have lured Hippolytus to bed,
      but to no harmonious bed,
    she was always an ill-omened bird for harmony.
She could have lured Penelope to wed
    with lewd Antinoüs,
    whispers of Ulysses alive notwithstanding.
At her will, the lodestone would unclamp iron,
    a bird abandon nestlings;
    and if she bring magic herbs to her ditch,
    then firm things dissolve into water.
She would enchant the moon
    with her brazen magical song;
  she would roam by night in a wolf's shape
      that husbands might be undone, deceit
    blinding their watch
      stretched out anxious through the night.
And with crow's eyes
    & the counsel of screech owls
  she sought my blood,
  and gathered potions for my seed
    from the effluence of pregnant mares.
And she kept at her work, underminer,
    like a mole in hard ground,
    & she would advise Cynthia thus:

[6] Ovid borrowed a good deal from this poem.

[220]

"If the dawn-gold shore of Dorozantum delights you,
   or the proud purple dye of Tyrian conch;
    if kingly Coan silk pleases you,
       and cut figurines languid with gold ornament,
     & gifts from palmy Thebes, & fired ceramic chalices
           out of Parthia,
then sidestep good faith; & for god's sake
        live in no odor of sanctity,
    make no ruinous covenant wth chastity.
And by no means rely on truth.
   Pretend you have hooked another man,
    use any device.
Love burns stronger if you scatter out his nights.
If he takes you by the hair in anger,
   make use of the anger,
        press him to buy back love's promise
         when he wants it,
      and then feign obliged abstinence
       for the overdue rites of Isis.
Have your servant inform you then
      of the upcoming Feast of Courtesans
        requiring celebration,
    & let another harp on your impending birthday;
    He will then pray your attention.
Sit and pretend to write someone;
   if he trembles,
     you know you have him.
Never hide the bites on your neck,
  & he will speculate as to what struggling produced them.
But avoid Medea's transgression—disdained
     for asking first.
Instead imitate worldly Menander's high-priced whore.
Change your custom with the man.

[221]

If he prides his singing,
    lift your voice to his sotted tune.
Have the doorman stand alert
    for those who bring gifts,
    but have him sleep through empty-handed knocks,
    have him sleep with the bolt drawn.
Take on soldiers when they come,
    even if as rough in love as war,
take sailors when they grip coppers
    in calloused hands;
Hell, take chalk-footed barbarians [7]
    who have danced in the slave market.
Examine carefully the gold,
not the hand the gold arrives in.
    And if you attend verses, what will you gain but words?
    'Why go forth in the streets
    with elegant coiffure, my love,
    moving in subtle curves of Coan vestment?'[8]
Hear no man who gives you Coan verses
    instead of Coan silk, & learn to grow deaf
    to the ungilded lyre.
Use your time while the blood pumps strong
and your beauty is unmarred by wrinkles,
    before that future morning
when your face will please no man.
I have beheld the blight, the burning of rose gardens
    under the morning wind out of Africa."
And while Acanthis thus twisted my Cynthia's soul,
    you could have counted my bones
    under my taut skin.

[7] It was customary to whiten the feet of slaves put up for sale.
  [8] This quotation is possibly an interpolation of the first three lines of
I.2.

But receive my gift in your fire, Queen Aphrodite,
I saw her cough harden in her wrinkled throat,
    bloody spittle in hollow teeth;
I saw her evil soul expire,
    a chill in the broken fireplace of her brothel.
Her funeral riches were two stolen headbands,
  a pale miter ruined by neglect,
     & that overwakeful dog of painful memory,
    always alert
       when my hands would unloose the grating.
Let this jade's grave marker be
    a cracked amphora;
  may the fig tree grow out of her ashes;
  and all you who love, whoever you are,
    fall on that sepulcher
      with stones and maledictions.

6

Let there be silence, that the sacrifice fall well;
    the heifer is struck down now
   before the fire of my altar,
      with properly inspired consecration.
Let the Roman wreath contend
     with the ivy berries of Philetas,
  let the jar splash me
       with Cyrenian water,[9] give me
        mild myrrh & alluring olibanum,
& wind the wool disk [10] 3 times round the fire;
   pour the ablution down,
     let the ivory flute
       ring a tuneful song
    here by the new altar;
Deception, depart; let evil float in another air.
  Smooth the singer's new path with laurel.
Muse, we will bring anew
    the story of Palatine Apollo's shrine; Calliope,
    the work deserves your favor.
I sing these songs in Caesar's name,
  & while Caesar is sung, I pray even Zeus be silent.
The scene: The Athamanian coast, the shore of Apollo,
    a sheltering bay out of Ionian sea rumble;
    Actium's sea, a relief to sailors,
    a memorial to Julian craft.
Here the fleets of the world assembled,
    great bulks of pine, stock-still on the water.
The bird of providence failed one side,
    one fleet to be ruined by Trojan Augustus,

---

[9] A reference to Callimachus
[10] A festoon of wool often seen carved on Roman altars.

for the shame of a Roman lance in the hands of a woman.
And under conquering insignia
sails tightened
in Jovian blessing,
& Nereus bent the twin ranks in a sharp crescent,
& the painted water shimmered
in the radiation of arms.
And Phoebus came out of Delos—now rooted in the sea
under his shield, though once floating
with the rage of the south wind—
stood above the august poop deck
with slanting torch fire,
a curved triple flame.
No loose hair then, no strung tortoise shell;
but he looked as he did when he shot death
through Agamemnon's camp,
& as when he broke the turning coils of the Python,
terror of pacific Muses.
"O Augustus," said he, "descended from Alba Longa,
Preserver of the world, renowned above Hector,
the land is yours, conquer now in sea wave.
My bow bends in your service,
the bolts at my shoulder favor you.
Unshackle the country from fear,
the country puts prayers on your keel.
If you should not defend Rome,
then the birds Romulus saw from the Palatine
portended evil for his walls.
The enemy rows too close.
Must Latin billows uphold a queen
while you are prince? Have no fear, though their fleet
move on winged oars,
those ships will move only to the sea floor.
Despite prows with centaurs & rock-wielding monsters,

you will prove them hollow timbers & painted terrors.
The strength of a soldier is broken or lifted
    by the strength of his cause,
      with no justice in his cause, a soldier's sword shakes in
        his hand.
Now it is time; for I create the time,
    commit your fleet, & I will lead it with the laurel bough."
And they felt the weight of his bow,
      and the bite of Caesar's lance,
& Rome came back victorious
    with Apollo's help; and that woman
    was brought to ruin; the Ionian floated broken scepters.
Augustus, from godly Caesar's blood, under Caesar's comet,
      was sung by Triton & Nereid,
    & they applauded the banners of liberty.
And the Queen pulled wickedly
    for the river Nile,
    the one goal she achieved,
      & she chose her own time to die.
Which is for the best; how would it look
    to lead a woman through the same streets
      Jugurtha came through?
Thus Actian Phoebus got his monument—
    pay for his boat-breaking projectiles.
I have sung sufficiently of war;
  Apollo would now hear my cithern;
    he lays down his sword for the quiet dance.
Let the glittering banquet pass into the grove,
    & alluring roses circle my neck.
Pour the Falernian, put perfume in my hair;
    & may the Muse inflame poets now heated only with
      drink—
Phoebus & Bacchus go well together.
Let's have some

poet
      retell the breaking of the Sycambri,
or sing of the black kingdom beyond the Nile,
      or the truce with the Parthians, thus:
"Bring home the Roman standards; they will lose their own
          soon enough.
      or if Caesar spares the East, it will be as a trophy
          for his grandsons.
Rejoice, Crassus, if the light has not yet left you
          in the black sands
      that we can now pass over the Euphrates
          to your graveyard."
Thus with libation the night passes,
    with Propertius as cheerleader,
until the morning sunray strikes my wineglass.

7[11]

Spirits float in the night
        liberated by death,
                that illusion of finality.
The shadowing ghost rises lurid
        from the smoking fire;
Cynthia, just buried in the murmur
        of her last road,
                came in the dark,
    a wraith at my bed, when sleep hovered
        in the wake of love's funeral,
                and I mourned in my cold-couched realm.
Her proud hair was as it once was
        and her eyes
             but her tunic was burnt
                & her beryl ring fire-blackened,
her lovely lips parched
        by the waters of Lethe.
Spirit and whispers
    were carried in her breath,
        fragile hands clicked their bones.
"Dishonest man,
        though you could be worse,
                has a hard sleep gripped you so soon?
Do you forget our intrigues
        in the watching Roman night,
do you forget my window
        polished by our midnight meetings,
            when I came down a rope
hand over hand, landing in your arms?
Oftentimes the two of us & love mingled at the crossroads,
        heartbeat to heartbeat,
        the road hot beneath our cloaks.

[11] This poem has been translated by Robert Lowell.

The southerly squalls sweep deaf to our silent love pact,
     those lies whipped off with the wind.
No man grieved as the light left my eyes,
   and had you prayed
      I might have seen one day more.
No night watchman rattled his cloven cane
     at my departure,
  and my head rested on a broken tile.
     Who saw you at the last,
       bowed at my burial,
    your toga black
      with hot tears?
If being seen in the street with my bier offended you,
       you might have had it carried to the door
     more slowly.
Why didn't you pray for a wind
      to fan the fire, ungracious man?
Why didn't the flame smoke with incense?
  And what a great burden
     the price of a few hyacinths would have been,
    a few flowers for the fire,
  and an offering from a broken flask.

"And let Lygdamus burn, let the iron grow incandescent
    for my slave, whose crime I sensed
as I paled at his wine;
  & let Nomas remove
     her hidden concoctions;
the cup burning with venom
     will brand her hands.
That doxy, the object of the public's gaze
   because of her price, which was cheap,
     now dusts the ground
with a golden gown. She repays the honest words
    of a servant who has praised my beauty

with heavier work;
& Petale is chained for carrying
a flower crown to my headstone;
& Lalage is hung up by her braided hair & whipped
for daring to say my name.
And you let her melt my golden image
so she might have a dowry from my flames.
Yet I will not press these complaints,
though you deserve to hear them,
for I reigned a long while
in the kingdom of your books.
Let the 3-headed dog howl more softly,
for I swear by the Fates, whose song cannot be undone,
that I was faithful,
and if I lie
may a snake coil hissing over my bones.
Hell allots two places
beside its black river
and all who come
must be rowed to one or the other,
through those clamoring waters.
One barge is stained by Clytemnestra's crime,
bears the monstrous carved horns
of Pasiphaë.
But behold the flowered yawl
sailing others to Elysium
where rich winds stir the roses gently,
where the lutes strum
& Cybele's bronze cymbals ring,
where mitered dancers move to the lyre.
Andromeda and Hypermnestra,
pure and blameless wives,
recount their adventures there;

Andromeda speaking of arms bruised by chains,
     hands wrongly locked to the cold rock;
And Hypermnestra of the bold crimes of her sisters
     & how she quailed at such evil.
Thus with the tears of death
     we heal life's loves.
But I keep your faithless ways secret still.
     But now see to these things,
        if your heart has stirred,
if the philters of your present whore
     have not laid hold of you:
Let my nurse Parthenie have
     whatever she might want
        in her trembling age;
She was neither harsh nor avaricious.
  Forbid my dear Latris
     to hold up the mirror to another mistress.
And burn the songs you wrote for me;
     cease to use my fame.
Dislodge the ivy from my tomb
    which twists its leaves and berries
       around my yielding bones.
And where the fruitful Anio
   curls through the orchards
     where ivory whitens with age,[12]
by order of Hercules,
     there, in Tibur, inscribe a song worthy of me
        in stone, but briefly,
       that it may be read
     from the running chariot
     by the traveler from the city:

[12] Ivory was thought to grow whiter with age in the air of Tibur.

HERE LIES GOLDEN CYNTHIA
IN HER TIBURTINE FIELDS
SHE ADDS TO THE ANIO'S GLORY

And do not fear these holy dreams;
        they come with truth.
Night frees us and we walk shadowy abroad,
        Cerberus himself howls straying in the night.
But the dawn requires our return
                to the marshes of hell
                        & we come and are counted by the ferryman.
Now may some other woman have you
for soon
                you will be mine again,
                        bone against polished bone."
Her reproaches ended then
        and her smoky image
        vanished as I embraced it.

8

Hear me, and learn
    what pulse of alarm
        struck through the night of the liquid Esquiline,[13]
propelling a fearful throng through the New Field gardens
    when a foul tumult agitated the darkness,[14]
        tumult in which I meant to be no contender,
       & in which my good name received certain injuries.
Lanuvium is from old times guarded by her tutelary snake,
      an ageless reptile; a pause there is worth your while,
      a pause for this distinguished attraction.
Sacred steps plunge down a black cleft there,
    down which his yearly sacrifice descends,
      when reptilian hunger requires propitiation
(Young woman, beware of such places)
      when his annual hisses curl from the hollow earth.
A pale virgin descends to lurid rites,
    hands held out rashly with provender
        for his honorable maw,
    canister clattering in fearful hands.
If she be chaste, she returns to her parents' arms
        & the farmers sing that it will be a prosperous year,
           a fertile year.
My Cynthia took herself there, wth gleaming horses,
      pleading Juno's worship, intending Aphrodite's,
her chariot hurtling over the rocks,
    wheels reckless on the Appian Way,
Cynthia suspended at the pole's head, a spectacular sight,
      whipping her way through the bad spots in the road
      with somewhat more daring than the average beardless

---

[13] The slopes of Esquiline Hill were marshy and full of springs.
[14] This line and the two that follow translate lines 19 and 20 of the Latin.

                    prodigal
in his carriage hung with Chinese silk
    & his necklaced poodle.[15]
Thus another of her absences from our bed,
    & I undertook a little diversion,
        & pitched camp elsewhere.
Two girls, Phyllis, who lives near the Aventine Diana;
    who lacks charm sober, although things improve when she
                    drinks;
    & Teia, who resides near the Tarpeian wood,
        a glowing beauty, & when she is fired by wine,
            half a dozen lovers are scarcely sufficient.
I invited these two, set up a small orgy
    to soothe the long night & renew the dormant rites
    of Aphrodite
                    with secret lubricity.
One couch in a hidden garden served for 3 of us,
    me between the two,
and Lygdamus manned the wine ladle,
    & our summertime equipage of chalices served for the
                                        wine,
        a Greek wine, odor of Methymna.
Flutist from the Nile, a treble flute was played that night,
    & Phyllis played the castanets, elegantly artless,
    pleased to receive roses of acclamation.
Magnus the dwarf hopped and waved his hardened hands
    to the fluted descant, song of the hollow boxwood.
The lantern was full; the flame wavered [16] in the night,
    the table had collapsed with its burden,
        & as the dice clattered I prayed for the Venus throw,
but always the damned dog leapt into the light;
And they sang to a deaf man, & bared their bodies

---

[15] A short Propertian digression following this line has been omitted.
[16] A wavering flame was an omen of impending arrival.

[234]

for a blind man,
for I was alone at the gates of Lanuvium.
Suddenly a hinge creak at the doorposts,
    loud and resonant, a light footfall at the Lares,
    & then Cynthia threw down the folding doors,
hair disheveled, in a fiery rage.
She smashed the cup from my fingers; my wine-stricken lips
                                    went white,
    her eyes glittered, female rage possessed her;
A city would burn less wildly than she did,
as she sank savage claws in Phyllis's face,
    & Teia's frightful wail floated into the watery environs;
        and the neighbors, aroused,
    raised torches and milled in the street,
& the paths of the night echoed with madness.
My two girls fled, hair torn & tunics loose,
        into the first tavern on the dark road.
Now Cynthia came back, victress, & took a menacing pleasure
            in the spoils she had captured, wounded my mouth
        with her nails & bloodied my neck with her teeth,
& undertook to darken my wandering eyes with her fists;
    & when her arms got tired with that she spied Lygdamus
            cowering by the sinister couch, & she dragged him into
                the light
        as he prayed that I protect him. How can *I* protect you,
Lygdamus, when she has me by the balls?
    With much supplication, she became more reasonable,
        though she would scarcely let me touch her feet.
"If you really want me to forgive this turpitude,
        then you will no longer go strolling
            in the shade of Pompey's colonnade, dressed in
        your best finery; you will abstain from attending
the games in the Forum; you won't loiter about eyeing the
                                curtainless

palanquins jog past; you will abstain also
from craning your neck at those attractions
   in the high tiers of the theater, and finally,
let Lygdamus, that great troublemaker, be sold;
let his ankle chains clank as he walks."
To all this I acceded, and she smiled proud in her sovereignty,
   and she perfumed the contamination of those others,
    & washed the threshold with clear water,
     had me change my mantle, and with a fire of sulfur
     touched my head 3 times;
and then with the sheets changed
    we ascended into the covers,
   & we rolled over the whole bed,
   & thus resolved our quarrel.

9[17]

In those days, Hercules came on his cattle drive
        out of Erythea,
   came with his stolen cows to the wild hill
      of the Palatine
    hill teeming with herds, and there, being tired
       he camped to graze his cattle & recover strength,
 there where the Velabrum widened its waters
      forming a pool,
   boats floating over future urbanity.
But there were no welcome guests, and no cows were safe
  with the monster Cacus abroad, polluting & thieving—
Cacus being a native of the place,
  a robber from a fearful hole, a giant with three rumbling
        mouths.
   Now Cacus, so the tracks should not betray him,
     & his plundering not be manifest,
   took the cows by their tails, pulled them
     into his cave backward.
   But their bellows gave him away,
     & the god found the robber's cave
   & in anger pulled down the brutal doors.
   And he laid Cacus out with 3 swings of his cudgel,
     one stroke per head.
And Hercules then took leave of his twice-plundered cattle,
   calling them the last work of his club:
  "Let your moos hallow the ox's field,
    & your pasture be the grandeur of the Forum."
But now thirst was afflicting his dry tongue,
    & swarming earth provided no water.
But laughter far off struck his ear, from women behind walls,

---

[17] This poem and IV.10 are perfunctory and bad, both in Latin and
in English, but they may have had a "stuffed-owl" humor for the
Romans.

from a coppice circling in a ring of shadows;
      the secret place of the Goddess of Women,
   where the rites were never laid bare without penalty.
The doors were out of the way, & purple ribbons veiled
     them,
    & the crumbling hut shone with perfumed fire,
     & a long-leafed poplar embellished the temple
      & hid birdsong in its shadows.
And he came down to the gate
       dust matting a dry beard, and cast these words
      less exalted than his godly character:
"I pray you, those of you who play
     in the sacred hollow of the grove,
  throw open your temple to a tired man looking for a
     drink.
    The waters sound around me as I walk.
     A cupped handful from the stream would do.
Has word not reached you
     of the man who lifted the world on his back?
I am that man, whom the earth calls Hercules.
Who hasn't heard of the great work
    of my stick & of the true aim
    of my beast-killing spear,
and how one man lit black hell?
Receive me; I am tired; this earth is scarcely open to me.
  Even if you serve the altar of bitter Juno,
     she never denied me water.
  If you fear the lion skin
And my hair burnt in African sun,
    remember I once worked as a woman
     with wool & distaff, and a soft breastband
      on my hairy chest,
    and I was a pretty apt girl."
Purple ribbon in her white hair, the priestess replied, in her

kindness:
"Let your eyes not light within
    this venerable grove, depart from it,
retire & go now, forsake these lintels
    for your own sake.
The altar that claims this secret shrine
    may be seen by no man, & is avenged by fearful
    law.
The seer Tiresias beheld great Pallas naked
    as she bathed, the Gorgon shield laid down;
    & he paid a great price.
May the gods show you another fountain. This ravine
    bears the secret stream
    of women only."
Thus the old hag.
    But the locked gates buckled under Hercules' thirsty rage,
    and his shoulders broke the doorposts down;
    and he sucked up the stream, to put out the fire.
And then with his lips wiped dry
    he founded a new altar:
"This corner of the world
    now receives me
    in the path of my fate.
Though I am fatigued, this land is hardly receptive.
I will consecrate this great altar to the
    rescue of my cattle,
    & the altar will be great by my hands.
But it will never be open to women,
    that Hercules' thirst be remembered
    in coming ages."
And because Hercules had cleansed the world,
    he was established in this altar
    by Tatian Cures.
Hail, father Herakles, whom wild Juno favors now;
    favor my book.

10

I will undertake now,
    to lay bare the beginnings
    of Feretrian [18] Jupiter;
the triple loot of weapons seized
    from three generals.
I climb the great road, but glory gives me the strength—
    no crown from an easy ridge can please me.
Romulus first knew the value of spoils;
    Romulus, you first brought plunder home,
    that time you broke Acron's army
        which would have seized our gates;
your lance point nailed him
    to his own horse.
    Acron, seed of Hercules, commander of Caenina's citadel,
        once carried fear to the borders of Rome;
    he wanted spoils from the shoulders of Romulus,
        but he was himself relieved of his armor,
            stained with his own blood.
They met before the hollow towers,
    spears balanced, & Romulus went first
        with spear & vow,
    "Zeus, today this sacrifice on your altar,"
    & Acron fell the spoil of Jupiter.
Father of Rome and of manly virtue,
    Romulus was used to conquest,
    coming from thin Lares & cold tents;
        as apt at the plow
        as at the bridle;
    his helmet was a wolf hide with a bushy crest;
his painted buckler shone

----

[18] This poem hinges on a pun on *Feretrius, fero,* and *ferire*. Like H. E. Butler, I cannot translate it.

with no overlay of bronze; his belt was uncured leather.
The sound of Roman war had not yet
        gone over the Tiber,
    the farthest conquest being Nomentum & 3 acres in Cora.
     Then came Cossus, who cut down Tolumnius of Veii,
       in the days when conquering Veii,
         was no small thing.
Ah, ancient Veii, you were then a kingdom
    with a gold throne in your market.
Now lazy shepherds bray on crooked horns
       among your walls, & farmers harvest among your
         bones.
Tolumnius stood above the gates,
     trusting in his fortress,
    while the ram struck the walls, with brassy horn,
     & the mantlet covered the siege line.
And Cossus shouted
  "Better for brave men to meet in open field"
      & soon
      two ranks stood poised on the plain.
And the gods came to the aid of the Latin side;
  Tolumnius' throat cut, his blood spattering Roman horses.
And after that,
    Claudius beat the enemy
    back over the Rhone they had overshot,
   & brought home the rude shield of Virdomarus,
      their general,
    who boasted his Rhenish origin.
Virdomarus drove a straight chariot
& wielded a Gaulish javelin;
  & he fell in his striped pants
    in mid march,
    the bent torque cut from his neck.

Now the shrine
      bears
      triple plunder, this, & the generals
        borne down
     by the sword, & the arms
       borne home,
bear the story of the temple's name.

11

Leave my tombstone dry, Paullus,
   no tears, no prayers,
   may bring down the black gate,
once we are laid under dust
      in hell's jurisdiction;
         the road is barred after by fired steel.
The Lord of Shadows in his black palace
        may hear your entreaties,
    even so, your tears will evaporate
    in the silences of his coasts.
Beseechments may move Olympia,
   but let the boatman get his copper coins
    and he will bolt and lock
      the unearthly gate
    on his cargo of shades for once and all.
Thus sang the dark tubas with the blaze
    of the somber funeral torch brought down
    as the flame flickered against the couch
      & underneath my head.
What good then was my wedding day,
   & my children with my glory in their faces;
   what worth had my proud ancestral chariots?
They did not keep me
   from the bitter Parcae,
     & I drift as dust through the fingers now.
I do not come to the nights of hell
    and wade in shallow swamps
      with guilt in my heart.
I died young,
and may Lord Death have mercy
   on this phantom of Cornelia.
If Aeacus sits magistrate by the urn of judgment

may he adjudge no punishment
  when my number comes up.
Judges, draw close, let the austere Eumenides align themselves
  by the Minoan throne, and the court be silent.
  Stay your boulder, Sisyphus,
    let Ixion be unslung from his rumbling wheel,
Tantalus, assuage your dry throat,
    rattle not your chain, Cerberus,
      leave these specters in peace.
I speak now in my own behalf
  & if I lie let me bear all the urns of the Danaïdes.
Does anciently won glory and ancestral honor count, my
      lords?
  My devices speak of Scipio Africanus,
    and my mother also
      was of good family,
  & my husband's house is thus well founded.
When the bridal torches lit
    my maidenly disrobing, and a new ribbon graced my
      hair, Paullus,
we were long ago united in that bedchamber
    I now am sundered from.
In cut stone read
            TO ONE ONLY WAS SHE A BRIDE
May the holy ashes of my great ancestors
    whose standards ruled in Africa,[19]
be my witnesses.

. . . .

Perses, Achilles in your heart and lineage,
    with Hercules your forebear also,
      who splintered the door of this smoky hall,
Bear witness that I loosened no covenant,

[19] A reference to Scipio Africanus.

no ordinance of my husband, Censor Paullus.
    Nor was our fire darkened by any shame.
Cornelia damned no won splendor of that house,
    her virtue shone out even in such splendor.
I lived
        without accusation, unchanged by the passing years,
        exemplary between the one torch and the other.
Nature ruled law into my marrow;
    I fear no judge,
    let any who will cast a ballot;
    any woman may consider herself undemeaned in my
                        company,
even you, Claudia, great priestess of the rondel crown;
      and you, Aemilia, votary of Vesta, rekindling
           from dead coals the flame
      with a bright flaxon wand.
Nor have I wounded your sweet head, mother Scribonia;
    what would you wish changed in me, but my present fate?
My mother's tears, and the city's lamentations,
      are my threnody;
My bones are interred with a groan from Caesar,
    & the god whispered that I was a becoming sister
        to his Julia, and went with liquid eye at my death.
I have earned my vestments of honor,[20]
I was not severed from a barren house.
Paullus and Lepidus, you soothe me, you bring solace
    even into hell. The light left my eyes in your bosom.
And I lived to see my brother [21]
    twice seated on the curule throne,
      & it was during the feast of his consulate

[20] I.e., she was awarded the stola of honor for having had more than
two children.
[21] P. Cornelius Scipio.

that his sister was taken from celebration.
Daughter, semblance of your father, born to his honors,
    have only one man, after my example.
And sustain our lineage, my children,
    & I will go willing when the boat of hell floats loose,
        having been a mother to such children.
This is my reward and my triumph,
    that the living should exalt my glory,
            lift voice in my praise
                as the pyre's smoke rises.
Now Paullus, I give you these children,
        tokens of our union,
        and this care burns in my bones.
You must discharge my duty to them,
    I bequeath you a crowd of dependents
            & you must bear that burden
        and kiss them for me;
        the house and its work I bequeath to you also.
If grief afflicts you, hide it; and when they come to you
    deceive them, kiss them with a tearless eye.
Often, Paullus, you will lie awake
            thinking of me;
there will be enough nights
    when my beauty will light your dreams;
    and when you speak to me in solitude,
            speak as if I should reply.
Children, if the marriage couch by the door should change
    and a cautious stepmother linger in my stead
uphold and praise your father's choice
    and your propriety will capture her heart.
Do not praise me too much, or she will turn in anger.
    Or if he endures mindful of my spirit
        and esteems my memory always,

take notice of age growing upon him
    and leave no way that care might afflict him
        in his solitude.
May the time death took from me
    be added to your years,
May my children be a delight to Paullus when he is old.
I am thankful, for never did I wear black
    for any child of mine,
        & they all came to my funeral.
I have spoken my case, witnesses,
Earth will return its reward for my life.
  Heaven is accessible to virtue,
    & may my bones be carried
        among my honored ancestors.

GLOSSARY

ACANTHIS. Procuress and friend of Cynthia.

ACHAEA. Greece.

ACHERON. River in hell, or hell itself.

ACHILLES. Foremost Greek hero of Trojan War.

ACRON. King of Caenina.

ACTIUM. Scene of battle in which Augustus defeated Antony in 31 B.C.

ADONIS. Young man beloved by Aphrodite and killed by a boar.

ADRASTUS. Leader of the Seven against Thebes and owner of a talking horse.

AEACUS. Judge in the underworld.

AEGIS. Athena's shield.

AEMILIA. Vestal virgin who, accused of letting the fire go out in the temple, relit it by placing her dress on the dead coals. Miraculously, the fabric caught fire and she was vindicated.

AEMILIUS. Early Roman general who defeated Demetrius of Pherae.

AENEAS. Refugee from Troy and legendary ancestor of the Romans.

AESCHYLUS. Founder of Greek drama.

AESON. Father of Jason.

AETHER. Personification of the sky.

AETNA. Sicilian volcano.

AGAMEMNON. Husband of Clytemnestra, who killed him when he returned from Troy.

AJAX. Here, Ajax Oileus, who violated Cassandra.

ALBA LONGA. Ancient city near site where Rome was later founded.

ALBANUS. Lake near town of Alba.

ALCESTIS. Faithful wife who gave up her life for her husband Admetus.

ALCMAEON. Killed his mother Eriphyle and was tormented in hell by the Furies.

ALCMENE. Mother of Hercules by Jupiter.

AMMON. Jupiter Ammon.

AMPHIARAUS. One of the Seven against Thebes, he was swallowed up in a crack in the earth.

AMPHION. Son of Antiope who with his lyre caused rocks to spring up and form the walls of Thebes.

AMYMONE. Daughter of Danaüs who agreed to sleep with Neptune if he would cause a spring to come forth during a drought.

AMYTHAON. Father of Melampus.

ANDROGEUS. Son of Minos killed in a war with Athens and brought back to life by Asclepius, god of medicine.

ANDROMACHE. Hector's wife who, after the fall of Troy, married Helenus.

ANDROMEDA. Daughter of Cassiope, on whose account she was bound to a rock to be eaten by a sea monster. She was rescued by Perseus, who married her.

ANIO. Tributary of the Tiber; the town of Tibur was on its banks beside a waterfall.

ANTAEUS. Lybian giant killed by Hercules.

ANTIGONE. Daughter of Oedipus, betrothed to Haemon.

ANTIMACHUS. Greek poet of Colophon.

ANTINOÜS. Chief suitor of Penelope.

ANTIOPE. Wife of Lycus, who put her away to marry Dirce. Antiope's sons killed Dirce.

ANTONIUS. Mark Antony.

ANUBIS. Egyptian god with head of a dog.

AONIA. Mythic name of Boeotia, where Helicon is situated.

See also HELICON

APELLES. Greek painter of fourth century B.C.

APOLLO. God of the sun and of poetry and music.

APPIAN WAY. Famous road leading south from Rome to Brundisium.

ARAXES. Armenian river.

ARCADIA. Mountainous district of Greece.

ARCHEMORUS. Son of the king of Nemea. The Nemean games originated in the funeral celebrations held after he was killed by a snake.

ARCHYTAS. Mathematician of the fourth century B.C.

ARETHUSA. Wife of Lycotas.

ARGO. Ship of the Greeks who sought the Golden Fleece.

ARGUS. Builder or steersman of the Argo.

ARGUS. Monster with a hundred eyes who was charged with keeping Io after she was changed into a heifer.

ARGYNNUS. Young man who drowned, loved by Agamemnon.

ARIADNE. Daughter of Minos, she was deserted by Theseus after helping him out of the labyrinth. Bacchus fell in love with her and carried her up to heaven.

ARION. Musician saved from the sea by a dolphin.

ARION. Talking horse.

ARRIA. Possibly a kinswoman of Propertius.

ASCANIUS. River in Mysia.

ASCLEPIUS. Greek god of medicine.

ASSISI. Probably Propertius' birthplace.

ATALANTA. Young woman famous for her prowess in the footrace. See also MILANION

ATHAMANIA. A district of ancient Epirus in present-day Albania.

ATLAS. Mauretanian king changed into a mountain on which heaven rested.

ATTICA. The province of Athens.

AUGUSTUS. Surname of Octavian after he became emperor, and of subsequent Roman emperors.

AURORA. Goddess of dawn.

AVERNUS. Lake near Naples said to be the gate of hell, and hence hell itself.

BACTRA. Ancient capital of Bactria, in Persia.

BAIAE. Resort on the Bay of Naples.

BASSUS. Friend of Propertius.

BISTONIA. Thrace.

BOÖTES. Northern constellation.

BOREAS. God of the north wind.

BRENNUS. Leader of Gallic horde that attacked Delphi in 279 B.C.

BRIMO. Proserpine.

BRISEIS. Daughter of Brises and prize of Achilles, from whom she was taken by Agamemnon.

BRUTUS. Early Roman leader who saved the city from kingship.

CACUS. Monster killed by Hercules for stealing cattle.

CADMUS. Founder of Boeotian Thebes.

CAENINA. Town in Latium.

CALAIS. Son of the north wind.

CALCHAS. Prophet who told the Greeks to sacrifice Iphigenia.

CALLIMACHUS. Alexandrian poet, born in Cyrene, greatly admired by Propertius.

CALLIOPE. Muse of epic and other poetry and greatest of the Muses.

CALLISTO. Nymph changed into the constellation Ursa Major.

CALVUS. Poet and friend of Catullus. See also QUINTILIA

CALYPSO. Goddess abandoned by Odysseus.

CAMILLUS. Roman general of an early period.

CAMPANIA. Fertile province in Italy.

CAMPUS. Campus Martius, a place of assembly, games, military drills, and so on, in Rome.

CANNAE. Site of a battle in which Hannibal defeated the Romans.

CAPANEUS. One of the Seven against Thebes, he was blighted by a thunderbolt for offending Zeus.

CAPENE GATE. City gate on the Appian Way.

CARPATHIAN. Part of the Mediterranean named the Carpathian Sea after the island Carpathus.

CASSIOPE. Greek port on the Ionian Sea.

CASTOR. See POLLUX

CATULLUS. Famous Roman poet.

CAŸSTER. River in Lydia which flows into the Aegean Sea near Ephesus.

CERAUNIA. Dangerous promontory near Epirus.

CERBERUS. Three-headed dog guarding entrance to hell.

CHARON. Ferryman of the underworld.

CHARYBDIS. Whirlpool between Italy and Sicily, personified as a female monster.

CHIRON. Centaur renowned for his knowledge of medicine.

CIRCE. Famous witch.

CITHAERON. Mountain in Greece sacred to Bacchus and the Muses.

CLAUDIA. Claudia Quinta, whose rescue of the statue of Cybele when the ship carrying it struck a sandbar cleared her of an accusation of unchastity.

CLAUDIUS. Conqueror of Syracuse in Second Punic War and ancestor of Marcellus.

CLITUMNUS. Small Umbrian river.

CLYTEMNESTRA. Wife and murderess of Agamemnon.

CONON. Greek astronomer.

CORA. Town in Latium.

CORINNA. Famous Greek poetess contemporary with Pindar.

CORNELIA. Daughter of Scribonia and Cornelius Scipio and wife of L. Aemilius Paullus, consul in 34 B.C. and censor in 22 B.C.

COS. Island off coast of Caria famous for its wine and cloth and as birthplace of the poet Philetas.

COSSUS. Early consul.

CRASSUS. General who lost his life, as did also his son, in the disaster at Carrhae in 53 B.C.

CREÜSA. Jason's wife, burned to death by a fiery robe which Medea sent her.

CROESUS. Lydian king renowned for his wealth.

CUMAE, SIBYL OF. Prophetess of the town of Cumae, renowned for her great age.

CURES. Ancient capital of the Sabines.

CURII, CURIATII. Three brothers from Alba who were slain by the Horatii, three brothers of Rome.

CURTIUS. Roman hero who rode his horse into a giant crack in the Forum to stop the earthquake that had opened up the chasm.

CYBELE. Phrygian goddess widely worshiped in Rome.

CYRENE. Birthplace of Callimachus.

CYTHEREAN. Sacred to Venus.

CYZICUS. Town on the Propontis.

DAHAN. Region east of the Caspian Sea.

DANAË. Mother of Perseus by Zeus, who impregnated her by coming to her as a shower of gold while she was locked up in a tower.

DANAÏAN. Greek.

DANAÏDES. The fifty daughters of Danaüs, each of whom, except Hypermnestra, murdered her husband. For this crime they were condemned to pour water perpetually into a broken cistern in hell.

DAPHNIS. Shepherd in Vergil's pastorals.

DECII. Three generals—father, son, and grandson—who were all patriotic martyrs.

DEIDAMIA. Achilles' girlfriend and mother by him of Pyrrhus.

DEMOPHOÖN. (1) Son of Theseus. (2) Friend of Propertius. See also PHYLLIS

DEMOSTHENES. Famous Greek orator.

DEUCALION. He and his wife were the only survivors of the legendary Greek flood.

DIANA. Italian goddess of the moon, virginity, childbirth, hunting, and magic, identified with the Greek Artemis.

DIONE. Here, Aphrodite.

DIRCE. Killed for unjustly persecuting Antiope. See also ANTIOPE; LYCUS.

DODONA. City in Epirus in northern Greece, site of a famous oracle of Zeus.

DORIS. Daughter of Oceanus who was the mother of 100 (sometimes 50) sea nymphs.

DOROZANTUM. Probably a corruption of a place-name.

ELECTRA. Sister of Orestes.

ELIS. Region in Greece famous for horse racing, where Olympic games were held.

ENDYMION. Beautiful youth who offended Zeus and was condemned to eternal sleep; beloved by Luna.

ENIPEUS. River and river-god of Thessaly, whose form Poseidon assumed in order to seduce Tyro.

ENNIUS. First great Roman poet.

EPICURUS. Greek philosopher.

EREBUS. God of darkness and, by extension, Hades.

ERINNA. Famous Greek poetess of Lesbos.

ERIPHYLE. Wife of Amphiaraus who, in return for a golden necklace from Polynices, persuaded her husband to join the Seven against Thebes.

ERYTHEA. Legendary western island where the Geryones lived.

ESQUILINE. One of the hills of Rome, on which Propertius lived.

EUBOEA. Island in the Aegean Sea.

EUMENIDES. "The gracious ones," a euphemism for the Furies.

EUROPA. Sister of Cadmus, and mother of Sarpedon and Minos by Jupiter, who came to her in the form of a bull.

EVADNE. Wife of Capaneus who threw herself into her husband's funeral fire.

EVANDER. Arcadian exile who settled where Rome was later built.

FABIUS. Roman general famous for his delaying tactics in Second Punic War.

FALERNIAN. Wine from the district of Falernus.

FERETRIAN JUPITER. Jupiter Feretrius, one of Jupiter's designations.

FORUM. Open place in Rome where affairs of state were conducted.

GALAESUS. River in lower Italy.

GALATEA. Sea nymph loved by Polyphemus.

GALLA. Aelia Galla, wife of Postumus.

GALLUS. (1) Friend of Propertius mentioned in I.5, I.10, I.13, and I.20. (2) Rome's first great elegiac poet, who celebrated his mistress Lycoris. (3) Son of Arria and perhaps related to Propertius; perhaps also the soldier mentioned in I.21.

GERYON. Spanish monster with three bodies whose oxen were stolen by Hercules.

GETAE. Scythian tribe.

GLAUCUS. Greek fisherman who was changed into a sea-god.

GORGON. Any one of the three daughters of Phorcus, but especially Medusa; the sight of a Gorgon turned the beholder to stone.

GYGAEUS. Lake near Sardis in Lydia.

HAEMON. Son of Creon who killed himself when Antigone died.

HAEMONIA. Old name of Thessaly; Achilles' horses were Haemonian.

HANNIBAL. Famous Carthaginian general.

HECATE. Goddess of crossroads and of enchantments, identified with Diana, Luna, and Proserpine.

HECTOR. Greatest of the Trojan warriors.

HELICON. Mountain sacred to the Muses and to Apollo.

HELLE. Daughter of Athamas who, escaping on the back of a winged golden ram, fell into the sea—named the Hellespont after her—and drowned.

HERA. Juno, Jupiter's wife.

HERCULES. Legendary Greek hero.

HERMIONE. Daughter of Helen and Menelaus.

HESIOD. Greek poet born at Ascra.

HESPERIDES. Nymphs who watched a garden of golden apples on a legendary island beyond Mount Atlas.

HESPERUS. The evening star.

HIPPOCRENE. Fountain on Helicon sprung from a blow of Pegasus' hoof.

HIPPODAMIA. Young woman won by Pelops after he defeated her father in a chariot race.

HIPPOLYTUS. Son of Theseus and Hippolyte. See also PHAEDRA

HORATII. See CURII.

HORATIO. Horatius Cocles, who defended a bridge single-handed against an Etruscan army.

HOROS. An astrologer.

HYLAEUS. Centaur who attacked Atalanta and wounded Milanion, who defended her.

HYLAS. Hercules' catamite.

HYMENAEUS. God of marriage.

HYPERMNESTRA. The only one of Danaüs' fifty daughters who did not kill her husband.

ICARIUS. Killed by peasants to whom he had given wine, he became the star Arcturus in the constellation Boötes.

IDA. Famous mountain where Paris judged the beauty contest in which Aphrodite, Hera, and Athena participated.

IDALIA. Mountain in Cyprus sacred to Aphrodite.

IDAS. Strove with Apollo for the love of Marpessa.

ILION, ILIUM. Troy.

ILLYRIA. Roman province on the Adriatic.

INO. Daughter of Cadmus who, caused to go mad by Hera, leapt into the sea and was changed into the sea-goddess Leucothoë.

IO. Loved by Zeus. Changed by Hera into a cow, she later became the goddess Isis.

IOPE. Either the wife of Theseus or the mother of Andromeda.

IPHIGENIA. Daughter of Agamemnon sacrificed in expiation for a crime committed by her father. In some accounts Diana saves her at the last moment by putting a deer on the altar in her stead.

IRUS. Beggar at Odysseus' palace.

ISMARA. City and mountain in southern Thrace.

ITYS. Son of Tereus and Procne, killed by his mother and served to his father as food in revenge for Tereus' rape and maiming of Procne's sister, Philomela.

IXION. Strapped to an eternally revolving wheel in hell for attempting to seduce Juno.

JANUS. God of doorways, represented with two faces.

JASON. Hero of the quest for the Golden Fleece.

JUGURTHA. Numidian king conquered by Marius.

JULIA. Augustus' daughter and Cornelia's half sister.

JULUS. Son of Aeneas, also called Ascanius.

LAIS. Name of two beautiful Corinthian prostitutes.

LALAGE. One of Cynthia's slaves.

LANUVIUM. Town near Rome.

LATRIS. One of Cynthia's slaves.

LAVINIUM. City Aeneas founded and named for his wife, Lavinia.

LECHAEUM. Western port of Corinth.

LEDA. Mother of Helen.

LEMNIAN QUEEN. Hypsipyle, abandoned by Jason.

LEPIDUS. One of Cornelia's sons.

LESBIA. Clodia, mistress of Catullus.

LETHE. River in hell whose waters brought forgetfulness to those who drank.

LEUCADIA. See VARRO

LEUCOTHOË. A sea-goddess, the deification of Ino.

LIBER. Bacchus.

LINUS. Taught the lyre to Orpheus and Hercules, the latter of whom killed him with a blow of the lyre.

LUCIFER. The morning star.

LUCINA. Juno Lucina, goddess of childbirth.

LUCUMO. Leader of one of the three tribes of Rome after the Sabine war.

LUPERCALIA. Ancient Roman festival held by the Luperci; possibly connected with Lupercus, who was sometimes identified with Faunus, a rural deity.

LUPERCUS. Here, a son of Arria.

LYCINNA. Initiated Propertius in the sexual arts.

LYCOTAS. Pseudonym for an acquaintance of Propertius, perhaps identical with Postumus.

LYCURGUS. Thracian king who, driven mad for opposing and jailing Dionysus, killed his own son.

LYCUS. King of Thebes who put away Antiope and married Dirce.

LYDIA. Region in Asia Minor.

LYGDAMUS. One of Cynthia's slaves.

LYNCEUS. Poet and friend of Propertius.

MACHAON. Greek physician.

MAEANDER. Winding river in Asia Minor.

MAECENAS. Friend of Augustus and patron of Vergil, Horace, and Propertius.

MAENADS. Bacchantes.

MAMURIUS. Legendary bronzeworker.

MARCELLUS. Nephew of Octavian who died at Baiae in 23 B.C.

MARCIAN AQUEDUCT. Aqueduct named after Quintus Marcius Rex.

MARIUS. Famous Roman general who defeated Jugurtha.

MARO. Here, a statue of the companion of Bacchus.

MAUSOLUS. King of Caria whose tomb, built for him by his widow at Halicarnassus, is one of the Seven Wonders of the World.

MEDEA. An enchantress who, betrayed by her lover Jason, whom she had helped to bring back the Golden Fleece, killed her children by Jason and caused his new bride to be burned to death.

MEDES. Inhabitants of ancient Media, bounded by Armenia, Assyria, and Parthia.

MELAMPUS. Famous physician and fortune-teller who tried unsuccessfully to steal the cattle of Iphiclus so that his brother Bias might marry Pero. Here Melampus himself may be the suitor.

MEMNON. Aurora's son, said to be black, killed by Achilles at Troy.

MENANDER. Greek comic playwright.

MENELAUS. Helen's husband.

METHYMNA. Town on island of Lesbos.

GLOSSARY

MEVANIA. Umbrian town.
MILANION. Successful wooer of Atalanta.
MIMNERMUS. Early Greek elegiac poet.
MINOS. King of Crete, later a judge in hell.
MINOTAUR. Monster born of Pasiphaë and a bull.
MISENUS. Aeneas' trumpet player, buried near Baiae.
MITHRIDATES. King of Pontus who committed suicide after being defeated by Pompey.
MUTINA. Site of a battle between Antony and Octavian.
MYRON. Athenian sculptor.
MYRRHA. Maiden who fell in love with her father and was transformed into a myrrh tree.
MYSIA. Region in Asia Minor, on the Hellespont and the Aegean Sea.

NAIADS. Water nymphs.
NAUPLIUS. To avenge the death of his son Palamedes, killed by the Greeks, he burned signal fires on a dangerous headland, thus shipwrecking the Greeks as they returned from Troy.
NAXOS. Island in the Aegean Sea famous for its wines.
NEMI. Lake in the Alban Hills.
NEREIDES. Sea nymphs, daughters of Doris and Nereus.
NESTOR. Greek king who was the oldest and wisest of the Greek heroes before Troy.
NEURI. Scythian tribe.
NEW FIELD GARDENS. Gardens built by Maecenas on the site of an old cemetery on the Esquiline.
NILE GODDESS. Isis.
NIOBE. For boasting that her children were more beautiful than Apollo and Artemis she was turned to stone and the children were killed.
NIREUS. Next to Achilles, most beautiful of the Greek heroes at siege of Troy.

NOMAS. One of Cynthia's slaves.

NOMENTUM. Town near Rome.

OCNUS. Figure in hell represented as eternally braiding a straw rope whose other end was being eaten by an ass.

OETA. Mountain between Thessaly and Aetolia, where Hercules died. He was taken from there to heaven and married Hebe.

OMPHALE. Lydian queen admired and served by Hercules disguised as a woman.

OREITHYIA. Daughter of Erechtheus who was carried off by Boreas.

ORICOS. Port in Greek Illyria.

ORONTES. River near Antioch.

OROPS. An astrologer.

ORPHEUS. Famous lyre player, husband of Eurydice.

ORTYGIA. Island of Delos.

PACTOLUS. River in Lydia famed for its gold-bearing sands.

PAETUS. Friend of Propertius who drowned at sea.

PAGASA. Thessalian port where the Argo was built.

PALATINE. One of the seven hills of Rome.

PANTHUS. One of Cynthia's slaves.

PARCAE. The Fates.

PARILIA. The festival of Pales on April 21.

PARIS. Priam's son who chose Aphrodite as the most beautiful of goddesses in a contest on Mount Ida and in exchange was enabled to carry off Helen, Menelaus' wife. This act started the Trojan War.

PARNASSUS. Mountain sacred to the Muses and to Apollo. Delphi and the Castalian spring were at its foot. The Gauls were driven from Delphi by storm and earthquake in 279 B.C.

PARTHENIE. Cynthia's nurse.

PARTHENIUS. Mountain in Arcadia.

PARTHIANS. Scythian nomads found north of the Caspian.

PASIPHAË. Seduced a bull by putting on wooden horns and thus became mother of the Minotaur.

PATROCLUS. Friend of Achilles, killed by Hector.

PAULLUS. L. Aemilius Paullus. See CORNELIA

PEGASUS. Winged horse sprung from the blood of Medusa.

PEGE. Mysian fountain.

PELEUS. Achilles' father.

PENELOPE. Wife of Odysseus.

PENTHEUS. King of Thebes who was discovered spying on the ceremonies of bacchantes, led by his mother, and was torn to bits by them.

PERGAMA. The citadel of Troy.

PERILLUS. Bronzeworker who made a hollow bull for the tyrant Phalaris, in which criminals were to be roasted alive. The sculptor was reputedly the first victim.

PERIMEDE. Legendary sorceress.

PERSEPHONE. Queen of hell, wife of Dis.

PERSES. Macedonian king who claimed descent from Achilles and Hercules; defeated by Cornelia's ancestor in 168 B.C.

PERSEUS. Greek hero who received winged shoes from Mercury, killed Medusa, and rescued and married Andromeda. Their son Perses was progenitor of the Persians.

PERUSIA. Town in Etruria besieged by Octavian.

PETALE. One of Cynthia's slaves.

PHAEDRA. Sister of Ariadne who fell in love with her son-in-law Hippolytus and killed herself. Propertius' story that she tried to poison Hippolytus is otherwise unknown.

PHAROS. Lighthouse near Alexandria.

PHASIS. River in Colchis emptying into the Black Sea.

PHILETAS. Famous Alexandrian poet from the island of Cos.

PHILIPPI. City in Macedonia where Octavian and Antony defeated Brutus and Cassius.

[263]

PHILOCTETES. Bitten by a snake on the way to Troy and abandoned because of the stench of the wound, but later retrieved and cured because an oracle told the Greeks they needed his bow (or arrows) to win. He later killed Paris.

PHINEUS. Thracian king blinded and tormented by the Harpies for having his sons blinded. In hell his food was defiled so as to be inedible.

PHOEBE. See POLLUX

PHOENIX. Companion of Achilles who was healed of blindness by Chiron.

PHRYNE. Athenian prostitute so rich she offered to rebuild Thebes.

PHYLLIS. (1) Daughter of Sithon of Thrace who, deserted by Demophoön, killed herself and was changed into an almond tree. (2) Mistress of Propertius' friend styled "Demophoön." (3) In IV.8, a prostitute.

PINDUS. Mountain in Thrace.

PIRAEUS. Port of Athens, about 5 miles away and connected by long walls.

PLEIADES. Seven daughters of Atlas and Pleione who were placed in the heavens as a constellation.

POLLUX. Son of Tyndareus and Leda, brother of Castor and Helen. Castor and Pollux carried off Hilaira and Phoebe.

POLYDORUS. Son of Priam who was killed by Polymnestor, his guardian, for his gold.

POLYPHEMUS. Cyclops blinded by Odysseus. Loved Galatea.

POMPEY. Famous Roman general and triumvir.

PONTICUS. Poet and acquaintance of Propertius.

POSTUMUS. Perhaps a pseudonym for Lycotas, friend of Propertius.

PRAENESTE. Town east of Rome, famous for its oracle; now Palestrina.

PRIAM. King of Troy.

PROMETHEUS. Created the human race out of clay and brought fire from heaven, for which he was punished by being tied to a mountain where vultures gnawed at his entrails.

PROPONTIS. Sea of Marmora, between the Hellespont and the Bosporus.

PROTESILAUS. First Greek killed at Troy, he was allowed to leave hell to visit his bride.

PTOLEMY. Name of a line of Egyptian rulers.

PYRRHUS. King of Epirus who invaded Italy in third century B.C.

PYTHON. Huge snake killed at Delphi by Apollo.

QUINTILIA. Mistress of Calvus.

REMUS. Brother of Romulus.

ROMULUS. Founder of Rome.

SATURN. The reign of Saturn was considered a golden age in Italy.

SCAEAN GATE. Gate of Troy where Achilles was killed.

SCIPIO. One of two Roman generals of the same name who conquered the Carthaginians.

SCIRON. Legendary robber on the cliff road between Corinth and Athens.

SCRIBONIA. Mother of Cornelia and later wife of Augustus.

SCYLLA. (1) Rock on Italian coast, opposite Charybdis, personified as a sea monster. (2) Daughter and betrayer of Nisus. Propertius confuses the two in IV.4.

SCYTHIA. Region north and east of the Black Sea inhabited by nomadic tribes.

SEMELE. Mother of Bacchus.

SEMIRAMIS. Babylonian queen.

SIBYL. Any of several female fortune-tellers and oracles, the most important of whom was the prophetess at Cumae.

SIDON. Phoenician city.

SILENUS. Lewd attendant of Bacchus.

SISYPHUS. Condemned in hell to push a huge boulder up a hill, which always rolled down when near the top.

STYX. River in hell.

SYCAMBRI. Teutonic people who defeated the Romans in Gaul in 16 B.C.

SYPHAX. Libyan king defeated and captured by Scipio in Second Punic War.

SYRTES. Two inlets on Mediterranean coast of northern Africa with dangerous sandbars.

TANTALUS. In Hades, tormented by hunger and thirst while fruit and water were close by but beyond his reach.

TARPEIA. Maiden who opened the city of Rome to the Sabines for "what they wore on their arms"; instead of giving her their bracelets, as she expected, they killed her by throwing their shields on her.

TARPEIAN HILL. A rock on the Capitoline, a hill sacred to Jupiter.

TARQUIN. Roman king.

TATIUS. Sabine king who fought Romulus and became coruler of Rome.

TAYGETUS. Mountain range in Sparta.

TEIA. Prostitute.

TELEGONUS. Son of Odysseus and Circe who founded Tusculum and Praeneste.

TELEPHUS. Wounded by Achilles' spear but cured by its rust.

TELLUS. Earth.

THAIS. Famous Athenian prostitute.

THAMYRAS. Thracian poet stricken blind for challenging the Muses to a contest of song.

THEBES. (1) Greek city founded by Cadmus. (2) In IV.5, Egyptian city.

THERMODON. River in Asia Minor, on whose banks lived the Amazons.

THESEUS. King of Athens who abandoned Ariadne after she helped him out of the labyrinth.

THETIS. Sea-goddess and mother of Achilles.

TIBUR. Town on the falls of the Anio, now Tivoli.

TIRESIAS. Theban who was blinded because he saw Pallas naked; later given the power of prophecy.

TISIPHONE. One of the Furies.

TITHONUS. Consort of Aurora, who gave him immortality but neglected to protect him against old age.

TITYOS. Giant punished for attempting to ravish Latona by being stretched out over 9 acres in Hades while vultures fed on his liver.

TOLUMNIUS. King of Veii.

TRITON. Here, a statue of the sea-god Triton.

TULLUS. Friend of Propertius.

TYRE. Chief city of Phoenicia.

TYRO. See ENIPEUS

VARRO. Elegiac poet who celebrated his mistress Leucadia and translated the *Argonautica* of Apollonius Rhodius.

VEII. Town in Etruria.

VELABRUM. Marshy ground beneath the Aventine which was once flooded.

VERGIL. Roman epic poet.

VERTUMNUS. God of change.

VIRDOMARUS. King of the Insubres who was killed fighting the Romans.

XERXES. King of Persia who tried to build a canal across the isthmus of Athos.

ZETES. Son of the north wind.

ZETHUS. Son of Antiope and twin brother of Amphion.

Sexti Properti Elegiarum

SEXTI PROPERTI
ELEGIARVM

LIBER PRIMVS

I

CYNTHIA prima suis miserum me cepit ocellis,
  contactum nullis ante cupidinibus.
tum mihi constantis deiecit lumina fastus
  et caput impositis pressit Amor pedibus,
donec me docuit castas odisse puellas
  improbus, et nullo vivere consilio.
et mihi iam toto furor hic non deficit anno,
  cum tamen adversos cogor habere deos.
Milanion nullos fugiendo, Tulle, labores
  saevitiam durae contudit Iasidos.   10
nam modo Partheniis amens errabat in antris,
  ibat et hirsutas ille videre feras;
ille etiam Hylaei percussus verbere [1] rami
  saucius Arcadiis rupibus ingemuit.
ergo velocem potuit domuisse puellam:
  tantum in amore preces et benefacta valent.
in me tardus Amor non ullas cogitat artes,
  nec meminit notas, ut prius, ire vias.

  [1] verbere *Baehrens:* vulnere *N:* arbore *A F.*

[271]

at vos, deductae quibus est fallacia lunae
    et labor in magicis sacra piare focis,   20
en agedum dominae mentem convertite nostrae,
    et facite illa meo palleat ore magis !
tunc ego crediderim vobis et sidera et amnes
    posse Cytaeines [1] ducere carminibus.
aut [2] vos, qui sero lapsum revocatis, amici,
    quaerite non sani pectoris auxilia.
fortiter et ferrum saevos patiemur et ignes,
    sit modo libertas quae velit ira loqui.
ferte per extremas gentes et ferte per undas,
    qua non ulla meum femina norit iter :   30
vos remanete, quibus facili deus annuit aure,
    sitis et in tuto semper amore pares.
in me nostra Venus noctes exercet amaras,
    et nullo vacuus tempore defit Amor.
hoc, moneo, vitate malum : sua quemque moretur
    cura, neque assueto mutet amore locum
quod si quis monitis tardas adverterit aures,
    heu referet quanto verba dolore mea !

II

Qvid iuvat ornato procedere, vita, capillo
    et tenues Coa veste movere sinus ?
aut quid Orontea crines perfundere murra,
    teque peregrinis vendere muneribus ;

---

[1] Cytaeines *Hertzberg :* cythalinis *etc. NAF.*
[2] aut *Hemsterhuys :* et *NAF.*

naturaeque decus mercato perdere cultu,
nec sinere in propriis membra nitere bonis?
crede mihi, non ulla tua est medicina figurae:
nudus Amor formae non amat artificem.
aspice quos summittat humus formosa colores;
ut veniant hederae sponte sua melius,   10
surgat et in solis formosius arbutus antris,
et sciat indociles currere lympha vias.
litora nativis persuadent picta lapillis,
et volucres nulla dulcius arte canunt.
non sic Leucippis succendit Castora Phoebe,
Pollucem cultu non Hilaira soror;
non, Idae et cupido quondam discordia Phoebo,
Eueni patriis filia litoribus;
nec Phrygium falso traxit candore maritum
avecta externis Hippodamia rotis: 20
sed facies aderat nullis obnoxia gemmis,
qualis Apelleis est color in tabulis.
non illis studium vulgo conquirere amantes:
illis ampla satis forma pudicitia.
non ego nunc verear? ne[1] sim tibi vilior istis:
uni si qua placet, culta puella sat est;
cum tibi praesertim Phoebus sua carmina donet
Aoniamque libens Calliopea lyram,
unica nec desit iucundis gratia verbis,
omnia quaeque Venus, quaeque Minerva probat. 30
his tu semper eris nostrae gratissima vitae,
taedia dum miserae sint tibi luxuriae.

[1] verear? ne *Jacob:* vereor ne *NAF.*

[273]

III

Qvalis Thesea iacuit cedente carina
  languida desertis Gnosia litoribus;
qualis et accubuit primo Cepheia somno
  libera iam duris cotibus Andromede;
nec minus assiduis Edonis fessa choreis
  qualis in herboso concidit Apidano:
talis visa mihi mollem spirare quietem
  Cynthia non certis nixa caput manibus,
ebria cum multo traherem vestigia Baccho,
  et quaterent sera nocte facem pueri.   10
hanc ego, nondum etiam sensus deperditus omnes,
  molliter impresso conor adire toro;
et quamvis duplici correptum ardore iuberent
  hac Amor hac Liber, durus uterque deus,
subiecto leviter positam temptare lacerto
  osculaque admota sumere avara [1] manu,
non tamen ausus eram dominae turbare quietem,
  expertae metuens iurgia saevitiae;
sed sic intentis haerebam fixus ocellis,
  Argus ut ignotis cornibus Inachidos.   20
et modo solvebam nostra de fronte corollas
  ponebamque tuis, Cynthia, temporibus;
et modo gaudebam lapsos formare capillos;
  nunc furtiva cavis poma dabam manibus;
omniaque ingrato largibar munera somno,
  munera de prono saepe voluta sinu;

1 avara *Baehrens :* et arma *NAF.*

[274]

et quotiens raro duxti [1] suspiria motu,
    obstupui vano credulus auspicio,
ne qua tibi insolitos portarent visa timores,
    neve quis invitam cogeret esse suam :   30
donec diversas praecurrens luna fenestras,
    luna moraturis sedula luminibus,
compositos levibus radiis patefecit ocellos.
    sic ait in molli fixa toro cubitum :
" tandem te nostro referens iniuria lecto
    alterius clausis expulit e foribus ?
namque ubi longa meae consumpsti tempora noctis,
    languidus exactis, ei mihi, sideribus ?
o utinam tales perducas, improbe, noctes,
    me miseram quales semper habere iubes !   40
nam modo purpureo fallebam stamine somnum,
    rursus et Orpheae carmine, fessa, lyrae ;
interdum leviter mecum deserta querebar
    externo longas saepe in amore moras :
dum me iucundis lapsam sopor impulit alis.
    illa fuit lacrimis ultima cura meis."

IV

QVID mihi tam multas laudando, Basse, puellas
    mutatum domina cogis abire mea ?
quid me non pateris vitae quodcumque sequetur
    hoc magis assueto ducere servitio ?
tu licet Antiopae formam Nycteidos, et tu
    Spartanae referas laudibus Hermionae,

           1 duxti ς : duxit *NAF*

[275]

et quascumque tulit formosi temporis aetas:
    Cynthia non illas nomen habere sinat:
nedum, si levibus fuerit collata figuris,
    inferior duro iudice turpis eat.   10
haec sed forma mei pars est extrema furoris;
    sunt maiora, quibus, Basse, perire iuvat:
ingenuus color et multis decus artibus, et quae
    gaudia sub tacita dicere veste libet.
quo magis et nostros contendis solvere amores,
    hoc magis accepta fallit uterque fide.
non impune feres : sciet haec insana puella
    et tibi non tacitis vocibus hostis erit;
nec tibi me post haec committet Cynthia nec te
    quaeret; erit tanti criminis illa memor,   20
et te circum omnes alias irata puellas
    differet: heu nullo limine carus eris.
nullas illa suis contemnet fletibus aras,
    et quicumque sacer, qualis ubique, lapis.
non ullo gravius temptatur Cynthia damno,
    quam sibi cum rapto cessat amore deus :
praecipue nostri.   maneat sic semper, adoro,
    nec quicquam ex illa quod querar inveniam

V

INVIDE, tu tandem voces compesce molestas
    et sine nos cursu, quo sumus, ire pares !
quid tibi vis, insane ?   meos sentire furores ?
    infelix, properas ultima nosse mala,

et miser ignotos vestigia ferre per ignes,
  et bibere e tota toxica Thessalia.
non est illa vagis similis collata puellis :
  molliter irasci non solet illa tibi.
quod si forte tuis non est contraria votis,
  at tibi curarum milia quanta dabit !   10
non tibi iam somnos, non illa relinquet ocellos :
  illa feros animis alligat una viros.
a, mea contemptus quotiens ad limina curres,
  cum tibi singultu fortia verba cadent,
et tremulus maestis orietur fletibus horror,
  et timor informem ducet in ore notam,
et quaecumque voles fugient tibi verba querenti,
  nec poteris, qui sis aut ubi, nosse miser.
tum grave servitium nostrae cogere puellae
  discere et exclusum quid sit abire domum ;   20
nec iam pallorem totiens mirabere nostrum,
  aut cur sim toto corpore nullus ego.
nec tibi nobilitas poterit succurrere amanti :
  nescit Amor priscis cedere imaginibus.
quod si parva tuae dederis vestigia culpae,
  quam cito de tanto nomine rumor eris !
non ego tum potero solacia ferre roganti,
  cum mihi nulla mei sit medicina mali ;
sed pariter miseri socio cogemur amore
  alter in alterius mutua flere sinu.   30
quare, quid possit mea Cynthia, desine, Galle,
  quaerere : non impune illa rogata venit.

VI

Non ego nunc Hadriae vereor mare noscere tecum,
    Tulle, neque Aegaeo ducere vela salo,
cum quo Rhipaeos possim conscendere montes
    ulteriusque domos vadere Memnonias;
sed me complexae remorantur verba puellae,
    mutatoque graves saepe colore preces.
illa mihi totis argutat noctibus ignes,
    et queritur nullos esse relicta deos;
illa meam mihi iam se denegat, illa minatur,
    quae solet irato tristis amica viro.   10
his ego non horam possum durare querelis:
    a pereat, si quis lentus amare potest!
an mihi sit tanti doctas cognoscere Athenas
    atque Asiae veteres cernere divitias,
ut mihi deducta faciat convicia puppi
    Cynthia et insanis ora notet manibus,
osculaque opposito dicat sibi debita vento,
    et nihil infido durius esse viro?
tu patrui meritas conare anteire secures,
    et vetera oblitis iura refer sociis.   20
nam tua non aetas umquam cessavit amori,
    semper et armatae cura fuit patriae;
et tibi non umquam nostros puer iste labores
    afferat et lacrimis omnia nota meis!
me sine, quem semper voluit fortuna iacere,
    hanc animam extremae reddere nequitiae.

[278]

multi longinquo periere in amore libenter,
    in quorum numero me quoque terra tegat.
non ego sum laudi, non natus idoneus armis :
    hanc me militiam fata subire volunt.   30
at tu seu mollis qua tendit Ionia, seu qua
    Lydia Pactoli tingit arata liquor ;
seu pedibus terras seu pontum carpere remis
    ibis, et accepti pars eris imperii :
tum tibi si qua mei veniet non immemor hora,
    vivere me duro sidere certus eris.

VII

Dvm tibi Cadmeae dicuntur, Pontice, Thebae
    armaque fraternae tristia militiae,
atque, ita sim felix, primo contendis Homero,
    (sint modo fata tuis mollia carminibus :)
nos, ut consuemus, nostros agitamus amores,
    atque aliquid duram quaerimus in dominam ;
nec tantum ingenio quantum servire dolori
    cogor et aetatis tempora dura queri.
hic mihi conteritur vitae modus, haec mea fama est,
    hinc cupio nomen carminis ire mei.   10
me laudent doctae solum placuisse puellae,
    Pontice, et iniustas saepe tulisse minas ;
me legat assidue post haec neglectus amator,
    et prosint illi cognita nostra mala.
te quoque si certo puer hic concusserit arcu,
    (quod nolim nostros evoluisse[1] deos)

[1] evoluisse *Beroaldus on alleged MS. authority :* eviolasse *NAF.*

longe castra tibi, longe miser agmina septem
    flebis in aeterno surda iacere situ ;
et frustra cupies mollem componere versum,
    nec tibi subiciet carmina serus Amor.   20
tum me non humilem mirabere saepe poetam,
    tunc ego Romanis praeferar ingeniis ;
nec poterunt iuvenes nostro reticere sepulcro
    " Ardoris nostri magne poeta, iaces."
tu cave nostra tuo contemnas carmina fastu :
    saepe venit magno faenore tardus Amor.

VIII

Tvne igitur demens, nec te mea cura moratur ?
    an tibi sum gelida vilior Illyria ?
et tibi iam tanti, quicumque est, iste videtur,
    ut sine me vento quolibet ire velis ?
tune audire potes vesani murmura ponti
    fortis, et in dura nave iacere potes ?
tu pedibus teneris positas fulcire pruinas,[1]
    tu potes insolitas, Cynthia, ferre nives ?
o utinam hibernae duplicentur tempora brumae,
    et sit iners tardis navita Vergiliis,   10
nec tibi Tyrrhena solvatur funis harena,
    neve inimica meas elevet aura preces !
atque ego non videam tales subsidere ventos,
    cum tibi provectas auferet unda rates,

---

1 pruinas *S* : ruinas *NAF*.

ut [1] me defixum vacua patiatur in ora
    crudelem infesta saepe vocare manu!
sed quocumque modo de me, periura, mereris,
    sit Galatea tuae non aliena viae:
utere [2] felici praevecta Ceraunia remo;
    accipiat placidis Oricos aequoribus.   20
nam me non ullae poterunt corrumpere, de te
    quin ego, vita, tuo limine acerba [3] querar;
nec me deficiet nautas rogitare citatos
    "Dicite, quo portu clausa puella mea est?"
et dicam "Licet Artaciis [4] considat in oris,
    et licet Hylaeis, illa futura mea est."

VIIIA [5]

HIC erat! hic iurata manet! rumpantur iniqui!
    vicimus: assiduas non tulit illa preces.
falsa licet cupidus deponat gaudia livor:
    destitit ire novas Cynthia nostra vias.   30
illi carus ego et per me carissima Roma
    dicitur, et sine me dulcia regna negat.
illa vel angusto mecum requiescere lecto
    et quocumque modo maluit esse mea,
quam sibi dotatae regnum vetus Hippodamiae,
    et quas Elis opes ante pararat equis.

[1] ut *Rothstein:* et *NAF.*
[2] utere *codd. Par. 7989, Voss. 117:* ut te *NAF.*
[3] acerba *Scaliger:* verba *NAF.*
[4] Artaciis *Palmer:* atraciis *et similia O.*
[5] *The MSS. mark no break; the separation is due to Lipsius.*

quamvis magna daret, quamvis maiora daturus,
  non tamen illa meos fugit avara sinus.
hanc ego non auro, non Indis flectere conchis,
  sed potui blandi carminis obsequio.   40
sunt igitur Musae, neque amanti tardus Apollo,
  quis ego fretus amo : Cynthia rara mea est !
nunc mihi summa licet contingere sidera plantis :
  sive dies seu nox venerit, illa mea est !
nec mihi rivalis firmos [1] subducit amores :
  ista meam norit gloria canitiem.

IX

DICEBAM tibi venturos, irrisor, amores,
  nec tibi perpetuo libera verba fore :
ecce iaces supplexque venis ad iura puellae,
  et tibi nunc quaevis imperat empta modo.
non me Chaoniae vincant in amore columbae
  dicere, quos iuvenes quaeque puella domet.
me dolor et lacrimae merito fecere peritum :
  atque utinam posito dicar amore rudis !
quid tibi nunc misero prodest grave dicere carmen
  aut Amphioniae moenia flere lyrae ?   10
plus in amore valet Mimnermi versus Homero :
  carmina mansuetus levia quaerit Amor.
i quaeso et tristes istos compone libellos,
  et cane quod quaevis nosse puella velit !
quid si non esset facilis tibi copia ?   nunc tu
  insanus medio flumine quaeris aquam.

[1] firmos *Rossberg :* certos *N :* summos *AF.*

necdum etiam palles, vero nec tangeris igni :
  haec est venturi prima favilla mali.
tum magis Armenias cupies accedere tigres
  et magis infernae vincula nosse rotae,   20
quam pueri totiens arcum sentire medullis
  et nihil iratae posse negare tuae.
nullus Amor cuiquam faciles ita praebuit alas,
  ut non alterna presserit ille manu.
nec te decipiat, quod sit satis illa parata :
  acrius illa subit, Pontice, si qua tua est,
quippe ubi non liceat vacuos seducere ocellos,
  nec vigilare alio nomine cedat Amor :
qui non ante patet, donec manus attigit ossa.
  quisquis es, assiduas a fuge [1] blanditias !   30
illis et silices et possint cedere quercus,
  nedum tu possis, spiritus iste levis.
quare, si pudor est, quam primum errata fatere :
  dicere quo pereas saepe in amore levat.

X

O IVCVNDA quies, primo cum testis amor
  affueram vestris conscius in lacrimis !
o noctem meminisse mihi iucunda voluptas,
  o quotiens votis illa vocanda meis,
cum te complexa morientem, Galle, puella
  vidimus et longa ducere verba mora !

---

[1] a fuge *Bolt :* aufuge *NAF.*

quamvis labentes premeret mihi somnus ocellos
    et mediis caelo Luna ruberet equis,
non tamen a vestro potui secedere lusu :
    tantus in alternis vocibus ardor erat.   10
sed quoniam non es veritus concedere nobis,
    accipe commissae munera laetitiae :
non solum vestros didici reticere dolores,
    est quiddam in nobis maius, amice, fide.
possum ego diversos iterum coniungere amantes,
    et dominae tardas possum aperire fores ;
et possum alterius curas sanare recentes,
    nec levis in verbis est medicina meis.
Cynthia me docuit semper quaecumque petenda
    quaeque cavenda forent : non nihil egit Amor. 20
tu cave ne tristi cupias pugnare puellae,
    neve superba loqui, neve tacere diu ;
neu, si quid petiit, ingrata fronte negaris,
    neu tibi pro vano verba benigna cadant.
irritata venit, quando contemnitur illa,
    nec meminit iustas ponere laesa minas :
at quo sis humilis magis et subiectus amori,
    hoc magis effecto saepe fruare bono.
is poterit felix una remanere puella,
    qui numquam vacuo pectore liber erit.   30

XI

Ecqvid te mediis cessantem, Cynthia, Bais,
 qua iacet Herculeis semita litoribus,
et modo Thesproti mirantem subdita regno
 et modo [1] Misenis aequora nobilibus,
nostri cura subit memores a! ducere [2] noctes?
 ecquis in extremo restat amore locus?
an te nescio quis simulatis ignibus hostis
 sustulit e nostris, Cynthia, carminibus?
atque utinam mage te remis confisa minutis
 parvula Lucrina cumba moretur aqua,   10
aut teneat clausam tenui Teuthrantis in unda
 alternae facilis cedere lympha manu,
quam vacet alterius blandos audire susurros
 molliter in tacito litore compositam!—
ut solet amota labi custode puella
 perfida, communes nec meminisse deos:
non quia perspecta non es mihi cognita fama,
 sed quod in hac omnis parte timetur amor.
ignosces igitur, si quid tibi triste libelli
 attulerint nostri: culpa timoris erit.   20
nam [3] mihi non maior carae custodia matris,
 aut sine te vitae cura sit ulla meae.
tu mihi sola domus, tu, Cynthia, sola parentes,
 omnia tu nostrae tempora laetitiae.
seu tristis veniam seu contra laetus amicis
 quicquid ero, dicam " Cynthia causa fuit.

---

[1] et modo *ς*: proxima *NAF*.   [2] a ! ducere *Scaliger :*
adducere *NAF*.   [3] nam *Keil :* an *NAF*.

tu modo quam primum corruptas desere Baias :
  multis ista dabunt litora discidium,
litora quae fuerant castis inimica puellis :
  a pereant Baiae, crimen amoris, aquae !   30

XII

Qvid mihi desidiae non cessas fingere crimen,
  quod faciat nobis, conscia Roma, moram ?
tam multa illa meo divisa est milia lecto,
  quantum Hypanis Veneto dissidet Eridano ;
nec mihi consuetos amplexu nutrit amores
  Cynthia, nec nostra dulcis in aure sonat.
olim gratus eram : non illo tempore cuiquam
  contigit ut simili posset amare fide.
invidiae fuimus : num [1] me deus obruit ?   an quae
  lecta Prometheis dividit herba iugis ?   10
non sum ego qui fueram : mutat via longa puellas.
  quantus in exiguo tempore fugit amor !
nunc primum longas solus cognoscere noctes
  cogor et ipse meis auribus esse gravis.
felix, qui potuit praesenti flere puellae ;
  non nihil aspersis gaudet Amor lacrimis :
aut si despectus potuit mutare calores,
  sunt quoque translato gaudia servitio.
mi neque amare aliam neque ab hac desciscere [2] fas est :
  Cynthia prima fuit, Cynthia finis erit.   20

   1 num *ς* : non *NAF.*
   2 desciscere *Heinsius :* desistere *F :* dissistere *AN.*

[286]

XIII

Tv, quod saepe soles, nostro laetabere casu,
    Galle, quod abrepto solus amore vacem.
at non ipse tuas imitabor, perfide, voces :
    fallere te numquam, Galle, puella velit.
dum tibi deceptis augetur fama puellis,
    certus et in nullo quaeris amore moram,
perditus in quadam tardis pallescere curis
    incipis, et primo lapsus abire [1] gradu.
haec erit illarum contempti poena doloris :
    multarum miseras exiget una vices.   10
haec tibi vulgares istos compescet amores,
    nec nova quaerendo semper amicus eris.
haec ego non rumore malo, non augure doctus ;
    vidi ego : me quaeso teste negare potes ?
vidi ego te toto vinctum languescere collo
    et flere iniectis, Galle, diu manibus,
et cupere optatis animam deponere verbis,
    et quae deinde meus celat, amice, pudor.
non ego complexus potui diducere vestros :
    tantus erat demens inter utrosque furor.   20
non sic Haemonio Salmonida mixtus Enipeo
    Taenarius facili pressit amore deus,
nec sic caelestem flagrans amor Herculis Heben
    sensit in Oetaeis gaudia prima iugis.
una dies omnes potuit praecurrere amantes :
    nam tibi non tepidas subdidit illa faces,

        1 abire *S* : adire *NAF*.

nec tibi praeteritos passa est succedere fastus,
    nec sinet abduci : te tuus ardor aget.
nec mirum, cum sit Iove digna et proxima Ledae
    et Ledae partu gratior, una tribus ;   30
illa sit Inachiis et blandior heroinis,
    illa suis verbis cogat amare Iovem.
tu vero quoniam semel es periturus amore,
    utere : non alio limine dignus eras.
quae tibi sit felix, quoniam novus incidit error ;
    et quodcumque [1] voles, una sit ista tibi.

XIV

Tv licet abiectus Tiberina molliter unda
    Lesbia Mentoreo vina bibas opere,
et modo tam celeres mireris currere lintres
    et modo tam tardas funibus ire rates ;
et nemus omne satas intendat vertice silvas,
    urgetur quantis Caucasus arboribus ;
non tamen ista meo valeant contendere amori.
    nescit Amor magnis cedere divitiis.
nam sive optatam mecum trahit illa quietem,
    seu facili totum ducit amore diem,   10
tum mihi Pactoli veniunt sub tecta liquores,
    et legitur Rubris gemma sub aequoribus ;
tum mihi cessuros spondent mea gaudia reges :
    quae maneant, dum me fata perire volent !
nam quis divitiis adverso gaudet Amore ?
    nulla mihi tristi praemia sint Venere !

      1 quodcumque *Volscus :* quocunque *NAF.*

illa potest magnas heroum infringere vires,
　　illa etiam duris mentibus esse dolor :
illa neque Arabium metuit transcendere limen
　　nec timet ostrino, Tulle, subire toro　　　　　　20
et miserum toto iuvenem versare cubili :
　　quid relevant variis serica textilibus ?
quae mihi dum placata aderit, non ulla verebor
　　regna vel Alcinoi munera despicere.

XV

Saepe ego multa tuae levitatis dura timebam,
　　hac tamen excepta, Cynthia, perfidia.
aspice me quanto rapiat fortuna periclo !
　　tu tamen in nostro lenta timore venis ;
et potes hesternos manibus componere crines
　　et longa faciem quaerere desidia,
nec minus Eois pectus variare lapillis,
　　ut formosa novo quae parat ire viro.
at non sic Ithaci digressu mota Calypso
　　desertis olim fleverat aequoribus :　　　　　　10
multos illa dies incomptis maesta capillis
　　sederat, iniusto multa locuta salo,
et quamvis numquam post haec visura, dolebat
　　illa tamen, longae conscia laetitiae.
nec sic Aesoniden rapientibus anxia ventis　　　17
　　Hypsipyle vacuo constitit in thalamo :　　　　18
Hypsipyle nullos post illos sensit amores,　　　19
　　ut semel Haemonio tabuit hospitio.　　　　　　20

[289]

Alphesiboea suos ulta est pro coniuge fratres 15
    sanguinis et cari vincula rupit amor.[1] 16
coniugis Euadne miseros elata per ignes 21
    occidit, Argivae fama pudicitiae.
quarum nulla tuos potuit convertere mores,
    tu quoque uti fieres nobilis historia.
desine iam revocare tuis periuria verbis,
    Cynthia, et oblitos parce movere deos;
audax a nimium nostro dolitura periclo,
    si quid forte tibi durius inciderit!
multa prius:[2] vasto labentur flumina ponto,
    annus et inversas duxerit ante vices, 30
quam tua sub nostro mutetur pectore cura:
    sis quodcumque voles, non aliena tamen.
tam tibi[3] ne viles isti videantur ocelli,
    per quos saepe mihi credita perfidia est!
hos tu iurabas, si quid mentita fuisses,
    ut tibi suppositis exciderent manibus:
et contra magnum potes hos attollere solem,
    nec tremis admissae conscia nequitiae?
quis te cogebat multos pallere colores
    et fletum invitis ducere luminibus? 40
quis ego nunc pereo, similes moniturus amantes
    "O nullis tutum credere blanditiis!"

---

1 *15, 16, Markland's transposition.*
2 *I give Rothstein's punctuation.* Without it **multa** *must be altered to* alta *or the like.*
3 tam tibi *Palmer:* quam tibi *NAF.*

XVI

QVAE fueram magnis olim patefacta triumphis,
    ianua Tarpeiae nota pudicitiae;
cuius inaurati celebrarunt limina currus,
    captorum lacrimis umida supplicibus;
nunc ego, nocturnis potorum saucia rixis,
    pulsata indignis saepe queror manibus,
et mihi non desunt turpes pendere corollae
    semper et exclusis signa iacere faces.
nec possum infamis dominae defendere noctes
    nobilis obscenis tradita carminibus;   10
nec tamen illa suae revocatur parcere famae
    turpior et saecli vivere luxuria.
has inter gravius cogor deflere querelas,[1]
    supplicis a longis tristior excubiis.
ille meos numquam patitur requiescere postes,
    arguta referens carmina blanditia:
" Ianua vel domina penitus crudelior ipsa,
    quid mihi iam duris clausa taces foribus?
cur numquam reserata meos admittis amores,
    nescia furtivas reddere mota preces?   20
nullane finis erit nostro concessa dolori,
    turpis et in tepido limine somnus erit?
me mediae noctes, me sidera prona[2] iacentem,
    frigidaque Eoo me dolet aura gelu:

---

[1] gravius . . . querelas *Scaliger:* gravibus . . . querelis
NAF.   [2] prona ς: plena *NAF.*

tu sola humanos numquam miserata dolores
    respondes tacitis mutua cardinibus.
o utinam traiecta cava mea vocula rima
    percussas dominae vertat in auriculas !
sit silice [1] et saxo patientior illa Sicano,
    sit licet et ferro durior et chalybe,   30
non tamen illa suos poterit compescere ocellos,
    surget et invitis spiritus in lacrimis.
nunc iacet alterius felici nixa lacerto,
    at mea nocturno verba cadunt Zephyro.
sed tu sola mei, tu maxima causa doloris,
    victa meis numquam, ianua, muneribus.
te non ulla meae laesit petulantia linguae,
    quae solet irato dicere pota ioco,[2]
ut me tam longa raucum patiare querela
    sollicitas trivio pervigilare moras.   40
at tibi saepe novo deduxi carmina versu,
    osculaque impressis nixa dedi gradibus.
ante tuos quotiens verti me, perfida, postes,
    debitaque occultis vota tuli manibus ! "
haec ille et si quae miseri novistis amantes,
    et matutinis obstrepit alitibus.
sic ego nunc dominae vitiis et semper amantis
    fletibus aeterna differor invidia.

[1] silice *cod. Voss. 81 :* licet *NAF.*
[2] pota ioco *Heinsius :* tota loco *NAF.*

XVII

Eт merito, quoniam potui fugisse puellam [1]
  nunc ego desertas alloquor alcyonas.
nec mihi Cassiope solito visura carinam,
  omniaque ingrato litore vota cadunt.
quin etiam absenti prosunt tibi, Cynthia, venti:
  aspice, quam saevas increpat aura minas.
nullane placatae veniet fortuna procellae?
  haecine parva meum funus harena teget?
tu tamen in melius saevas converte querelas:
  sat tibi sit poenae nox et iniqua vada.   10
an poteris siccis mea fata reposcere [1] ocellis,
  ossaque nulla tuo nostra tenere sinu?
a pereat, quicumque rates et vela paravit
  primus et invito gurgite fecit iter!
nonne fuit levius dominae pervincere mores
  (quamvis dura, tamen rara puella fuit),
quam sic ignotis circumdata litora silvis
  cernere et optatos quaerere Tyndaridas?
illic si qua meum sepelissent fata dolorem,
  ultimus et posito staret amore lapis,   20
illa meo caros donasset funere crines,
  molliter et tenera poneret ossa rosa;
illa meum extremo clamasset pulvere nomen,
  ut mihi non ullo pondere terra foret.
at vos, aequoreae formosa Doride natae,
  candida felici solvite vela choro:
si quando vestras labens Amor attigit undas,
  mansuetis socio parcite litoribus.

1 reposcere *Baehrens*: reponere *NAF*.

[293]

XVIII

HAEC certe deserta loca et taciturna querenti,
    et vacuum Zephyri possidet aura nemus.
hic licet occultos proferre impune dolores,
    si modo sola queant saxa tenere fidem.
unde tuos primum repetam, mea Cynthia, fastus?
    quod mihi das flendi, Cynthia, principium?
qui modo felices inter numerabar amantes,
    nunc in amore tuo cogor habere notam.
quid tantum merui? quae te mihi carmina mutant?
    an nova tristitiae causa puella tuae?   10
sic mihi te referas, levis, ut non altera nostro
    limine formosos intulit ulla pedes.
quamvis multa tibi dolor hic meus aspera debet,
    non ita saeva tamen venerit ira mea
ut tibi sim merito semper furor, et tua flendo
    lumina deiectis turpia sint lacrimis.
an quia parva damus mutato signa colore?
    et non ulla meo clamat in ore fides?
vos eritis testes, si quos habet arbor amores,
    fagus et Arcadio pinus amica deo.   20
a quotiens teneras resonant mea verba sub umbras,
    scribitur et vestris Cynthia corticibus!
a! tua quot[1] peperit nobis iniuria curas,
    quae solum tacitis cognita sunt foribus?
omnia consuevi timidus perferre superbae
    iussa neque arguto facta dolore queri.

---

1 a! tua quot ς : an tua quod *NAF*.

pro quo divini [1] fontes et frigida rupes
  et datur inculto tramite dura quies ;
et quodcumque meae possunt narrare querelae,
  cogor ad argutas dicere solus aves.   30
sed qualiscumque es resonent mihi " Cynthia " silvae,
  nec deserta tuo nomine saxa vacent.

XIX

NoN ego nunc tristes vereor, mea Cynthia, Manes,
  nec moror extremo debita fata rogo ;
sed ne forte tuo careat mihi funus amore,
  hic timor est ipsis durior exsequiis.
non adeo leviter noster puer haesit ocellis,
  ut meus oblito pulvis amore vacet.
illic Phylacides iucundae coniugis heros
  non potuit caecis immemor esse locis,
sed cupidus falsis attingere gaudia palmis
  Thessalus antiquam venerat umbra domum.   10
illic quidquid ero, semper tua dicar imago :
  traicit et fati litora magnus amor.
illic formosae veniant chorus heroinae,
  quas dedit Argivis Dardana praeda viris;
quarum nulla tua fuerit mihi, Cynthia, forma
  gratior, et (Tellus hoc ita iusta sinat)
quamvis te longae remorentur fata senectae,
  cara tamen lacrimis ossa futura meis.
quae tu viva mea possis sentire favilla '
  tum mihi non ullo mors sit amara loco.   20

---

[1] Divini *probably corrupt.* di I nivei *Lachmann.*

quam vereor, ne te contempto, Cynthia, busto
  abstrahat ei![1] nostro pulvere iniquus Amor,
cogat et invitam lacrimas siccare cadentes!
  flectitur assiduis certa puella minis.
quare, dum licet, inter nos laetemur amantes:
  non satis est ullo tempore longus amor.

XX

Hoc pro continuo te, Galle, monemus amore.
  (id tibi ne vacuo detluat ex animo)
saepe imprudenti fortuna occurrit amanti:
  crudelis Minyis dixerit Ascanius.
est tibi non infra speciem, non nomine dispar,
  Theiodamanteo proximus ardor Hylae:
hunc tu, sive leges Vmbrae sacra[2] flumina silvae,
  sive Aniena tuos tinxerit unda pedes,
sive Gigantea spatiabere litoris ora,
  sive ubicumque vago fluminis hospitio,   10
Nympharum semper cupidas defende rapinas
  (non minor Ausoniis est amor Adryasin[3]);
ne tibi sit duros[4] montes et frigida saxa,
  Galle, neque experto[5] semper adire lacus:
quae miser ignotis error perpessus in oris
  Herculis indomito fleverat Ascanio.

1 ci *Aldina 1515* : e *NAF.*
2 Vmbrae sacra *Hoeufft :* umbrosae *NAF.*
3 Adryasin *Struvius :* adriacis *NAF.*
4 sit duros *Lipsius :* sint duri *NAF.*
5 experto *Livineius :* expertos *NAF.*

namque ferunt olim Pagasae navalibus Argon
 egressum [1] longe Phasidos isse viam,
et iam praeteritis labentem Athamantidos undis
 Mysorum scopulis applicuisse ratem.   20
hic manus heroum, placidis ut constitit oris,
 mollia composita litora fronde tegit.
at comes invicti iuvenis processerat ultra
 raram sepositi quaerere fontis aquam.
hunc duo sectati fratres, Aquilonia proles,
 hunc super et Zetes, hunc super et Calais,
oscula suspensis instabant carpere palmis,
 oscula et alterna ferre supina fuga.
ille sub extrema pendens secluditur ala
 et volucres ramo summovet insidias.   30
iam Pandioniae cessit [2] genus Orithyiae:
 a dolor! ibat Hylas, ibat Hamadryasin.
hic erat Arganthi Pege sub vertice montis
 grata domus Nymphis umida Thyniasin,
quam supra nullae pendebant debita curae
 roscida desertis poma sub arboribus,
et circum irriguo surgebant lilia prato
 candida purpureis mixta papaveribus.
quae modo decerpens tenero pueriliter ungui
 proposito florem praetulit officio,   40
et modo formosis incumbens nescius undis
 errorem blandis tardat imaginibus.
tandem haurire parat demissis flumina palmis
 innixus dextro plena trahens umero.

1 egressum *Ellis:* egressam *NAF.*
2 cessit *ς*: cesset *NAF:* cessat *ς*.

cuius ut accensae Dryades candore puellae
  miratae solitos destituere choros,
prolapsum leviter facili traxere liquore:
  tum sonitum rapto corpore fecit Hylas;
cui procul Alcides iterat responsa, sed illi
  nomen ab extremis fontibus aura refert.   50
his, o Galle, tuos monitus servabis amores,
  formosum Nymphis credere visus Hylan.

XXI

"Tv, qui consortem properas evadere casum,
  miles ab Etruscis saucius aggeribus,
quid nostro gemitu turgentia lumina torques?
  pars ego sum vestrae proxima militiae.
sic te servato, ut possint gaudere parentes,
  ne soror acta tuis sentiat e lacrimis:
Gallum per medios ereptum Caesaris enses
  effugere ignotas non potuisse manus;
et quaecumque [1] super dispersa invenerit ossa
  montibus Etruscis, nesciat [2] esse mea."   10

1 quaecunque *NAF*: quicunque *S*.
2 nesciat *Phillimore*: haec sciat *NAF*.

XXII

QVALIS et unde genus, qui sint mihi, Tulle, Penates,
    quaeris pro nostra semper amicitia.
si Perusina tibi patriae sunt nota sepulcra,
    Italiae duris funera temporibus,
cum Romana suos egit discordia civis ;
    (sic, mihi praecipue, pulvis Etrusca, dolor,
tu proiecta mei perpessa es membra propinqui,
    tu nullo miseri contegis ossa solo)
proxima supposito contingens Vmbria campo
    me genuit terris fertilis uberibus.   10

LIBER SECVNDVS

I

QVAERITIS, unde mihi totiens scribantur amores,
    unde meus veniat mollis in ore liber.
non haec Calliope, non haec mihi cantat Apollo,
    ingenium nobis ipsa puella facit.
sive illam Cois fulgentem incedere cogis,
    hoc totum e Coa veste volumen erit ;
seu vidi ad frontem sparsos errare capillos,
    gaudet laudatis ire superba comis ;
sive lyrae carmen digitis percussit eburnis,
    miramur, faciles ut premat arte manus ;   10
seu cum poscentes somnum declinat ocellos,
    invenio causas mille poeta novas ;
seu nuda erepto mecum luctatur amictu,
    tum vero longas condimus Iliadas ;
seu quidquid fecit sive est quodcumque locuta,
    maxima de nihilo nascitur historia.
quod mihi si tantum, Maecenas, fata dedissent,
    ut possem heroas ducere in arma manus,
non ego Titanas canerem, non Ossan Olympo
    impositam, ut caeli Pelion esset iter,   20

[301]

nec veteres Thebas, nec Pergama nomen Homeri,
  Xerxis et imperio bina coisse vada,
regnave prima Remi aut animos Carthaginis altae,
  Cimbrorumque minas et benefacta Mari :
bellaque resque tui memorarem Caesaris, et tu
  Caesare sub magno cura secunda fores.
nam quotiens Mutinam aut civilia busta Philippos
  aut canerem Siculae classica bella fugae,
eversosque focos antiquae gentis Etruscae,
  et Ptolomaeei litora capta Phari,   30
aut canerem Aegyptum et Nilum, cum atratus [1]
  in urbem
  septem captivis debilis ibat aquis,
aut regum auratis circumdata colla catenis,
  Actiaque in Sacra currere rostra Via ;
te mea Musa illis semper contexeret armis,
  et sumpta et posita pace fidele caput :
  .   .   .   .[2]

Theseus infernis, superis testatur Achilles,
  hic Ixioniden, ille Menoetiaden.
sed neque Phlegraeos Iovis Enceladique tumultus
  intonet angusto pectore Callimachus,   40
nec mea conveniunt duro praecordia versu
  Caesaris in Phrygios condere nomen avos.
navita de ventis, de tauris narrat arator,
  enumerat [3] miles vulnera, pastor oves ;

---

1 atratus *Baehrens :* attractus *N :* attractatus *F :* tractus ς.
2 *A couplet seems to have been lost, since something is needed
to introduce the mythological parallels for the friendship of
Augustus and Maecenas.*
3 enumerat *AF :* et numerat *N.*

nos contra angusto versantes proelia lecto :
　qua pote quisque, in ea conterat arte diem.
laus in amore mori : laus altera, si datur uno
　posse frui : fruar o solus amore meo!
si memini, solet illa leves culpare puellas,
　et totam ex Helena non probat Iliada.   50
seu mihi sunt tangenda novercae pocula
　　Phaedrae,
　pocula privigno non nocitura suo
seu mihi Circaeo pereundum est gramine, sive
　Colchis Iolciacis [1] urat aena focis,
una meos quoniam praedata est femina sensus,
　ex hac ducentur funera nostra domo.
omnes humanos sanat medicina dolores :
　solus amor morbi non amat artificem.
tarda Philoctetae sanavit crura Machaon,
　Phoenicis Chiron lumina Phillyrides,   60
et deus exstinctum Cressis Epidaurius herbis
　restituit patriis Androgeona focis,
Mysus et Haemonia iuvenis qua cuspide vulnus
　senserat, hac ipsa cuspide sensit opem.
hoc si quis vitium poterit mihi demere, solus
　Tantaleae [2] poterit tradere poma manu ;
dolia virgineis idem ille repleverit urnis,
　ne tenera assidua colla graventur aqua ;
idem Caucasia solvet de rupe Promethei
　bracchia et a medio pectore pellet avem.   70

1 Iolciacis *Scaliger :* Colchiacis *NAF.*
2 Tantaleae *Beroaldus :* Tantalea *NF.*

quandocumque igitur vitam mea fata reposcent,
  et breve in exiguo marmore nomen ero,
Maecenas, nostrae spes invidiosa iuventae,
  et vitae et morti gloria iusta meae,
si te forte meo ducet via proxima busto,
  esseda caelatis siste Britanna iugis,
taliaque illacrimans mutae iace verba favillae:
  " Huic misero fatum dura puella fuit."

II

LIBER eram et vacuo meditabar vivere lecto ;
  at me composita pace fefellit Amor.
cur haec in terris facies humana moratur?
  Iuppitur, ignosco [1] pristina furta tua.
fulva coma est longaeque manus, et maxima toto
  corpore, et incedit vel Iove digna soror,
aut cum Dulichias Pallas spatiatur ad aras,
  Gorgonis anguiferae pectus operta comis;
qualis et Ischomache Lapithae genus heroine,
  Centauris medio grata rapina mero;   10
Mercurio et sacris [2] fertur Boebeidos undis
  virgineum Brimo [3] composuisse latus.
cedite iam, divae, quas pastor viderat olim
  Idaeis tunicas ponere verticibus !
hanc utinam faciem nolit mutare senectus,
  etsi Cumaeae saecula vatis aget !

----

[1] ignosco *n :* ignoro *NF.*
[2] et sacris *Butler :* sacris *cod. Barberinus :* satis *NF.*
[3] Brimo *Turnebus :* primo *NF.*

III

Qvi nullum tibi dicebas iam posse nocere,
    haesisti, cecidit spiritus ille tuus !
vix unum potes, infelix, requiescere mensem,
    et turpis de te iam liber alter erit.
quaerebam, sicca si posset piscis harena
    nec solitus ponto vivere torvus aper ;
aut ego si possem studiis vigilare severis :
    differtur, numquam tollitur ullus amor.
nec me tam facies, quamvis sit candida, cepit
    (lilia non domina sint magis alba mea ;   10
ut Maeotica nix minio si certet Hibero,
    utque rosae puro lacte natant folia),
nec de more comae per levia colla fluentes,
    non oculi, geminae, sidera nostra, faces,
nec si qua Arabio lucet bombyce puella
    (non sum de nihilo blandus amator ego) :
quantum quod posito formose saltat Iaccho,
    egit ut euhantes dux Ariadna choros,
et quantum, Aeolio cum temptat carmina plectro,
    par Aganippeae ludere docta lyrae ;   20
et sua cum antiquae committit scripta Corinnae,
    carminaque Erinnes [1] non putat aequa suis.
non tibi nascenti primis, mea vita, diebus
    candidus [2] argutum sternuit omen Amor ?
haec tibi contulerunt caelestia munera divi,
    haec tibi ne matrem forte dedisse putes.

---

[1] -que Erinnes *Volscus, Beroaldus :* quae lyrines μυ : quae
quivis *NF.*   [2] candidus *Macrobius :* ardidus *NF.*

non non humani partus sunt talia dona :
   ista decem menses non peperere bona.
gloria Romanis una es tu nata puellis :
   Romana accumbes prima puella Iovi,   30
nec semper nobiscum humana cubilia vises ;
   post Helenam haec terris forma secunda redit.
hac ego nunc mirer si flagret nostra iuventus ?
   pulchrius hac fuerat, Troia, perire tibi.
olim mirabar, quod tanti ad Pergama belli
   Europae atque Asiae causa puella fuit :
nunc, Pari, tu sapiens et tu, Menelae, fuisti,
   tu quia poscebas, tu quia lentus eras.
digna quidem facies, pro qua vel obiret Achilles ;
   vel Priamo belli causa probanda fuit.   40
si quis vult fama tabulas anteire vetustas,
   hic dominam exemplo ponat in arte meam :
sive illam Hesperiis, sive illam ostendet Eois,
   uret et Eoos, uret et Hesperios.
his saltem ut tenear iam finibus ! aut mihi si quis,
   acrius ut moriar, venerit alter amor !
ac veluti primo taurus detractat aratra,
   post venit assueto mollis ad arva iugo,
sic primo iuvenes trepidant in amore feroces,
   dehinc domiti post haec aequa et iniqua ferunt. 50
turpia perpessus vates est vincla Melampus,
   cognitus Iphicli surripuisse boves ;
quem non lucra, magis Pero formosa coegit,
   mox Amythaonia nupta futura domo.

IV

MVLTA prius dominae delicta queraris oportet,
    saepe roges aliquid, saepe repulsus eas,
et saepe immeritos corrumpas dentibus ungues,
    et crepitum dubio suscitet ira pede !
nequiquam perfusa meis unguenta capillis,
    ibat et expenso planta morata gradu.
non hic herba valet, non hic nocturna Cytaeis,
    non Perimedeae [1] gramina cocta manus ;
quippe ubi nec causas nec apertos cernimus ictus,
    unde tamen veniant tot mala caeca via est ;   10
non eget hic medicis, non lectis mollibus aeger,
    huic nullum caeli tempus et aura nocet ;
ambulat—et subito mirantur funus amici !
    sic est incautum, quidquid habetur amor.
nam cui non ego sum fallaci praemia vati ?
    quae mea non decies somnia versat anus ?
hostis si quis erit nobis, amet ille puellas :
    gaudeat in puero, si quis amicus erit.
tranquillo tuta descendis flumine cumba :
    quid tibi tam parvi litoris unda nocet ?   20
alter saepe uno mutat praecordia verbo,
    altera vix ipso sanguine mollis erit.

---

[1] Perimedeae *Beroaldus on the authority of "some MSS."*:
per medeae *NF.*

V

Hoc verum est, tota te ferri, Cynthia, Roma,
    et non ignota vivere nequitia?
haec merui sperare? dabis mihi, perfida, poenas;
    et nobis aliquo,[1] Cynthia, ventus erit.
inveniam tamen e multis fallacibus unam,
    quae fieri nostro carmine nota velit,
nec mihi tam duris insultet moribus et te
    vellicet: heu sero flebis amata diu.
nunc est ira recens, nunc est discedere tempus:
    si dolor afuerit, crede, redibit amor.   10
non ita Carpathiae variant Aquilonibus undae,
    nec dubio nubes vertitur atra Noto,
quam facile irati verbo mutan ur amantes:
    dum licet, iniusto subtrahe colla iugo.
nec tu non aliquid, sed prima nocte, dolebis;
    omne in amore malum, si patiare, leve est.
at tu per dominae Iunonis dulcia iura
    parce tuis animis, vita, nocere tibi.
non solum taurus ferit uncis cornibus hostem,
    verum etiam instanti laesa repugnat ovis.   20
nec tibi periuro scindam de corpore vestes,
    nec mea praeclusas fregerit ira fores,
nec tibi conexos iratus carpere crines,
    nec duris ausim laedere pollicibus:
rusticus haec aliquis tam turpia proelia quaerat,
    cuius non hederae circuiere caput.

        1 aliquo *Bosscha:* aquilo *NF.*

scribam igitur, quod non umquam tua deleat aetas,
  "Cynthia, forma potens; Cynthia, verba levis."
crede mihi, quamvis contemnas murmura famae,
  hic tibi pallori, Cynthia, versus erit.   30

VI

Non ita complebant Ephyreae Laidos aedes,
  ad cuius iacuit Graecia tota fores;
turba Menandreae fuerat nec Thaidos olim
  tanta, in qua populus lusit Erichthonius;
nec quae deletas potuit componere Thebas,
  Phryne tam multis facta beata viris.
quin etiam falsos fingis tibi saepe propinquos,
  oscula nec desunt qui tibi iure ferant.
me iuvenum pictae facies, me nomina laedunt,
  me tener in cunis et sine voce puer;   10
me laedet, si multa tibi dabit oscula mater,
  me soror et cum quae ¹ dormit amica simul:
omnia me laedent: timidus sum (ignosce timori)
  et miser in tunica suspicor esse virum.
his olim, ut fama est, vitiis ad proelia ventum est,
  his Troiana vides funera principiis;
aspera Centauros eadem dementia iussit
  frangere in adversum pocula Pirithoum.
cur exempla petam Graium?   tu criminis auctor
  nutritus duro, Romule, lacte lupae: 20
tu rapere intactas docuisti impune Sabinas:
  per te nunc Romae quidlibet audet Amor.

¹ quae *Dousa:* qua *NF.*

[309]

felix Admeti coniunx et lectus Vlixis,
  et quaecumque viri femina limen amat!
templa Pudicitiae quid opus statuisse puellis,
  si cuivis nuptae quidlibet esse licet?
quae manus obscenas depinxit prima tabellas
  et posuit casta turpia visa domo,
illa puellarum ingenuos corrupit ocellos
  nequitiaeque suae noluit esse rudes.   30
a gemat, in terris ista qui protulit arte
  iurgia sub tacita condita laetitia!
non istis olim variabant tecta figuris :
  tum paries nullo crimine pictus erat.
sed non immerito velavit aranea fanum
  et mala desertos occupat herba deos.
quos igitur tibi custodes, quae limina ponam,
  quae numquam supra pes inimicus eat ?
nam nihil invitae tristis custodia prodest :
  quam peccare pudet, Cynthia, tuta sat est.   40
nos uxor numquam, numquam seducet [1] amica :
  semper amica mihi, semper et uxor eris.

VII

Gavisa est certe sublatam Cynthia legem,
  qua quondam edicta flemus [2] uterque diu,
ni nos divideret : quamvis diducere amantes
  non queat invitos Iuppiter ipse duos.

[1] seducet *Rothstein :* me ducet *NF.*
[2] flemus *cod. Beroaldi :* stemus *NF.*

"At magnus Caesar." sed magnus Caesar in
    armis :
  devictae gentes nil in amore valent.
nam citius paterer caput hoc discedere collo
  quam possem nuptae perdere more faces,
aut ego transirem tua limina clausa maritus,
  respiciens udis prodita luminibus.   10
a mea tum quales caneret tibi tibia somnos,
  tibia, funesta tristior illa tuba !
unde mihi patriis natos praebere triumphis ? [1]
  nullus de nostro sanguine miles erit.
quod si vera meae comitarem [2] castra puellae,
  non mihi sat magnus Castoris iret equus.
hinc etenim tantum meruit mea gloria nomen,
  gloria ad hibernos lata Borysthenidas.
tu mihi sola places : placeam tibi, Cynthia, solus :
  hic erit et patrio nomine [3] pluris amor.   20

VIII

ERIPITVR nobis iam pridem cara puella
  et tu me lacrimas fundere, amice, vetas ?
nullae sunt inimicitiae nisi amoris acerbae :
  ipsum me iugula, lenior hostis ero.
possum ego in alterius positam spectare lacerto
  nec mea dicetur, quae modo dicta mea est ?

---

[1] *A new elegy in NF.*
[2] comitarem *ς* : comitarent *NF.*
[3] nomine *Postgate :* sanguine *NF.*

[311]

omnia vertuntur   certe vertuntur amores :
    vinceris aut vincis, haec in amore rota est.
magni saepe duces, magni cecidere tyranni,
    et Thebae steterant altaque Troia fuit.   10
munera quanta dedi vel qualia carmina feci!
    illa tamen numquam ferrea dixit " Amo." [1]

VIIIᴀ

Eʀɢᴏ iam multos nimium temerarius annos,
    improba, qui tulerim teque tuamque domum,
ecquandone tibi liber sum visus ?   an usque
    in nostrum iacies verba superba caput ?
sic igitur prima moriere aetate, Properti ?
    sed morere ; interitu gaudeat illa tuo !
exagitet nostros Manes, sectetur et umbras,
    insultetque rogis, calcet et ossa mea !   20
[quid ?   non Antigonae tumulo Boeotius Haemon
    corruit ipse suo saucius ense latus,
et sua cum miserae permiscuit ossa puellae,
    qua sine Thebanam noluit ire domum ? [2]]
sed non effugies : mecum moriaris oportet ;
    hoc eodem ferro stillet uterque cruor.

----

[1] *The MSS. mark no break at this point.   But 1–12 can stand
by themselves and clearly do not belong to what follows.   I there-
fore mark a new elegy.*
[2] *Lines 21–24 cannot belong to their present context ; the
simile is too irrelevant.   Housman would place them after*
xxviii. *40, perhaps rightly.*

[312]

quamvis ista mihi mors est inhonesta futura :
   mors inhonesta quidem, tu moriere tamen.[1]

    ·   ·   ·   ·   ·

ille etiam abrepta desertus coniuge Achilles
   cessare in tectis pertulit arma sua.   30
viderat ille fugas, tractos in litore Achivos,
   fervere et Hectorea Dorica castra face;
viderat informem multa Patroclon harena
   porrectum et sparsas caede iacere comas,
omnia formosam propter Briseida passus :
   tantus in erepto saevit amore dolor.
at postquam sera captiva est reddita poena,
   fortem illum Haemoniis Hectora traxit equis.
inferior multo cum sim vel matre [2] vel armis,
   mirum, si de me iure triumphat Amor?   40

IX

Iste quod est, ego saepe fui : sed fors et in hora
   hoc ipso eiecto [3] carior alter erit.
Penelope poterat bis denos salva per annos
   vivere, tam multis femina digna procis;
coniugium falsa poterat differre Minerva,
   nocturno solvens texta diurna dolo;
visura et quamvis numquam speraret Vlixen,
   illum exspectando facta remansit anus.

---

[1] *Some lines seem to have been lost at this point, if, indeed,*
29–40 can be regarded as belonging at all to what precedes.
[2] matre, *a MS. of L. Valla :* marte *NF.*
[3] eiecto ς : electo *NF.*

nec non exanimem amplectens Briseis Achillen
    candida vesana verberat ora manu ;   10
et dominum lavit maerens captiva cruentum,
    propositum fulvis [1] in Simoenta vadis,
foedavitque comas, et tanti corpus Achilli
    maximaque in parva sustulit ossa manu ;
cum tibi nec Peleus aderat nec caerula mater,
    Scyria nec viduo Deidamia toro.[2]
tunc igitur veris gaudebat Graecia natis,
    tunc etiam felix inter et arma pudor.
at tu non una potuisti nocte vacare,
    impia, non unum sola manere diem !   20
quin etiam multo duxistis pocula risu :
    forsitan et de me verba fuere mala.
hic etiam petitur, qui te prius ante reliquit :
    di faciant, isto capta fruare viro !
haec mihi vota tuam propter suscepta salutem,
    cum capite hoc Stygiae iam poterentur aquae,
et lectum flentes circum staremus amici ?
    hic ubi tum, pro di, perfida, quisve fuit ?
quid si longinquos retinerer miles ad Indos,
    aut mea si staret navis in Oceano ?   30
sed vobis facile est verba et componere fraudes :
    hoc unum didicit femina semper opus.
non sic incerto mutantur flamine Syrtes,
    nec folia hiberno tam tremefacta Noto,
quam cito feminea non constat foedus in ira,
    sive ea causa gravis sive ea causa levis.

     1 fulvis *ς* : fluviis *NF.*   2 toro *Itali :* viro *NF.*

nunc, quoniam ista tibi placuit sententia, cedam :
   tela, precor, pueri, promite acuta magis,
figite certantes atque hanc mihi solvite vitam !
   sanguis erit vobis maxima palma meus.   40
sidera sunt testes et matutina pruina
   et furtim misero ianua aperta mihi,
te nihil in vita nobis acceptius umquam :
   nunc quoque eris, quamvis sic inimica mihi.
nec domina ulla meo ponet vestigia lecto :
   solus ero, quoniam non licet esse tuum.
atque utinam, si forte pios eduximus annos,
   ille vir in medio fiat amore lapis ! [1]

    •   •   •   •

non ob regna magis diris cecidere sub armis
   Thebani media non sine matre duces :   50
quam, mihi si media liceat pugnare puella
   mortem ego non fugiam morte subire tua.

X

SED tempus lustrare aliis Helicona choreis,
   et campum Haemonio iam dare tempus equo.
iam libet et fortes memorare ad proelia turmas
   et Romana mei dicere castra ducis.
quod si deficiant vires, audacia certe
   laus erit : in magnis et voluisse sat est.

---

[1] *Some lines have clearly been lost at this point, and I there-fore mark a gap with Lachmann. Housman would insert* VIII.
3, 4.

aetas prima canat Veneres, extrema tumultus :
  bella canam, quando scripta puella mea est.
nunc volo subducto gravior procedere vultu,
  nunc aliam citharam me mea Musa docet.   10
surge, anima ; ex humili iam carmine sumite vires,
  Pierides : magni nunc erit oris opus.
iam negat Euphrates equitem post terga tueri
  Parthorum et Crassos se tenuisse dolet :
India quin,[1] Auguste, tuo dat colla triumpho,
  et domus intactae te tremit Arabiae ;
et si qua extremis tellus se subtrahit oris,
  sentiat illa tuas postmodo capta manus.
haec ego castra sequar ; vates tua castra canendo
  magnus ero : servent hunc mihi fata diem !   20
ut caput in magnis ubi non est tangere signis,
  ponitur hac imos ante corona pedes,
sic nos nunc, inopes laudis conscendere carmen,
  pauperibus sacris vilia tura damus.
nondum etiam Ascraeos norunt mea carmina fontes,
  sed modo Permessi flumine lavit Amor.

XI

SCRIBANT de te alii vel sis ignota licebit :
  laudet, qui sterili semina ponit humo.
omnia, crede mihi, tecum uno munera lecto
  auferet extremi funeris atra dies ;

1 quin *Beroaldus :* quis *NF.*

[316]

et tua transibit contemnens ossa viator,
    nec dicet " Cinis hic docta puella fuit."

XII

Qvicvmqve ille fuit, puerum qui pinxit Amorem,
    nonne putas miras hunc habuisse manus?
is primum vidit sine sensu vivere amantes,
    et levibus curis magna perire bona.
idem non frustra ventosas addidit alas,
    fecit et humano corde volare deum :
scilicet alterna quoniam iactamur in unda,
    nostraque non ullis permanet aura locis.
et merito hamatis manus est armata sagittis,
    et pharetra ex umero Gnosia utroque iacet :   10
ante ferit quoniam, tuti quam cernimus hostem,
    nec quisquam ex illo vulnere sanus abit.
in me tela manent, manet et puerilis imago :
    sed certe pennas perdidit ille suas ;
evolat ei nostro quoniam de pectore nusquam,
    assiduusque meo sanguine bella gerit.
quid tibi iucundum est siccis habitare medullis?
    si pudor est, alio traice duella tua ! [1]
intactos isto satius temptare veneno :
    non ego, sed tenuis vapulat umbra mea.   20
quam si perdideris, quis erit qui talia cantet,
    (haec mea Musa levis gloria magna tua est),
qui caput et digitos et lumina nigra puellae,
    et canat ut soleant molliter ire pedes?

[1] pudor *v :* puer *NF.* duella *Lipsius :* puella *NF.*   tua *ς :*
tuo *NF.*

XIII

Non tot Achaemeniis armatur Erythra[1] sagittis,
    spicula quot nostro pectore fixit Amor.
hic me tam graciles vetuit contemnere Musas,
    iussit et Ascraeum sic habitare nemus,
non ut Pieriae quercus mea verba sequantur,
    aut possim Ismaria ducere valle feras,
sed magis ut nostro stupefiat Cynthia versu :
    tunc ego sim Inachio notior arte Lino.
non ego sum formae tantum mirator honestae,
    nec si qua illustres femina iactat avos :   10
me iuvet in gremio doctae legisse puellae,
    auribus et puris scripta probasse mea.
haec ubi contigerint, populi confusa valeto
    fabula : nam domina iudice tutus ero.
quae si forte bonas ad pacem verterit aures,
    possum inimicitias tunc ego ferre Iovis.

XIIIa

Qvandocvmqve igitur nostros mors claudet ocellos
    accipe quae serves funeris acta mei.
nec mea tunc longa spatietur imagine pompa,
    nec tuba sit fati vana querela mei ;   20
nec mihi tunc fulcro sternatur lectus eburno,
    nec sit in Attalico mors mea nixa toro.

    1 Erythra *Housman :* Etrusca *NF.*

desit odoriferis ordo mihi lancibus, adsint
  plebei parvae funeris exsequiae.
sat mea sit magno,[1] si tres sint pompa libelli,
  quos ego Persephonae maxima dona feram.
tu vero nudum pectus lacerata sequeris,
  nec fueris nomen lassa vocare meum,
osculaque in gelidis pones suprema labellis,
  cum dabitur Syrio munere plenus onyx.   30
deinde, ubi suppositus cinerem me fecerit ardor,
  accipiat Manes parvula testa meos,
et sit in exiguo laurus super addita busto,
  quae tegat exstincti funeris umbra locum,
et duo sint versus: QVI NVNC IACET HORRIDA PVLVIS,
  VNIVS HIC QVONDAM SERVVS AMORIS ERAT.
nec minus haec nostri notescet fama sepulcri,
  quam fuerant Phthii busta cruenta viri.
tu quoque si quando venies ad fata, memento,
  hoc iter ad lapides cana veni memores.   40
interea cave sis nos aspernata sepultos:
  non nihil ad verum conscia terra sapit.
atque utinam primis animam me ponere cunis
  iussisset quaevis de Tribus una Soror!
nam quo tam dubiae servetur spiritus horae?
  Nestoris est visus post tria saecla cinis:
cui si tam longae[2] minuisset fata senectae
  Gallicus[3] Iliacis miles in aggeribus,

---

[1] magno *Phillimore :* magna *NF.*
[2] cui si tam longae *Livineius :* quis tam longaevae *NF.*
[3] Gallicus *NF, probably corrupt :* bellicus *Behot :* Ilius
Lachmann.

[319]

non ille Antilochi vidisset corpus humari,
    diceret aut "O mors, cur mihi sera venis?"   50
tu tamen amisso non numquam flebis amico:
    fas est praeteritos semper amare viros.
testis, qui niveum quondam percussit Adonem
    venantem Idalio vertice durus aper;
illis formosus [1] iacuisse paludibus, illuc
    diceris effusa tu, Venus, isse coma.
sed frustra mutos revocabis, Cynthia, Manes:
    nam mea qui poterunt ossa minuta loqui?

XIV

Non ita Dardanio gavisus Atrida triumpho est,
    cum caderent magnae Laomedontis opes;
nec sic errore exacto laetatus Vlixes,
    cum tetigit carae litora Dulichiae;
nec sic Electra, salvum cum aspexit Oresten,
    cuius falsa tenens fleverat ossa soror;
nec sic incolumem Minois Thesea vidit,
    Daedalium lino cum duce rexit iter;
quanta ego praeterita collegi gaudia nocte:
    immortalis ero, si altera talis erit.   10
at dum demissis supplex cervicibus ibam,
    dicebar sicco vilior esse lacu.
nec mihi iam fastus opponere quaerit iniquos,
    nec mihi ploranti lenta sedere potest.

[1] formosus *Postgate:* formosum *NF.*

atque utinam non tam sero mihi nota fuisset
    condicio! cineri nunc medicina datur.
ante pedes caecis lucebat semita nobis:
    scilicet insano nemo in amore videt.
hoc sensi prodesse magis: contemnite, amantes!
    sic hodie veniet, si qua negavit heri.   20
pulsabant alii frustra dominamque vocabant:
    mecum habuit positum lenta puella caput.
haec mihi devictis potior victoria Parthis,
    haec spolia, haec reges, haec mihi currus erunt.
magna ego dona tua figam, Cytherea, columna,
    taleque sub nostro nomine carmen erit:
HAS PONO ANTE TVAS TIBI, DIVA, PROPERTIVS AEDES
    EXVVIAS, TOTA NOCTE RECEPTVS AMANS.
nunc ad te, mea lux, veniet mea litore navis
    servata. an mediis sidat onusta vadis?   30
quod si forte aliqua nobis mutabere culpa,
    vestibulum iaceam mortuus ante tuum!

XV

O ME felicem! o nox mihi candida! et o tu
    lectule deliciis facte beate meis!
quam multa apposita narramus verba lucerna,
    quantaque sublato lumine rixa fuit!
nam modo nudatis mecum est luctata papillis,
    interdum tunica duxit operta moram.
illa meos somno lassos patefecit ocellos
    ore suo et dixit "Sicine, lente, iaces?

[321]

quam vario amplexu mutamus bracchia ! quantum
    oscula sunt labris nostra morata tuis !   10
non iuvat in caeco Venerem corrumpere motu :
    si nescis, oculi sunt in amore duces.
ipse Paris nuda fertur periisse Lacaena,
    cum Menelaeo surgeret e thalamo ;
nudus et Endymion Phoebi cepisse sororem
    dicitur et nudae concubuisse deae.
quod si pertendens animo vestita cubaris,[1]
    scissa veste meas experiere manus :
quin etiam, si me ulterius provexerit ira,
    ostendes matri bracchia laesa tuae.   20
necdum inclinatae prohibent te ludere mammae :
    viderit haec, si quam iam peperisse pudet.
dum nos fata sinunt, oculos satiemus amore :
    nox tibi longa venit, nec reditura dies.
atque utinam haerentes sic nos vincire catena
    velles, ut numquam solveret ulla dies !
exemplo vinctae tibi sint in amore columbae,
    masculus et totum femina coniugium.
errat, qui finem vesani quaerit amoris :
    verus amor nullum novit habere modum.   30
terra prius falso partu deludet arantes,
    et citius nigros Sol agitabit equos,
fluminaque ad caput incipient revocare liquores,
    aridus et sicco gurgite piscis erit,
quam possim nostros alio transferre dolores :
    huius ero vivus, mortuus huius ero.

        1 cubaris *Muretus :* cubares *O.*

quod mihi si secum tales concedere noctes
   illa velit, vitae longus et annus erit.
si dabit haec multas, fiam immortalis in illis :
   nocte una quivis vel deus esse potest.   40
qualem si cuncti cuperent decurrere vitam
   et pressi multo membra iacere mero,
non ferrum crudele neque esset bellica navis,
   nec nostra Actiacum verteret ossa mare,
nec totiens propriis circum oppugnata triumphis
   lassa foret crines solvere Roma suos.
haec certe merito poterunt laudare minores :
   laeserunt nullos pocula nostra deos.
tu modo, dum lucet, fructum ne desere vitae !
   omnia si dederis oscula, pauca dabis.   50
ac veluti folia arentes liquere corollas,
   quae passim calathis strata natare vides,
sic nobis, qui nunc magnum speramus amantes,
   forsitan includet craslina fata dies.

XVI

Praetor ab Illyricis venit modo, Cynthia, terris,
   maxima praeda tibi, maxima cura mihi.
non potuit saxo vitam posuisse Cerauno ?
   a, Neptune, tibi qualia dona darem !
nunc sine me plena fiunt convivia mensa,
   nunc sine me tota ianua nocte patet.
quare, si sapis, oblatas ne desere messes
   et stolidum pleno vellere carpe pecus ;

deinde, ubi consumpto restabit munere pauper,
    dic alias iterum naviget Illyrias!   10
Cynthia non sequitur fasces nec curat honores,
    semper amatorum ponderat una sinus.
at tu nunc nostro, Venus, o succurre dolori,
    rumpat ut assiduis membra libidinibus!
ergo muneribus quivis mercatur amorem?
    Iuppiter, indigna merce puella perit.
semper in Oceanum mittit me quaerere gemmas,
    et iubet ex ipsa tollere dona Tyro.
atque utinam Romae nemo esset dives, et ipse
    straminea posset dux habitare casa!   20
numquam venales essent ad munus amicae,
    atque una fieret cana puella domo.
numquam septenas noctes seiuncta cubares,[1]
    candida tam foedo bracchia fusa viro,
non quia peccarim (testor te), sed quia vulgo
    formosis levitas semper amica fuit.
barbarus exclusis [2] agitat vestigia lumbis—
    et subito felix nunc mea regna tenet!
aspice quid donis Eriphyla invenit amaris,
    arserit et quantis nupta Creusa malis.   30
nullane sedabit nostros iniuria fletus?
    an dolor hic vitiis nescit abesse tuis? [3]
tot iam abiere dies, cum me nec cura theatri
    nec tetigit Campi, nec mea mensa iuvat.
at pudeat certe, pudeat!—nisi forte, quod aiunt,
    turpis amor surdis auribus esse solet.

---

[1] numquam . . . cubares *Itali:* non quia . . . cubaris *NF.*
[2] excussis *S.*   [3] tuis *S* : suis *NF.*

cerne ducem, modo qui fremitu complevit inani
    Actia damnatis aequora militibus :
hunc infamis amor versis dare terga carinis
    iussit et extremo quaerere in orbe fugam.   40
Caesaris haec virtus et gloria Caesaris haec est :
    illa, qua vicit, condidit arma manu.
sed quascumque tibi vestes, quoscumque smaragdos,
    quosve dedit flavo lumine chrysolithos,
haec videam rapidas in vanum ferre procellas :
    quae tibi terra, velim, quae tibi fiat aqua.
non semper placidus periuros ridet amantes
    Iuppiter et surda neglegit aure preces.
vidistis toto sonitus percurrere caelo,
    fulminaque aetheria desiluisse domo :   50
non haec Pleiades faciunt neque aquosus Orion,
    nec sic de nihilo fulminis ira cadit;
periuras tunc ille solet punire puellas,
    deceptus quoniam flevit et ipse deus.
quare ne tibi sit tanti Sidonia vestis,
    ut timeas, quotiens nubilus Auster erit.

XVII

MENTIRI noctem, promissis ducere amantem,
    hoc erit infectas sanguine habere manus !
horum ego sum vates, quotiens desertus amaras
    explevi noctes, fractus utroque toro.

[325]

vel tu Tantalea moveare ad flumina sorte,
  ut liquor arenti fallat ab ore sitim;
vel tu Sisyphios licet admirere labores,
  difficile ut toto monte volutet onus;
durius in terris nihil est quod vivat amante,
  nec, modo si sapias, quod minus esse velis.   10
quem modo felicem invidia admirante ferebant,
  nunc decimo admittor vix ego quoque die.
nunc iacere e duro corpus iuvat, impia, saxo,
  sumere et in nostras trita venena manus;
nec licet in triviis sicca requiescere luna,
  aut per rimosas mittere verba fores.
quod quamvis ita sit, dominam mutare cavebo:
  tum flebit, cum in me senserit esse fidem.

XVIII [1]

Assidvae multis odium peperere querelae:
  frangitur in tacito femina saepe viro.
si quid vidisti, semper vidisse negato!
  aut si quid doluit forte, dolere nega!

XVIIIA

Qvid mea si canis aetas canesceret annis,
  et faceret scissas languida ruga genas?
at non Tithoni spernens Aurora senectam
  desertum Eoa passa iacere domo est:

---

[1] *I have given these verses, which, as Rossberg pointed out are
alien to their context, the rank of a separate elegy.*

illum saepe suis decedens fovit in undis
    quam prius adiunctos sedula lavit equos;   10
illum ad vicinos cum amplexa quiesceret Indos,
    maturos iterum est questa redire dies;
illa deos currum conscendens dixit iniquos,
    invitum et terris praestitit officium.
cui maiora senis Tithoni gaudia vivi,
    quam gravis amisso Memnone luctus erat.
cum sene non puduit talem dormire puellam
    et canae totiens oscula ferre comae.
at tu etiam iuvenem odisti me, perfida, cum sis
    ipsa anus haud longa curva futura die.   20
quin ego deminuo curam, quod saepe Cupido
    huic malus esse solet, cui bonus ante fuit.

XVIIIʙ[1]

Nvnc etiam infectos demens imitare Britannos,
    ludis et externo tincta nitore caput?
ut natura dedit, sic omnis recta figura est:
    turpis Romano Belgicus ore color.
illi sub terris fiant mala multa puellae,
    quae mentita suas vertit inepta comas!
deme: mihi certe poteris formosa videri;
    mi formosa satis, si modo saepe venis.   30
an si caeruleo quaedam sua tempora fuco
    tinxerit, idcirco caerula forma bona est?
cum tibi nec frater nec sit tibi filius ullus,
    frater ego et tibi sim filius unus ego.

    [1] *Separated from the preceding by Kuinoel.*

ipse tuus semper tibi sit custodia lectus,
    nec nimis ornata fronte sedere velis.
credam ego narranti, noli committere, famae :
    et terram rumor transilit et maria.

XIX

ETSI me invito discedis, Cynthia, Roma,
    laetor quod sine me devia rura colis.
nullus erit castis iuvenis corruptor in agris,
    qui te blanditiis non sinat esse probam ;
nulla neque ante tuas orietur rixa fenestras,
    nec tibi clamatae somnus amarus erit.
sola eris et solos spectabis, Cynthia, montes
    et pecus et fines pauperis agricolae.
illic te nulli poterunt corrumpere ludi,
    fanaque peccatis plurima causa tuis.   10
illic assidue tauros spectabis arantes,
    et vitem docta ponere falce comas ;
atque ibi rara feres inculto tura sacello,
    haedus ubi agrestes corruet ante focos ;
protinus et nuda choreas imitabere sura ;
    omnia ab externo sint modo tuta viro.
ipse ego venabor : iam nunc me sacra Dianae
    suscipere et Veneri ponere vota iuvat.
incipiam captare feras et reddere pinu
    cornua et audaces ipse monere canes ;   20
non tamen ut vastos ausim temptare leones
    aut celer agrestes comminus ire sues.

haec igitur mihi sit lepores audacia molles
  excipere et stricto figere avem calamo,
qua formosa suo Clitumnus flumina luco
  integit, et niveos abluit unda boves.
tu quotiens aliquid conabere, vita, memento
  venturum paucis me tibi Luciferis.
sic me nec solae poterunt avertere silvae,
  nec vaga muscosis flumina fusa iugis,   30
quin ego in assidua mutem tua nomina lingua :
  absenti nemo non nocuisse velit.

XX

Qvid fles abducta gravius Briseide ? quid fles
  anxia captiva tristius Andromacha ?
quidve mea de fraude deos, insana, fatigas ?
  quid quereris nostram sic cecidisse fidem ?
non tam nocturna volucris funesta querela
  Attica Cecropiis obstrepit in foliis,
nec tantum Niobe bis sex ad busta superba [1]
  sollicito lacrimas defluit a Sipylo.
me licet aeratis astringant bracchia nodis,
  sint mea vel Danaes condita membra domo,   10
in te ego et aeratas rumpam, mea vita, catenas,
  ferratam Danaes transiliamque domum.
de te quodcumque ad surdas mihi dicitur aures :
  tu modo ne dubita de gravitate mea.
ossa tibi iuro per matris et ossa parentis
  (si fallo, cinis heu sit mihi uterque gravis !)

          1 superba *Beroaldus :* superbe *NF.*

[329]

me tibi ad extremas mansurum, vita, tenebras:
  ambos una fides auferet, una dies.
quod si nec nomen nec me tua forma teneret,
  posset servitium mite tenere tuum.   20
septima iam plenae deducitur orbita lunae,
  cum de me et de te compita nulla tacent:
interea nobis non numquam[1] ianua mollis,
  non numquam[1] lecti copia facta tui.
nec mihi muneribus nox ulla est empta beatis:
  quidquid eram, hoc animi gratia magna tui.
cum te tam multi peterent, tu me una petisti:
  possum ego naturae non meminisse tuae?
tum me vel tragicae vexetis Erinyes, et me
  inferno damnes, Aeace, iudicio,   30
atque inter Tityi volucres mea poena vagetur,
  tumque ego Sisyphio saxa labore geram!
nec tu supplicibus me sis venerata tabellis:
  ultima talis erit quae mea prima fides.
hoc mihi perpetuo ius est, quod solus amator
  nec cito desisto nec temere incipio.

XXI

A QVANTVM de me Panthi tibi pagina finxit,
  tantum illi Pantho ne sit amica Venus!
sed tibi iam videor Dodona verior augur.
  uxorem ille tuus pulcher amator habet!

----

[1] non numquam *F:* non unquam *N.*

tot noctes periere ?   nihil pudet ?   aspice, cantat
   liber : tu nimium credula, sola iaces.
et nunc inter eos tu sermo es, te ille superbus
   dicit se invito saepe fuisse domi.
dispeream, si quicquam aliud quam gloria de te
   quaeritur : has laudes ille maritus habet.   10
Colchida sic hospes quondam decepit Iason :
   eiecta est (tenuit[1] namque Creusa) domo.
sic a Dulichio iuvene est elusa Calypso :
   vidit amatorem pandere vela suum.
a nimium faciles aurem praebere puellae,
   discite desertae non temere esse bonae !
huic quoque, qui restet,[2] iam pridem quaeritur alter :
   experta in primo, stulta, cavere potes.
nos quocumque loco, nos omni tempore tecum
   sive aegra pariter sive valente sumus.   20

XXII

Scis here mi multas pariter placuisse puellas ;
   scis mihi, Demophoon, multa venire mala.
nulla meis frustra lustrantur compita plantis ;
   o nimis exitio nata theatra meo,
sive aliquis molli diducit candida gestu
   bracchia, seu varios incinit ore modos !
interea nostri quaerunt sibi vulnus ocelli,
   candida non tecto pectore si qua sedet,

1 tenuit *ς* : tenuis *NFL.*
2 restet *Phillimore :* restat *NFL.*

sive vagi crines puris in frontibus errant,
    Indica quos medio vertice gemma tenet.   10
quae si forte aliquid vultu mihi dura negarat,
    frigida de tota fronte cadebat aqua.
quaeris, Demophoon, cur sim tam mollis in omnis?
    quod quaeris, "quare" non habet ullus amor.
cur aliquis sacris laniat sua bracchia cultris
    et Phrygis insanos caeditur ad numeros?
uni cuique dedit vitium natura creato:
    mi fortuna aliquid semper amare dedit.
me licet et Thamyrae cantoris fata sequantur,
    numquam ad formosas, invide, caecus ero.   20
sed tibi si exiles videor tenuatus in artus,
    falleris: haud umquam est culta labore Venus.
percontere licet: saepe est experta puella
    officium tota nocte valere meum.
Iuppiter Alcmenae geminas requieverat Arctos,
    et caelum noctu bis sine rege fuit;
nec tamen idcirco languens ad fulmina venit:
    nullus amor vires eripit ipse suas.
quid, cum e complexu Briseidos iret Achilles?
    num[1] fugere minus Thessala tela Phryges?   30
quid, ferus Andromachae lecto cum surgeret Hector?
    bella Mycenaeae non timuere rates?
ille vel hic, classes poterant vel perdere muros:
    hic ego Pelides, hic ferus Hector ego.
aspice uti caelo modo sol modo luna ministret:
    sic etiam nobis una puella parum est.

1 num *FL:* non *N.*

[332]

altera me cupidis teneat foveatque lacertis,
  altera si quando non sinit esse locum ;
aut si forte irata meo sit facta ministro,
  ut sciat esse aliam, quae velit esse mea !   40
nam melius duo defendunt retinacula navim,
  tutius et geminos anxia mater alit.

XXIIₐ¹

Avt si es dura, nega : sin es non dura, venito !
  quid iuvat at ² nullo ponere verba loco ?
hic unus dolor est ex omnibus acer amanti,
  speranti subito si qua venire negat.
quanta illum toto versant suspiria lecto,
  cum recipi, quem non noverit ille, necat ! ³
et rursus puerum quaerendo audita fatigat,
  quem, quae ⁴ scire timet, quaerere fata iubet.   50

XXIII

Cvi fuit indocti fugienda haec ⁵ semita vulgi,
  ipsa petita lacu nunc mihi dulcis aqua est.
ingenuus quisquam alterius dat munera servo,
  ut promissa suae verba ferat dominae ?
et quaerit totiens " Quaenam nunc porticus illam
  integit ? " et " Campo quo movet illa pedes ? "

---

¹ *Separated from the preceding by Renaissance scholars.*
² at *Baehrens :* et *NFL.*
³ cum *v :* cur *NFL.* quem *ς :* quae *NFL.* necat *Heinsius :*
vetat *NFL.*   ⁴ quem quae *F :* quae quoque *L : om. N.*
⁵ haec *ς :* et *NLF.*

deinde, ubi pertuleris, quos dicit fama labores
   Herculis, ut scribat " Muneris ecquid habes ? "
cernere uti possis vultum custodis amari,
   captus et immunda saepe latere casa,   10
quam care semel in toto nox vertitur anno !
   a pereant, si quos ianua clausa iuvat !
contra, reiecto quae libera vadit amictu,
   custodum et nullo saepta timore, placet ?
cui saepe immundo Sacra conteritur Via socco,
   nec sinit esse moram, si quis adire velit ;
differet haec numquam, nec poscet garrula, quod te
   astrictus ploret saepe dedisse pater,
nec dicet " Timeo, propera iam surgere, quaeso :
   infelix, hodie vir mihi rure venit."   20
et quas Euphrates et quas mihi misit Orontes,
   me iuerint : nolim furta pudica tori ;
libertas quoniam nulli iam restat amanti :
   si quis liber erit, nullus[1] amare volet.

XXIV

" Tv loqueris, cum sis[2] iam noto fabula libro
   et tua sit toto Cynthia lecta foro ? "
cui non his verbis aspergat tempora sudor ?
   aut pudor ingenuus, aut reticendus amor ?
quod si tam facilis spiraret Cynthia nobis,
   non ego nequitiae dicerer esse caput,

1 si quis . . . nullus *Foster :* nullus . . . si quis *NFL.*
2 sis ς : sit *NFL.*

[334]

nec sic per totam infamis traducerer urbem,
  urerer et quamvis non bene,[1] verba darem.
quare ne tibi sit mirum me quaerere viles :
  parcius infamant : num tibi causa levis ?   10

   •   •   •   •   .[2]

et modo pavonis caudae flabella superbae
  et manibus dura frigus habere pila,
et cupit iratum talos me poscere eburnos,
  quaeque nitent Sacra vilia dona Via.
a peream, si me ista movent dispendia, sed [3] me
  fallaci dominae iam pudet esse iocum !

XXIVa [4]

Hoc erat in primis quod me gaudere iubebas ?
  tam te formosam non pudet esse levem ?
una aut altera nox nondum est in amore peracta,
  et dicor lecto iam gravis esse tuo.   20
me modo laudabas et carmina nostra legebas :
  ille tuus pennas tam cito vertit amor ?
contendat mecum ingenio, contendat et arte,
  in primis una discat amare domo :
si libitum tibi erit, Lernaeas pugnet ad hydras
  et tibi ab Hesperio mala dracone ferat,
taetra venena libens et naufragus ebibat undas,
  et numquam pro te deneget esse miser :

1 urerer *ς* : ureret *NFL.* non bene *Housman :* nomine *NFL*
2 *Some verses have clearly been lost here.*   3 sed *ς :* si *NFL*
4 *17–52 separated by Scaliger.*

(quos utinam in nobis, vita, experiare labores!)
    iam tibi de timidis iste protervus erit,   30
qui nunc se in tumidum iactando venit honorem:
    discidium vobis proximus annus erit.
at me non aetas mutabit tota Sibyllae,
    non labor Alcidae, non niger ille dies.
tu mea compones et dices "Ossa, Properti,
    haec tua sunt: eheu tu mihi certus eras,
certus eras eheu, quamvis nec sanguine avito
    nobilis et quamvis non ita [1] dives eras."
nil ego non patiar, numquam me iniuria mutat:
    ferre ego formosam nullum onus esse puto.   40
credo ego non paucos ista periisse figura,
    credo ego sed multos non habuisse fidem.
parvo dilexit spatio Minoida Theseus,
    Phyllida Demophoon, hospes uterque malus.
iam tibi Iasonia nota est Medea carina
    et modo servato [2] sola relicta viro.
dura est quae multis simulatum fingit amorem,
    et se plus uni si qua parare potest.
noli nobilibus, noli conferre beatis:
    vix venit, extremo qui legat ossa die.   50
hi tibi nos erimus: sed tu potius precor ut me
    demissis plangas pectora nuda comis.

[1] non ita *Pontanus :* navita *NFL.*
[2] servato *N : om. FL.*

XXV

Vnica nata meo pulcherrima cura dolori,
  excludit quoniam sors mea "saepe veni,"
ista meis fiet notissima forma libellis,
  Calve, tua venia, pace, Catulle, tua.
miles depositis annosus secubat armis,
  grandaevique negant ducere aratra boves,
putris et in vacua requiescit navis harena,
  et vetus in templo bellica parma vacat:
at me ab amore tuo deducet nulla senectus,
  sive ego Tithonus sive ego Nestor ero.   10
nonne fuit satius duro servire tyranno
  et gemere in tauro, saeve Perille, tuo?
Gorgonis et satius fuit obdurescere vultu,
  Caucasias etiam si pateremur aves.
sed tamen obsistam.   teritur robigine mucro
  ferreus et parvo saepe liquore silex:
at nullo dominae teritur sub limine amor, qui
  restat et immerita sustinet aure minas.
ultro contemptus rogat, et peccasse fatetur
  laesus, et invitis ipse redit pedibus.   20
tu quoque, qui pleno fastus assumis amore,
  credule, nulla diu femina pondus habet.
an quisquam in mediis persolvit vota procellis,
  cum saepe in portu fracta carina natet?
aut prius infecto deposcit praemia cursu,
  septima quam metam triverit ante rota?

[337]

me:.daces ludunt flatus in amore secundi :
    si qua venit sero, magna ruina venit.
tu tamen interea, quamvis te diligat illa,
    in tacito cohibe gaudia clausa sinu.   30
namque in amore suo semper sua maxima cuique
    nescio quo pacto verba nocere solent.
quamvis te persaepe vocet, semel ire memento :
    invidiam quod habet, non solet esse diu.
at si saecla forent antiquis grata puellis,
    essem ego quod nunc tu : tempore vincor ego.
non tamen ista meos mutabunt saecula mores :
    unus quisque sua noverit ire via.
at, vos qui officia in multos revocatis amores,
    quantum sic cruciat lumina vestra [1] dolor !   40
vidistis pleno teneram candore puellam,
    vidistis fusco, ducit [2] uterque color ;
vidistis quandam Argivam prodente [3] figura,
    vidistis nostras, utraque forma rapit.
illaque plebeio vel sit sandycis amictu :
    haec atque illa mali vulneris una via est.
cum satis una tuis insomnia portet ocellis,
    una sit et cuivis femina multa mala.

XXVI

Vidi te in somnis fracta, mea vita, carina
    Ionio lassas ducere rore manus,

[1] vestra ς : nostra *NFL*.   [2] ducit *N :* dulcis *F :* lucus *L*.
[3] Argivam *Baehrens :* argiva *NFL*. prodente *FL :* prodire *N*.

et quaecumque in me fueras mentita fateri,
   nec iam umore graves tollere posse comas,
qualem purpureis agitatam fluctibus Hellen,
   aurea quam molli tergore vexit ovis.
quam timui, ne forte tuum mare nomen haberet,
   atque tua labens navita fleret aqua !
quae tum ego Neptuno, quae tum cum Castore
     fratri,
   quaeque tibi excepi, iam dea, Leucothoe !   10
at tu vix primas extollens gurgite palmas
   saepe meum nomen iam peritura vocas.
quod si forte tuos vidisset Glaucus ocellos,
   esses Ionii facta puella maris,
et tibi ob invidiam Nereides increpitarent,
   candida Nesaee, caerula Cymothoe.
sed tibi subsidio delphinum currere vidi,
   qui, puto, Arioniam vexerat ante lyram.
iamque ego conabar summo me mittere saxo,
   cum mihi discussit talia visa metus.   20

XXVIᴀ[1]

Nvnc admirentur quod tam mihi pulchra puella
   serviat et tota dicar in urbe potens !
non, si Cambysae redeant et flumina Croesi,
   dicat " De nostro surge, poeta, toro."

        [1] *Separated by Burmann.*

[339]

nam mea cum recitat, dicit se odisse beatos :
    carmina tam sancte nulla puella colit.
multum in amore fides, multum constantia prodest :
    qui dare multa potest, multa et amare potest.
seu mare per longum mea cogitet ire puella,
    hanc sequar, et fidos una aget aura duos ;   30
unum litus erit sopitis unaque tecto
    arbor, et ex una saepe bibemus aqua ;
et tabula una duos poterit componere amantis,
    prora cubile mihi seu mihi puppis erit.
omnia perpetiar : saevus licet urgeat Eurus ;
    velaque in incertum frigidus Auster agat ;
quicumque et venti miserum vexastis Vlixen,
    et Danaum Euboico litore mille rates ;
et qui movistis duo litora, cum ratis Argo
    dux erat ignoto missa columba mari.   40
illa meis tantum non umquam desit ocellis,
    incendat navem Iuppiter ipse licet.
certe isdem nudi pariter iactabimur oris :
    me licet unda ferat, te modo terra tegat.
sed non Neptunus tanto crudelis amori,
    Neptunus fratri par in amore Iovi.
testis Amymone, latices dum ferret, in arvis [1]
    compressa, et Lernae pulsa tridente palus.
iam deus amplexu votum persolvit, at illi
    aurea divinas urna profudit aquas.   50
crudelem et Borean rapta Orithyia negavit :
    hic deus et terras et maria alta domat.

    1 dum *N :* cum *FL.* arvis *O :* Argis *ς, perhaps rightly.*

crede mihi, nobis mitescet Scylla, nec umquam
  alternante vacans [1] vasta Charybdis aqua;
ipsaque sidera erunt nullis obscura tenebris,
  purus et Orion, purus et Haedus erit.
quid mihi si ponenda tuo sit corpore vita?
  exitus hic nobis non inhonestus erit.

XXVII

At vos incertam, mortales, funeris horam
  quaeritis, et qua sit mors aditura via;
quaeritis et caelo, Phoenicum inventa, sereno,
  quae sit stella homini commoda quaeque mala!
seu pedibus Parthos sequimur seu classe Britannos,
  et maris et terrae caeca pericla viae.
rursus et obiectum fles tu caput esse tumultu [2]
  cum Mavors dubias miscet utrimque manus;
praeterea domibus flammam domibusque ruinas,
  neu subeant labris pocula nigra tuis.   10
solus amans novit, quando periturus et a qua
  morte, neque hic Boreae flabra neque arma
    timet.
iam licet et Stygia sedeat sub harundine remex,
  cernat et infernae tristia vela ratis:
si modo clamantis revocaverit aura puellae,
  concessum nulla lege redibit iter.

  [1] vacans *Ayrmann:* vorans *NFL.*
  [2] fles tu *Housman:* fletus *N:* flemus *FL.* caput *NF:* capiti
L. tumultu *cod. Mus. Brit. 23766:* tumultum *NFL.*

[341]

XXVIII

IVPPITER, affectae tandem miserere puellae:
   tam formosa tuum mortua crimen erit.
venit enim tempus, quo torridus aestuat aer,
   incipit et sicco fervere terra Cane.
sed non tam ardoris culpa est neque crimina caeli,
   quam totiens sanctos non habuisse deos.
hoc perdit miseras, hoc perdidit ante puellas:
   quidquid iurarunt, ventus et unda rapit.
num [1] sibi collatam doluit Venus? illa peraeque
   prae se formosis invidiosa dea est.   10
an contempta tibi Iunonis templa Pelasgae?
   Palladis aut oculos ausa negare bonos?
semper, formosae, non nostis parcere verbis.
   hoc tibi lingua nocens, hoc tibi forma dedit.
sed tibi vexatae per multa pericula vitae
   extremo venit mollior hora die.
Io versa caput primos mugiverat annos:
   nunc dea, quae Nili flumina vacca bibit.
Ino etiam prima terris aetate vagata est:
   hanc miser implorat navita Leucothoen.   20
Andromede monstris fuerat devota marinis:
   haec eadem Persei nobilis uxor erat.
Callisto Arcadios erraverat ursa per agros:
   haec nocturna suo sidere vela regit.
quod si forte tibi properarint fata quietem,
   illa sepulturae fata beata tuae,

1 num *FL:* non *N.*

[342]

narrabis Semelae, quo sit formosa periclo,
 credet et illa, suo docta puella malo;
et tibi Maeonias omnes heroidas inter
 primus erit nulla non tribuente locus.   30
nunc, utcumque potes, fato gere saucia morem:
 et deus et durus vertitur ipse dies.
hoc tibi vel poterit coniunx ignoscere Iuno:
 frangitur et Iuno, si qua puella perit.
[1] deficiunt magico torti sub carmine rhombi,
 et iacet exstincto laurus adusta foco;
et iam Luna negat totiens descendere caelo,
 nigraque funestum concinit omen avis.
una ratis fati nostros portabit amores
 caerula ad infernos velificata lacus.   40
sed [2] non unius quaeso, miserere duorum!
 vivam, si vivet: si cadet illa, cadam.
pro quibus optatis sacro me carmine damno:
 scribam ego " Per magnum est salva puella Iovem";
ante tuosque pedes illa ipsa operata sedebit,
 narrabitque sedens longa pericla sua.

XXVIIIᴀ [3]

Haec tua, Persephone, maneat clementia, nec tu,
 Persephonae coniunx, saevior esse velis.
sunt apud infernos tot milia formosarum:
 pulchra sit in superis, si licet, una locis!   50

[1] *A new elegy in Nμ, no break in FL.*
[2] sed *N :* si *FL.*
[3] *Separated by Lachmann.*

[343]

vobiscum est Iope, vobiscum candida Tyro,
    vobiscum Europe nec proba Pasiphae,
et quot Troia [1] tulit vetus et quot Achaia formas,
    et Phoebi et Priami diruta regna senis :
et quaecumque erat in numero Romana puella,
    occidit : has omnes ignis avarus habet.
nec forma aeternum aut cuiquam est fortuna
    perennis :
    longius aut propius mors sua quemque manet.
tu quoniam es, mea lux, magno dimissa periclo,
    munera Dianae debita redde choros,   60
redde etiam excubias divae nunc, ante iuvencae ;
    votivas noctes et mihi solve decem.

XXIX

Hesterna, mea lux, cum potus nocte vagarer,
    nec me servorum duceret ulla manus,
obvia nescio quot pueri mihi turba minuta
    venerat (hos vetuit me numerare timor) ;
quorum alii faculas, alii retinere sagittas,
    pars etiam visa est vincla parare mihi.
sed nudi fuerant.   quorum lascivior unus,
    " Arripite hunc," inquit, "iam [2] bene nostis eum :
hic erat, hunc mulier nobis irata locavit."
    dixit, et in collo iam mihi nodus erat.   10
hic alter iubet in medium propellere, at alter,
    " Intereat, qui nos non putat esse deos !

---

[1] Troia *NFL, perhaps corrupt :* Phthia *Huschke.*
[2] iam *N :* nam *FL.*

haec te non meritum totas exspectat in horas :
   at tu nescio quas quaeris, inepte, fores.
quae cum Sidoniae nocturna ligamina mitrae
   solverit atque oculos moverit illa graves,
afflabunt tibi non Arabum de gramine odores,
   sed quos ipse suis fecit Amor manibus.
parcite iam, fratres, iam certos spondet amores ;
   et iam ad mandatam venimus ecce domum."   20
atque ita me in tectum duxerunt rursus amicae : [1]
   " I nunc et noctes disce manere domi."

XXIXa [2]

MANE erat, et volui, si sola quiesceret illa,
   visere : at in lecto Cynthia sola fuit.
obstipui : non illa mihi formosior umquam
   visa, neque ostrina cum fuit in tunica,
ibat et hinc castae narratum somnia Vestae,
   neu sibi neve mihi quae nocitura forent :
talis visa mihi somno dimissa recenti.
   heu quantum per se candida forma valet !   30
" Quid ? [3] tu matutinus," ait " speculator amicae,
   me similem vestris moribus esse putas ?
non ego tam facilis : sat erit mihi cognitus unus,
   vel tu vel si quis verior esse potest.
apparent non ulla toro vestigia presso,
   signa volutantis [4] nec iacuisse duos.

---

[1] in tectum duxerunt . . . amicae *G. Fischer :* in lecto
duxerunt . . . amictu *NFL.*   [2] *Separated by Guyetus.*
   [3] quid *S :* quod *NFL.*   [4] volutantis *L :* voluntatis *NF.*

aspice ut in toto nullus mihi corpore surgat
spiritus admisso notus adulterio."
dixit, et opposita propellens savia dextra
prosilit in laxa nixa pedem solea.　　　　　40
sic ego tam sancti custos retrudor [1] amoris :
ex illo felix nox [2] mihi nulla fuit.

XXX

Nvnc tu, dure,[3] paras Phrygias nunc ire per undas　19
et petere Hyrcani litora nauta [4] maris ?　　　　20
[spargere et [5] alterna communis caede Penates　21
et ferre ad patrios praemia dira Lares ?]　　　　22
quo fugis a demens ? nulla est fuga : tu licet usque　1
ad Tanain fugias, usque sequetur Amor.
non si Pegaseo vecteris in aere dorso,
nec tibi si Persei moverit ala pedes ;
vel si te sectae rapiant talaribus aurae,
nil tibi Mercurii proderit alta via.
instat semper Amor supra caput, instat amanti,
et gravis ipse super libera colla sedet.
excubat ille acer custos et tollere numquam
te patietur humo lumina capta semel.　　　　10
et iam si pecces, deus exorabilis ille est,
si modo praesentes viderit esse preces.

----

[1] custos *ς* : custode *NL* : custodis *F*.　retrudor *Postgate* :
reludor *N* : rector *FL*.　　　　[2] nox *ς* : non *NFL*.
[3] dure *cod. vet. Beroaldi* : dura *FL* : non tamen immerito *N*.
[4] nauta *Hertzberg* : nota *NFL*.
[5] spargere et *N* : spargereque *FL*.

[346]

ista senes licet accusent convivia duri :
   nos modo propositum, vita, teramus iter.
illorum antiquis onerantur legibus aures :
   hic locus est in quo, tibia docta, sones,
quae non iure vado Maeandri iacta natasti,
   turpia cum faceret Palladis ora tumor.   18
una contentum pudeat me vivere amica ?   23
   hoc si crimen erit, crimen Amoris erit :
mi nemo obiciat.   libeat tibi, Cynthia, mecum
   rorida muscosis antra tenere iugis.
illic aspicies scopulis haerere Sorores
   et canere antiqui dulcia furta Iovis,
ut Semela est combustus, ut est deperditus Io,
   denique ut ad Troiae tecta volarit avis ;   30
(quod si nemo exstat qui vicerit Alitis arma,
   communis culpae cur reus unus agor ?)
nec tu Virginibus reverentia moveris ora :
   hic quoque non nescit quid sit amare chorus ;
si tamen Oeagri quaedam compressa figura
   Bistoniis olim rupibus accubuit.
hic ubi te [1] prima statuent in parte choreae,
   et medius docta cuspide Bacchus erit,
tum capiti sacros patiar pendere corymbos :
   nam sine te nostrum non valet ingenium   40

[1] te *ς* : me *O.*

XXXI [1]

Qvaeris, cur veniam tibi tardior? aurea Phoebi
  Porticus a magno Caesare aperta fuit;
tanta erat in speciem Poenis digesta columnis,
  inter quas Danai femina turba senis.   4
tum medium claro surgebat marmore templum,   9
  et patria Phoebo carius Ortygia: 10
et duo Solis erant [2] supra fastigia currus;
  et valvae, Libyci nobile dentis opus,
altera deiectos Parnasi vertice Gallos,
  altera maerebat funera Tantalidos.
deinde inter matrem deus ipse interque sororem
  Pythius in longa carmina veste sonat.   16
hic equidem Phoebo visus mihi pulchrior ipso   5
  marmoreus tacita carmen hiare lyra: 6
atque aram circum steterant armenta Myronis,   7
  quattuor artificis, vivida signa, boves.[3]   8

XXXII [4]

Qvi videt, is peccat: qui te non viderit ergo,
  non cupiet: facti lumina crimen [5] habent.
nam quid Praenesti dubias, o Cynthia, sortes,
  quid petis Aeaei moenia Telegoni?

---

1 *A new elegy in* μ, *no break in NFL.*
2 et duo . . . erant *Hertzberg:* et quo . . . erat *NFL.*
3 *5–8 transposed to follow 16 by Dousa.*
4 *No break in NFL, separated by Beroaldus.*
5 lumina crimen Ϛ: crimina lumen *NFL.*

cur tua te [1] Herculeum deportant esseda Tibur?
  Appia cur totiens te via Lanuvium? [2]
hoc utinam spatiere loco, quodcumque vacabis,
  Cynthia! sed tibi me credere turba vetat,
cum videt accensis devotam currere taedis
  in nemus et Triviae lumina ferre deae.   10
scilicet umbrosis sordet Pompeia columnis
  Porticus, aulaeis nobilis Attalicis,
et platanis creber pariter surgentibus ordo,
  flumina sopito quaeque Marone cadunt,
et leviter nymphis tota crepitantibus urbe
  cum subito Triton ore recondit aquam.
falleris, ista tui furtum via monstrat amoris:
  non urbem, demens, lumina nostra fugis!
nil agis, insidias in me componis inanes,
  tendis iners docto retia nota mihi.   20
sed de me minus est: famae iactura pudicae
  tanta tibi miserae, quanta meretur,[3] erit.
nuper enim de te nostras maledixit [4] ad aures
  rumor, et in tota non bonus urbe fuit.
sed tu non debes inimicae credere linguae:
  semper formosis fabula poena fuit.
non tua deprenso damnata est fama veneno:
  testis eris puras, Phoebe, videre manus.
sin autem longo nox una aut altera lusu
  consumpta est, non me crimina parva movent.   30

---

[1] cur tua te *Baehrens:* curva te *N:* cur vatem *FL.*
[2] Lanuvium *Jortin:* dicit anum *N:* ducit anum *FL.*
[3] meretur *N:* mereris *FL.*   [4] nostras *f:* nostra *NFL.*
maledixit *Schneidewin:* me ledit *FLN.*

Tyndaris externo patriam mutavit amore,
    et sine decreto viva reducta domum est.
ipsa Venus fertur [1] corrupta libidine Martis,
    nec minus in caelo semper honesta fuit.
quamvis Ida Parim pastorem dicat amasse
    atque inter pecudes accubuisse deam,
hoc et Hamadryadum spectavit turba sororum
    Silenique senes [2] et pater ipse chori;
cum quibus Idaeo legisti poma sub antro,
    supposita excipiens, Nai, caduca [3] manu.   40
an quisquam in tanto stuprorum examine quaerit
    "Cur haec tam dives?   quis dedit?   unde dedit?"
o nimium nostro felicem tempore Romam,
    si contra mores una puella facit!
haec eadem ante illam impune et Lesbia fecit:
    quae sequitur, certe est invidiosa minus.
qui quaerit Tatios veteres durosque Sabinos,
    hic posuit nostra nuper in urbe pedem.
tu prius et fluctus poteris siccare marinos,
    altaque mortali deligere astra manu,   50
quam facere, ut nostrae nolint peccare puellae:
    hic mos Saturno regna tenente fuit,
et cum Deucalionis aquae fluxere per orbem;
    at [4] post antiquas Deucalionis aquas,
dic mihi, quis potuit lectum servare pudicum,
    quae dea cum solo vivere sola deo?

[1] fertur *N:* quamvis *FL.*
[2] senes *Beroaldus:* senis *NFL.*
[3] Nai, caduca *Scaliger:* naica dona *NFL.*
[4] at *Palmer:* et *NFL.*

uxorem quondam magni Minois, ut aiunt,
  corrupit torvi candida forma bovis;
nec minus aerato Danae circumdata muro
  non potuit magno casta negare Iovi.   60
quod si tu Graias es tuque [1] imitata Latinas,
  semper vive meo libera iudicio!

XXXIII

TRISTIA iam redeunt iterum sollemnia nobis:
  Cynthia iam noctes est operata decem.
atque utinam pereant, Nilo quae sacra tepente
  misit matronis Inachis Ausoniis!
quae dea tam cupidos totiens divisit amantes,
  quaecumque illa fuit, semper amara fuit.
tu certe Iovis occultis in amoribus, Io,
  sensisti multas quid sit inire vias,
cum te iussit habere puellam cornua Iuno
  et pecoris duro perdere verba sono.   10
a quotiens quernis laesisti frondibus ora,
  mandisti et stabulis arbuta [2] pasta tuis!
an, quoniam agrestem detraxit ab ore figuram
  Iuppiter, idcirco facta superba dea es?
an tibi non satis est fuscis Aegyptus alumnis?
  cur tibi tam longa Roma petita via?
quidve tibi prodest viduas dormire puellas?
  sed tibi, crede mihi, cornua rursus erunt,

---

1 es tuque *Baehrens:* tuque es *NFL.*
2 mandisti *Palmer:* mansisti *NFL.* et *Heinsius:* om. *NFL.*
arbuta *Palmer:* abdita *NFL.*

aut nos e nostra te, saeva, fugabimus urbe:
cum Tiberi Nilo gratia nulla fuit.   20
at tu, quae nostro nimium placata dolore es,
noctibus his vacui ter faciamus iter.
non audis et verba sinis mea ludere, cum iam
flectant Icarii sidera tarda boves.
lenta bibis : mediae nequeunt te frangere noctes?
an nondum est talos mittere lassa manus?
a pereat, quicumque meracas repperit uvas
corrupitque bonas nectare primus aquas!
Icare, Cecropiis merito iugulate colonis,
pampineus nosti quam sit amarus odor!   30
tuque o Eurytion vino Centaure peristi,
nec non Ismario tu, Polypheme, mero.
vino forma perit, vino corrumpitur aetas,
vino saepe suum nescit amica virum.
me miserum, ut multo nihil est mutata Lyaeo!
iam bibe : formosa es : nil tibi vina nocent,
cum tua praependent demissae in pocula sertae,[1]
et mea deducta carmina voce legis.
largius effuso madeat tibi mensa Falerno,
spumet et aurato mollius in calice.   40
nulla tamen lecto recipit se sola libenter :
est quiddam, quod vos [2] quaerere cogat Amor.
semper in absentes felicior aestus amantes :
elevat assiduos copia longa viros.

[1] demissae . . . sertae *N, Charisius:* demissa . . . serta
FL.
[2] vos *N :* nos *FL.*

XXXIV [1]

CVR quisquam faciem dominae iam credat [2] Amori?
　sic erepta mihi paene puella mea est.
expertus dico, nemo est in amore fidelis:
　formosam raro non sibi quisque petit.
polluit ille deus cognatos, solvit amicos,
　et bene concordes tristia ad arma vocat.
hospes in hospitium Menelao venit adulter:
　Colchis et ignotum nonne secuta virum est?
Lynceu, tune meam potuisti, perfide, curam
　tangere? nonne tuae tum cecidere manus?　　10
quid si non constans illa et tam certa fuisset?
　posses in tanto vivere flagitio?
tu mihi vel ferro pectus vel perde veneno:
　a domina tantum te modo tolle mea.
te socium vitae, te corporis esse licebit,
　te dominum admitto rebus, amice, meis:
lecto te solum, lecto te deprecor uno:
　rivalem possum non ego ferre Iovem.
ipse meas solus, quod nil est, aemulor umbras,
　stultus, quod nullo [3] saepe timore tremo.　　20
una tamen causa est, cur crimina tanta remitto,
　errabant multo quod tua verba mero.
sed numquam vitae fallet me ruga severae:
　omnes iam norunt quam sit amare bonum.

---

[1] *No break in NFL, separated by Beroaldus.*
[2] iam credat *N:* non credit *FL.*
[3] nullo *Heinsius:* stulto *NFL.*

Lynceus ipse meus seros insanit amores !

    solum te nostros laetor adire deos.

quid tua Socraticis tibi nunc sapientia libris

    proderit aut rerum dicere posse vias ?

aut quid Erechthei tibi prosunt carmina plectri ? [1]

    nil iuvat in magno vester amore senex.   30

tu satius Meropem Musis [2] imitere Philetan

    et non inflati somnia Callimachi.

nam rursus licet Aetoli referas Acheloi

    fluxerit ut magno fractus [3] amore liquor,

atque etiam ut Phrygio fallax Maeandria campo

    errat et ipsa suas decipit unda vias,

qualis et Adrasti fuerit vocalis Arion,

    tristis ad Archemori funera victor equus :

Amphiarea tibi non prosint [4] fata quadrigae

    aut Capanei magno grata ruina Iovi.   40

desine et Aeschyleo componere verba coturno,

    desine, et ad molles membra resolve choros.

incipe iam angusto versus includere torno,

    inque tuos ignes, dure poeta, veni.

tu non Antimacho, non tutior ibis Homero :

    despicit et magnos recta puella deos.

sed non ante gravis taurus succumbit aratro,

    cornua quam validis haeserit in laqueis,

---

[1] erecthei *μ* : erechti *N·*: erethei *FL*.   plectri *Palmer :* lecta *NFL*.

[2] Meropem Musis *Bergk, Schneidewin :* memorem musis *N :* m sis memorem *FL*.

[3] fractus *ς* : tactus *NFL*.

[4] Amphiarea tibi nil prosint *Postgate :* non amphiareae prosint tibi *NFL*.

nec tu tam[1] duros per te patieris amores :
    trux tamen a nobis ante domandus eris.   50
harum nulla solet rationem quaerere mundi,
    nec cur fraternis Luna laboret equis,
nec si post Stygias aliquid rest arbiter undas,[2]
    nec si consulto fulmina missa tonent.
aspice me, cui parva domi fortuna relicta est
    nullus et antiquo Marte triumphus avi,
ut regnem mixtas inter conviva puellas
    hoc ego, quo tibi nunc elevor, ingenio !
mi lubet hesternis posito[3] languere corollis,
    quem tetigit iactu certus ad ossa deus ;   60
Actia Vergilio custodis litora Phoebi,
    Caesaris et fortes dicere posse rates,
qui nunc Aeneae Troiani suscitat arma
    iactaque Lavinis moenia litoribus.
cedite Romani scriptores, cedite Grai !
    nescio quid maius nascitur Iliade.
tu canis umbrosi subter pineta Galaesi
    Thyrsin et attritis Daphnin harundinibus,
utque decem possint corrumpere mala puellas
    missus et impressis haedus ab uberibus.   70
felix, qui viles pomis mercaris amores !
    huic licet ingratae Tityrus ipse canat.
felix intactum Corydon qui temptat Alexin
    agricolae domini carpere delicias !

---

[1] tam *FL :* iam *N.*
[2] rest arbiter undas *Munro :* restabit *NFL.* erumpnas *FL.*
om. *N.*
[3] mi lubet . . . posito *Housman :* me iuvet . . . positum
NFL. hesternis *v :* externis *N :* aeternis *FL.*

[355]

quamvis ille sua lassus requiescat avena,
    laudatur faciles inter Hamadryadas.
tu canis Ascraei veteris praecepta poetae,
    quo seges in campo, quo viret uva iugo.
tale facis carmen docta testudine quale
    Cynthius impositis temperat articulis.   80
non tamen haec ulli venient ingrata legenti,
    sive in amore rudis sive peritus erit.
nec minor hic animis, ut sit minor ore,[1] canorus
    anseris indocto carmine cessit olor.
haec quoque perfecto ludebat Iasone Varro,
    Varro Leucadiae maxima flamma suae;
haec quoque lascivi cantarunt scripta Catulli,
    Lesbia quis ipsa notior est Helena;
haec etiam docti confessa est pagina Calvi,
    cum caneret miserae funera Quintiliae.   90
et modo formosa qui[2] multa Lycoride Gallus
    mortuus inferna vulnera lavit aqua!
Cynthia quin etiam versu laudata Properti,
    hos inter si me ponere Fama volet.

---

[1] hic *Housman:* his *NFL.* animis *N:* animi *FL.* ut sit
minor *Housman:* aut sim minor *NFL* (minor ore canorus
om. N).
[2] qui *ς* : quam *NFL.*

LIBER TERTIVS

I

CALLIMACHI Manes et Coi sacra Philetae,
  in vestrum, quaeso, me sinite ire nemus.
primus ego ingredior puro de fonte sacerdos
  Itala per Graios orgia ferre choros.
dicite, quo pariter carmen tenuastis in antro?
  quove pede ingressi? quamve bibistis aquam?
a valeat, Phoebum quicumque moratur in armis!
  exactus tenui pumice versus eat,—
quo me Fama levat terra sublimis, et a me
  nata coronatis Musa triumphat equis,   10
et mecum in curru parvi vectantur Amores,
  scriptorumque meas turba secuta rotas.
quid frustra missis in me certatis habenis?
  non datur ad Musas currere lata via.
multi, Roma, tuas laudes annalibus addent,
  qui finem imperii Bactra futura canent;
sed, quod pace legas, opus hoc de monte Sororum
  detulit intacta pagina nostra via.
mollia, Pegasides, date vestro serta poetae:
  non faciet capiti dura corona meo   20

at mihi quod vivo detraxerit invida turba,
post obitum duplici faenore reddet Honos; [1]
omnia post obitum fingit maiora vetustas : [2]
maius ab exsequiis nomen in ora venit.
nam quis equo pulsas abiegno nosceret arces,
fluminaque Haemonio comminus isse viro,
Idaeum Simoenta, Iovis cum prole Scamandro, [3]
Hectora per campos ter maculasse rotas ?
Deiphobumque Helenumque et Pulydamanta et
in armis
qualemcumque Parim vix sua nosset humus.   30
exiguo sermone fores nunc, Ilion, et tu
Troia bis Oetaei numine capta dei.
nec non ille tui casus memorator Homerus
posteritate suum crescere sensit opus.
meque inter seros laudabit Roma nepotes :
illum post cineres auguror ipse diem.
ne mea contempto lapis indicet ossa sepulcro
provisum est Lycio vota probante deo.

IJ

Carminis interea nostri redeamus in orbem ;
gaudeat in solito tacta puella sono.
Orphea delenisse [4] feras et concita dicunt
flumina Threicia sustinuisse lyra ;

[1] reddet *f :* reddit *NFL.*   honos *ς :* onus *NFL.*
[2] omnia *FL :* famae *N.*   vetustas *FL :* vetustae *N.*
[3] cum prole Scamandro *G. Wolff :* cunabula parvi *FL :* om. *N.*
[4] delenisse *Ayrmann :* detinuisse *NL :* detenuisse *F.*

saxa Cithaeronis Thebas agitata per artem
    sponte sua in muri [1] membra coisse ferunt;
quin etiam, Polypheme, fera Galatea sub Aetna
    ad tua rorantes carmina flexit equos.
miremur, nobis et Baccho et Apolline dextro,
    turba puellarum si mea verba colit ?   10
quod non Taenariis domus est mihi fulta columnis,
    nec camera auratas inter eburna trabes,
nec mea Phaeacas aequant pomaria silvas,
    non operosa rigat Marcius antra liquor;
at Musae comites et carmina cara legenti,
    nec [2] defessa choris Calliopea meis.
fortunata, meo si qua est celebrata libello!
    carmina erunt formae tot monumenta tuae.
nam neque Pyramidum sumptus ad sidera ducti,
    nec Iovis Elei caelum imitata domus,   20
nec Mausolei dives fortuna sepulcri
    mortis ab extrema condicione vacant.
aut illis flamma aut imber subducit honores,
    annorum aut ictus pondere [3] victa ruent.
at non ingenio quaesitum nomen ab aevo
    excidet: ingenio stat sine morte decus.

[1] in muri *5* : in numeri *NL :* immineri *F.*
[2] nec *Baehrens :* et *FL :* omitted by *N.*
[3] ictus *L :* ictu *NF.* pondere *NL :* pondera *F*

III

Visvs eram molli recubans Heliconis in umbra,
  Bellerophontei qua fluit umor equi,
reges, Alba, tuos et regum facta tuorum,
  tantum operis, nervis hiscere posse meis ;
parvaque tam magnis admoram fontibus ora,
  unde pater sitiens Ennius ante bibit ;
et cecinit Curios fratres et Horatia pila,
  regiaque Aemilia vecta tropaea rate,
victricesque moras Fabii pugnamque sinistram
  Cannensem et versos ad pia vota deos,   10
Hannibalemque Lares Romana sede fugantes,
  anseris et tutum voce fuisse Iovem :
cum me Castalia speculans ex arbore Phoebus
  sic ait aurata nixus ad antra lyra :
" Quid tibi cum tali, demens, est flumine ?   quis te
  carminis heroi tangere iussit opus ?
non hinc ulla tibi speranda est fama, Properti :
  mollia sunt parvis prata terenda rotis ;
ut tuus in scamno iactetur saepe libellus,
  quem legat exspectans sola puella virum.   20
cur tua praescripto sevecta est pagina gyro ?
  non est ingenii cumba gravanda tui.
alter remus aquas alter tibi radat harenas,
  tutus eris : medio maxima turba mari est."
dixerat, et plectro sedem mihi monstrat eburno,
  qua nova muscoso semita facta solo est.

hic erat affixis viridis spelunca lapillis,
    pendebantque cavis tympana pumicibus,
orgia [1] Musarum et Sileni patris imago
    fictilis et calami, Pan Tegeaee, tui ;   30
et Veneris dominae volucres, mea turba, columbae
    tingunt Gorgoneo punica rostra lacu ;
diversaeque novem sortitae rura Puellae
    exercent teneras in sua dona manus :
haec hederas legit in thyrsos, haec carmina nervis
    aptat, at illa manu texit utraque rosam.
e quarum numero me contigit una dearum
    (ut reor a facie, Calliopea fuit) :
" Contentus niveis semper vectabere cycnis,
    nec te fortis equi ducet ad arma sonus.   40
nil tibi sit rauco praeconia classica cornu
    flare, nec Aonium tinguere Marte nemus ;
aut quibus in campis Mariano proelia signo
    stent et Teutonicas Roma refringat opes,
barbarus aut Suevo perfusus sanguine Rhenus
    saucia maerenti corpora vectet aqua.
quippe coronatos alienum ad limen amantes
    nocturnaeque canes ebria signa fugae,
ut per te clausas sciat excantare puellas,
    qui volet austeros arte ferire viros."   50
talia Calliope, lymphisque a fonte petitis
    ora Philetaea nostra rigavit aqua.

            [1] orgia *Heinsius :* ergo *NFL.*

IV

ARMA deus Caesar dites meditatur ad Indos,
    et freta gemmiferi findere classe maris.
magna, viri, merces: parat ultima terra triumphos,
    Thybris, et Euphrates sub tua iura fluet; [1]
sera, sed Ausoniis veniet provincia virgis;
    assuescent Latio Partha tropaea Iovi.
ite agite, expertae bello date lintea prorae,
    et solitum armigeri ducite munus equi!
omina fausta cano. Crassos clademque piate!
    ite et Romanae consulite historiae!   10
Mars pater, et sacrae fatalia lumina Vestae,
    ante meos obitus sit precor illa dies,
qua videam spoliis oneratos Caesaris axes,
    ad vulgi plausus saepe resistere equos,
inque sinu carae nixus spectare puellae
    incipiam et titulis oppida capta legam,
tela fugacis equi et bracati militis arcus,
    et subter captos arma sedere duces!
ipsa tuam serva prolem, Venus: hoc sit in aevum,
    cernis ab Aenea quod superesse caput.   20
praeda sit haec illis, quorum meruere labores:
    mi sat erit Sacra [2] plaudere posse Via.

---

[1] Thybris . . . fluet *Housman:* Tigris . . . fluent *NFL.*
[2] mi *ς:* me *NFL.*   sacra *N: om. L:* media *F.*

V

Pacis Amor deus est, pacem veneramur amantes:
    sat [1] mihi cum domina proelia dura mea.
nec tantum [2] inviso pectus mihi carpitur auro,
    nec bibit e gemma divite nostra sitis,
nec mihi mille iugis Campania pinguis aratur,
    nec, miser, aera paro clade, Corinthe, tua.
o prima infelix fingenti terra Prometheo!
    ille parum caute pectoris egit opus.
corpora disponens mentem non vidit in arte:
    recta animi primum debuit esse via.   10
nunc maris in tantum vento iactamur, et hostem
    quaerimus, atque armis nectimus arma nova.
haud ullas portabis opes Acherontis ad undas:
    nudus ad infernas, stulte, vehere rates.
victor cum victis pariter miscebitur umbris:
    consule cum Mario, capte Iugurtha, sedes.
Lydus Dulichio non distat Croesus ab Iro:
    optima mors, carpta quae venit acta [3] die.
me iuvat in prima coluisse Helicona iuventa
    Musarumque choris implicuisse manus: 20
me iuvet et multo mentem vincire Lyaeo,
    et caput in verna semper habere rosa.

[1] sat *Livineius :* stant *NFL.*
[2] tantum *Lachmann :* tamen *NFL.*
[3] carpta *Baehrens :* parca *NFL.* acta *NL :* apta *F.*

atque ubi iam Venerem gravis interceperit aetas,
    sparserit et nigras[1] alba senecta comas,
tum mihi naturae libeat perdiscere mores,
    quis deus hanc mundi temperet arte domum,
qua venit exoriens, qua deficit, unde coactis
    cornibus in plenum menstrua luna redit,
unde salo superant venti, quid flamine captet
    Eurus, et in nubes unde perennis aqua;   30
sit ventura dies mundi quae subruat arces,
    purpureus pluvias cur bibit arcus aquas,
aut cur Perrhaebi tremuere cacumina Pindi,
    solis et atratis luxerit orbis equis,
cur serus versare boves et plaustra Bootes,[2]
    Pleiadum spisso cur coit igne chorus,
curve suos finis altum non exeat aequor,
    plenus et in partis quattuor annus eat;
sub terris sint iura deum et tormenta Gigantum,
    Tisiphones atro si furit angue caput,   40
aut Alcmaeoniae furiae aut ieiunia Phinei,
    num rota, num scopuli, num sitis inter aquas,
num tribus infernum custodit faucibus antrum
    Cerberus, et Tityo iugera pauca novem,
an ficta in miseras descendit fabula gentis,
    et timor haud ultra quam rogus esse potest.
exitus hic vitae superest mihi: vos, quibus arma
    grata magis, Crassi signa referte domum.

---

[1] sparserit et *N :* sparsit et *FL.* nigras ς : integras *NFL.*
[2] plaustra Bootes ς : flamma palustra *FL :* flamma boon *N.*

VI

Dic mihi de nostra, quae sentis, vera puella :
    sic tibi sint dominae, Lygdame, dempta iuga.
num [1] me laetitia tumefactum fallis inani,
    haec referens, quae me credere velle putas ?
omnis enim debet sine vano nuntius esse,
    maioremque timens servus habere fidem.
nunc mihi, si qua tenes, ab origine dicere prima
    incipe : suspensis auribus ista bibam.
sic, ut eam [2] incomptis vidisti flere capillis,
    illius ex oculis multa cadebat aqua ?   10
nec speculum strato vidisti, Lygdame, lecto ?
    ornabat niveas nullane gemma manus ?
ac maestam teneris vestem pendere lacertis,
    scriniaque ad lecti clausa iacere pedes ?
tristis erat domus, et tristes sua pensa ministrae
    carpebant, medio nebat et ipsa loco,
umidaque impressa siccabat lumina lana,
    rettulit et querulo iurgia nostra sono ?
" Haec te teste mihi promissa est, Lygdame, merces ?
    est poenae servo rumpere teste fidem.   20
ille potest nullo miseram me linquere facto,
    et qualem nolo [3] dicere habere domo !
gaudet me vacuo solam tabescere lecto.
    si placet, insultet, Lygdame, morte mea.

[1] num *ς* : non *N :* dum *FL.*
[2] sic, ut eam *Butler :* sicut eam *FL :* si că *N.*
[3] et qualem nolo *Palmer :* et qualem nullo *N :* aequalem nulla *FL.*

non me moribus illa, sed herbis improba vicit :
    staminea rhombi ducitur ille rota.
illum turgentis ranae portenta rubetae
    et lecta exuctis [1] anguibus ossa trahunt,
et strigis inventae per busta iacentia plumae,
    cinctaque funesto lanea vitta viro.   30
si non vana canunt mea somnia, Lygdame, testor,
    poena erit ante meos sera sed ampla pedes ;
putris et in vacuo texetur aranea lecto :
    noctibus illorum dormiet ipsa Venus.''
quae tibi si veris animis est questa puella,
    hac eadem rursus, Lygdame, curre via,
et mea cum multis lacrimis mandata reporta
    iram, non fraudes esse in amore meo,
me quoque consimili impositum torquerier igni :
    iurabo bis sex integer esse dies.   40
quod mihi si e tanto [2] felix concordia bello
    exstiterit, per me, Lygdame, liber eris.

VII

ERGO sollicitae tu causa, pecunia, vitae !
    per te immaturum mortis adimus iter ;
tu vitiis hominum crudelia pabula praebes ;
    semina curarum de capite orta tuo.
tu Paetum ad Pharios tendentem lintea portus
    obruis insano terque quaterque mari.

---

[1] exuctis *Burmann :* exectis *NL :* exactis *F.*
[2] e tanto *Lachmann :* tanto *NFL.*

nam dum te sequitur, primo miser excidit aevo
  et nova longinquis piscibus esca natat ;
et mater non iusta piae dare debita terrae
  nec pote cognatos inter humare rogos ;   10
sed tua nunc volucres astant super ossa marinae,
  nunc tibi pro tumulo Carpathium omne mare est.
infelix Aquilo, raptae timor Orithyiae,
  quae spolia ex illo tanta fuere tibi ?
aut quidnam fracta gaudes, Neptune, carina ?
  portabat sanctos alveus ille viros.
Paete, quid aetatem numeras ?   quid cara natanti
  mater in ore tibi est ?   non habet unda deos
nam tibi nocturnis ad saxa ligata procellis
  omnia detrito vincula fune cadunt.   20
reddite corpus humo, posita est in gurgite vita ; 25
  Paetum sponte tua, vilis arena, tegas ;
et quotiens Paeti transibit nauta sepulcrum,
  dicat " Et audaci tu timor esse potes."
ite, rates curvate,[1] et leti texite causas :
  ista per humanas mors venit acta manus.   30
terra parum fuerat fatis, adiecimus undas :
  fortunae miseras auximus arte vias.
ancora te teneat, quem non tenuere penates ?
  quid meritum dicas, cui sua terra parum est ?
ventorum est, quodcumque paras : haud ulla carina
  consenuit, fallit portus et ipse fidem.
natura insidians pontum substravit avaris :
  ut tibi succedat, vix semel esse potest.

[1] curvate *Lendrum :* curvae *NFL.*

sunt Agamemnonias testantia litora curas, 21
  qua notat Argynni poena Mimantis aquas.[1] 22
hoc iuvene amisso classem non solvit Atrides, 23
  pro qua mactata est Iphigenia mora.[2] 24
saxa triumphales fregere Capharea puppes, 39
  naufraga cum vasto Graecia tracta salo est. 40
paulatim socium iacturam flevit Vlixes,
  in mare cui solum [3] non valuere doli.
quod si contentus patrio bove verteret agros,
  verbaque duxisset pondus habere mea,
viveret ante suos dulcis conviva Penates,
  pauper, at in terra nil nisi fleret opes.[4]
non tulit haec Paetus, stridorem audire procellae
  et duro teneras laedere fune manus ;
sed Chio thalamo aut Oricia terebintho
  et fultum pluma versicolore caput. 50
huic fluctus vivo radicitus abstulit ungues,
  et miser invisam traxit hiatus aquam ;
hunc parvo ferri vidit nox improba ligno :
  Paetus ut occideret, tot coiere mala.
flens tamen extremis dedit haec mandata querelis,
  cum moribunda niger clauderet ora liquor :
" Di maris Aegaei quos sunt penes aequora,
    venti,
  et quaecumque meum degravat unda caput,

---

[1] Argynni *v :* agynni *N :* argioni *FL.* Mimantis aquas *Ellis :* minantis aquae *NFL.*
[2] *21-24 transposed by Scaliger after 38.*
[3] solum ʃ : soli *NFL.*
[4] nisi ʃ : ubi *NFL.* fleret opes *Baehrens :* flere potest *NFL.*

quo rapitis miseros primae lanuginis annos ?
   attulimus nocuas [1] in freta vestra manus ?   60
a miser alcyonum scopulis affligar acutis !
   in me caeruleo fuscina sumpta deo est.
at saltem Italiae regionibus evehat aestus :
   hoc de me sat erit si modo matris erit.''
subtrahit haec fantem torta vertigine fluctus ;
   ultima quae Paeto voxque diesque fuit.
o centum aequoreae Nereo genitore puellae,
   et tu materno tracta dolore Thetis ;
vos decuit lasso supponere bracchia mento :
   non poterat vestras ille gravare manus :   70
at tu, saeve Aquilo, numquam mea vela videbis :
   ante fores dominae condar oportet iners.

VIII

DVLCIS ad hesternas fuerat mihi rixa lucernas,
   vocis et insanae tot maledicta tuae.
cum [2] furibunda mero mensam propellis et in me
   proicis insana cymbia plena manu.
tu vero nostros audax invade capillos
   et mea formosis unguibus ora nota,
tu minitare oculos subiecta exurere flamma,
   fac mea rescisso pectora nuda sinu !
nimirum veri dantur mihi signa caloris :
   nam sine amore gravi femina nulla dolet.   10

[1] nocuas *Housman :* longas *NFL.*
[2] cum *Beroaldus :* cur *NFL.*

[369]

quae mulier rabida [1] iactat convicia lingua,
 haec [2] Veneris magnae volvitur ante pedes,
custodum gregibus circa se stipat euntem,
 seu sequitur medias, Maenas ut icta, vias,
seu timidam crebro dementia somnia terrent,
 seu miseram in tabula picta puella movet:
his ego tormentis animi sum verus haruspex,
 has didici certo saepe in amore notas.
non est certa fides, quam non in iurgia vertas: [3]
 hostibus eveniat lenta puella meis.   20
in morso aequales videant mea vulnera collo:
 me doceat livor mecum habuisse meam.
aut in amore dolere volo aut audire dolentem,
 sive tuas lacrimas sive videre meas, [4]
tecta superciliis si quando verba remittis,
 aut tua cum digitis scripta silenda notas.
odi ego quae numquam pungunt suspiria somnos:
 semper in irata pallidus esse velim.
dulcior ignis erat Paridi, cum Graia [5] per arma
 Tyndaridi poterat gaudia ferre suae: 30
dum vincunt Danai, dum restat barbarus Hector,
 ille Helenae in gremio maxima bella gerit.
aut tecum aut pro te mihi cum rivalibus arma
 semper erunt: in te pax mihi nulla placet.

[1] rabida *Scaliger:* gravida *NFL.*
[2] haec *Livineius:* et *NFL.*
[3] iniurgia *N:* iniuria *FL.*   vertas *Vahlen:* versat *NL:* vertat *F.*
[4] tuas . . . meas *Sandstrom:* meas . . . tuas *NFL.*
[5] Graia *Fruter:* grata *NFL.*

VIIIa [1]

GAVDE, quod nulla est aeque formosa : doleres,
   si qua foret : nunc sis iure superba licet.
at tibi, qui nostro nexisti [2] retia lecto,
   sit socer aeternum nec sine matre domus !
cui nunc si qua data est furandae copia noctis,
   offensa illa mihi, non tibi amica, dedit.   40

IX

MAECENAS, eques Etrusco de sanguine regum,
   intra fortunam qui cupis esse tuam,
quid me scribendi tam vastum mittis in aequor ?
   non sunt apta meae grandia vela rati.
turpe est, quod nequeas, capiti committere pondus
   et pressum inflexo mox dare terga genu.
omnia non pariter rerum sunt omnibus apta,
   palma [3] nec ex aequo ducitur ulla iugo.
gloria Lysippo est animosa effingere signa ;
   exactis Calamis se mihi iactat equis ;   10
in Veneris tabula summam sibi poscit Apelles ;
   Parrhasius parva vindicat arte locum :
argumenta magis sunt Mentoris addita formae ;
   at Myos exiguum flectit acanthus iter ;

---

[1] *No break in NFL, separated by Butler.*
[2] nexisti *Priscianus and Diomedes :* tendisti *NFL.*
[3] palma 5 : flamma *NFL.*

Phidiacus signo se Iuppiter ornat eburno ;
    Praxitelen Triopos venditat [1] urbe lapis.
est quibus Eleae concurrit palma quadrigae,
    est quibus in celeres gloria nata pedes ;
hic satus ad pacem, hic castrensibus utilis armis :
    naturae sequitur semina quisque suae.   20
at tua, Maecenas, vitae praecepta recepi,
    cogor et exemplis te superare tuis.
cum tibi Romano dominas in honore secures
    et liceat medio ponere iura foro ;
vel tibi Medorum pugnaces ire per hastas,[2]
    atque onerare tuam fixa per arma domum ;
et tibi ad effectum vires det Caesar, et omni
    tempore tam faciles insinuentur opes ;
parcis et in tenues humilem te colligis umbras :
    velorum plenos subtrahis ipse sinus.   30
crede mihi, magnos aequabunt ista Camillos
    iudicia, et venies tu quoque in ora virum,
Caesaris et famae vestigia iuncta tenebis :
    Maecenatis erunt vera tropaea fides.
non ego velifera tumidum mare findo carina : [3]
    tota sub exiguo flumine nostra mora est.
non flebo in cineres arcem sedisse paternos
    Cadmi nec septem proelia clade pari ;
nec referam Scaeas et Pergama Apollinis arces,
    et Danaum decimo vere redisse rates,   40

---

[1] Triopos *Richmond :* propria *NFL.*   venditat *Burmann :*
vindicat *NFL.*
[2] hastas *Markland :* hostes *NFL.*
[3] 35 om. *N.*

moenia cum Graio Neptunia pressit aratro
 victor Palladiae ligneus artis equus.
inter Callimachi sat erit placuisse libellos
 et cecinisse modis, Dore [1] poeta, tuis.
haec urant pueros, haec urant scripta puellas,
 meque deum clament et mihi sacra ferant !
te duce vel Iovis arma canam caeloque minantem
 Coeum et Phlegraeis Eurymedonta [2] iugis ;
eductosque pares silvestri ex ubere reges,   51
 ordiar et caeso moenia firma Remo,   50
celsaque Romanis decerpta palatia tauris [3]   49
 crescet et ingenium sub tua iussa meum !
prosequar et currus utroque ab litore ovantes,
 Parthorum astutae tela remissa fugae,
castraque Pelusi Romano subruta ferro,
 Antonique graves in sua fata manus.
mollis tu coeptae fautor cape lora iuventae,
 dexteraque immissis da mihi signa rotis.
hoc mihi, Maecenas, laudis concedis, et a te est
 quod ferar in partes ipse fuisse tuas.   60

---

[1] Dore *Scriverius :* dure *NFL.*
[2] Eurymedonta *Huschke :* oromedonta *NFL.*
[3] *49 and 51 transposed by Peiper.*

X

MIRABAR, quidnam misissent mane Camenae,
    ante meum stantes sole rubente torum.
natalis nostrae signum misere puellae
    et manibus faustos ter crepuere sonos.
transeat hic sine nube dies, stent aere venti,
    ponat et in sicco molliter unda minax.
aspiciam nullos hodierna luce dolentes,
    et Niobae lacrimas supprimat ipse lapis,
alcyonum positis requiescant ora querelis,
    increpet absumptum nec sua mater Ityn.   10
tuque, o cara mihi, felicibus edita pennis,
    surge et poscentes iusta precare deos.
ac primum pura somnum tibi discute lympha,
    et nitidas presso pollice finge comas :
dein qua primum oculos cepisti veste Properti
    indue, nec vacuum flore relinque caput;
et pete, qua polles, ut sit tibi forma perennis,
    inque meum semper stent tua regna caput.
inde coronatas ubi ture piaveris aras,
    luxerit et tota flamma secunda domo,   20
sit mensae ratio, noxque inter pocula currat,
    et crocino nares murreus ungat onyx.
tibia nocturnis succumbat rauca choreis,
    et sint nequitiae libera verba tuae,
dulciaque ingratos adimant convivia somnos,
    publica vicinae perstrepat aura viae :

[374]

sit sors et nobis talorum interprete iactu,
  quem gravibus pennis verberet ille puer.
cum fuerit multis exacta trientibus hora,
  noctis et instituet sacra ministra Venus,   30
annua solvamus thalamo sollemnia nostro,
  natalisque tui sic peragamus iter.

XI

Qvid mirare, meam si versat femina vitam
  et trahit addictum sub sua iura virum,
criminaque ignavi capitis mihi turpia fingis,
  quod nequeam fracto rumpere vincla iugo?
venturam melius praesagit navita mortem,[1]
  vulneribus didicit miles habere metum.
ista ego praeterita iactavi verba iuventa:
  tu nunc exemplo disce timere meo.
Colchis flagrantes adamantina sub iuga tauros
  egit et armigera proelia sevit humo,   10
custodisque feros clausit serpentis hiatus,
  iret ut Aesonias aurea lana domos.
ausa ferox ab equo quondam oppugnare sagittis
  Maeotis Danaum Penthesilea rates;
aurea cui postquam nudavit cassida frontem,
  vicit victorem candida forma virum.
Omphale in tantum formae processit honorem,
  Lydia Gygaeo tincta puella lacu,

---

[1] venturam *NFL, perhaps corrupt:* ventorum *S. G. Owen.*
mortem *NFL:* motum *S. G. Owen.*

[375]

ut, qui pacato statuisset in orbe columnas,
  tam dura traheret mollia pensa manu.   20
Persarum statuit Babylona Semiramis urbem,
  ut solidum cocto tolleret aggere opus,
et duo in adversum mitti [1] per moenia currus
  nec possent tacto stringere ab axe latus;
duxit et Euphratem medium, quam condidit, arcis,[2]
  iussit et imperio subdere [3] Bactra caput.
nam quid ego heroas, quid raptem in crimine
    divos?
  Iuppiter infamat seque suamque domum.
quid, modo quae nostris opprobria vexerit armis
  et famulos inter femina trita suos,   30
coniugis obsceni pretium Romana poposcit
  moenia et addictos in sua regna Patres?
noxia Alexandria, dolis aptissima tellus,
  et totiens nostro Memphi cruenta malo,
tris ubi Pompeio detraxit harena triumphos!
  tollet nulla dies hanc tibi, Roma, notam.
issent Phlegraeo melius tibi funera campo,
  vel tua si socero colla daturus eras.
scilicet incesti meretrix regina Canopi,
  una Philippeo sanguine adusta nota,   40
ausa Iovi nostro latrantem opponere Anubim,
  et Tiberim Nili cogere ferre minas,
Romanamque tubam crepitanti pellere sistro,
  baridos et contis rostra Liburna sequi,

1 mitti *Tyrrell :* missi *NFL.*
2 quam *FL :* qua *N.*   arcis *Baehrens :* arcus *NFL.*
3 subdere *Burmann :* surgere *NFL.*

foedaque Tarpeio conopia tendere saxo,
    iura dare et statuas inter et arma Mari.   46
septem urbs alta iugis, toto quae praesidet orbi,   57
    femineas [1] timuit territa Marte minas.[2]   58
quid nunc Tarquinii fractas iuvat esse secures,   47
    nomine quem simili vita superba notat,
si mulier patienda fuit ?   cape, Roma, triumphum
    et longum Augusto salva precare diem !   50
fugisti tamen in timidi vaga [3] flumina Nili :
    accepere tuae Romula vincla manus.
bracchia spectavi sacris admorsa colubris,
    et trahere occultum membra soporis iter.
" Non hoc, Roma, fui [4] tanto tibi cive verenda !"
    dixit et assiduo lingua sepulta mero.   56
Curtius expletis statuit monumenta lacunis,   61
    at Decius misso proelia rupit equo,
Coclitis abscissos testatur semita pontes,
    est [5] cui cognomen corvus habere dedit :
haec di condiderant, haec di quoque moenia
    servant :
    vix timeat salvo Caesare Roma Iovem.
nunc ubi Scipiadae classes, ubi signa Camilli,
    aut modo Pompeia Bospore capta manu,   68
Hannibalis spolia et victi monumenta Syphacis,   59
    et Pyrrhi ad nostros gloria fracta pedes ? [6]   60

---

[1] femineo *Postgate :* femineas *NFL.*
[2] *57, 58 transposed by Butler after 46.*   *58 om. N.*
[3] vaga *ς :* vada *NFL.*   [4] fui *ς :* fuit *NFL.*
[5] est *Puccius :* et *NFL.*
[6] *59, 60 transposed by Passerat after 68.*

Leucadius versas acies memorabit Apollo : 69
    tantum operis belli sustulit una dies. 70
at tu, sive petes portus seu, navita, linques,
    Caesaris in toto sis memor Ionio.

XII

POSTVME, plorantem potuisti linquere Gallam,
    miles et Augusti fortia signa sequi ?
tantine ulla fuit spoliati gloria Parthi,
    ne faceres [1] Galla multa rogante tua ?
si fas est, omnes pariter pereatis avari,
    et quisquis fido praetulit arma toro !
tu tamen iniecta [2] tectus, vesane, lacerna
    potabis galea fessus Araxis aquam.
illa quidem interea fama tabescet inani,
    haec tua ne virtus fiat amara tibi, 10
neve tua Medae laetentur caede sagittae,
    ferreus aurato neu cataphractus equo,
neve aliquid de te flendum referatur in urna :
    sic redeunt,[3] illis qui cecidere locis.
ter quater in casta felix, o Postume, Galla !
    moribus his alia coniuge dignus eras !
quid faciet nullo munita puella timore,
    cum sit luxuriae Roma magistra suae ? [4]
sed securus eas : Gallam non munera vincent,
    duritiaeque tuae non erit illa memor. 20

1 faceres *N :* facias *FL.*   2 iniecta *Itali :* intecta *NFL.*
3 sic redeunt *ς :* si credunt *N :* si credent *FL.*
4 suae *ς :* tuae *NFL.*

nam quocumque die salvum te fata remittent,
   pendebit collo Galla pudica tuo.
Postumus alter erit miranda coniuge Vlixes :
   non illi longae tot nocuere morae,
castra decem annorum, et Ciconum mons Ismara,
      Calpe,
   exustaeque tuae mox, Polypheme, genae,
et Circae fraudes, lotosque herbaeque tenaces,
   Scyllaque et alternas scissa Charybdis aquas,
Lampeties Ithacis veribus mugisse iuvencos
   (paverat hos Phoebo filia Lampetie),   30
et thalamum Aeaeae flentis fugisse puellae,
   totque hiemis noctes totque natasse dies,
nigrantesque domos animarum intrasse silentum,
   Sirenum surdo remige adisse lacus,
et veteres arcus leto renovasse procorum,
   errorisque sui sic statuisse modum.
nec frustra, quia casta domi persederat uxor.
   vincit Penelopes Aelia [1] Galla fidem.

XIII

QVAERITIS, unde avidis nox sit pretiosa puellis,
   et Venerem exhaustae damna querantur opes.
certa quidem tantis causa et manifesta ruinis :
   luxuriae nimium libera facta via est.
Inda cavis aurum mittit formica metallis,
   et venit e Rubro concha Erycina salo,

   [1] Aelia *Passerat :* laelia *NFL.*

et Tyros ostrinos praebet Cadmea colores,
    cinnamon et multi pastor odoris Arabs :
haec etiam clausas expugnant arma pudicas,
    quaeque gerunt [1] fastus, Icarioti, tuos.   10
matrona incedit census induta nepotum
    et spolia opprobrii nostra per ora trahit.
nulla est poscendi, nulla est reverentia dandi,
    aut si qua est, pretio tollitur ipsa mora.
felix Eois lex funeris una maritis,
    quos Aurora suis rubra colorat equis !
namque ubi mortifero iacta est fax ultima lecto,
    uxorum fusis stat pia turba comis,
et certamen habent leti, quae viva sequatur
    coniugium : pudor est non licuisse mori.   20
ardent victrices et flammae pectora praebent,
    imponuntque suis ora perusta viris.
hoc genus infidum nuptarum, hic nulla puella
    nec fida Euadne nec pia Penelope.
felix agrestum quondam pacata iuventus,
    divitiae quorum messis et arbor erant !
illis munus erant decussa [2] Cydonia ramo,
    et dare puniceis plena canistra rubis,
nunc violas tondere manu, nunc mixta referre
    lilia virgineos lucida per calathos,   30
et portare suis vestitas frondibus uvas
    aut variam plumae versicoloris [3] avem.
his tum blanditiis furtiva per antra puellae
    oscula silvicolis empta dedere viris.

[1] gerunt *Scioppius :* terunt *NFL.*
[2] decussa *FL :* discussa *N.*
[3] versicoloris *ς :* viricoloris *NFL :* vitricoloris *Ellis.*

hinnulei [1] pellis totos operibat amantis,

    altaque nativo creverat herba toro,

pinus et incumbens laetas [2] circumdabat umbras ;

    nec fuerat nudas poena videre deas ;

corniger atque dei vacuam pastoris in aulam

    dux aries saturas ipse reduxit oves ;   40

dique deaeque omnes, quibus est tutela per agros,

    praebebant nostris [3] verba benigna focis :

" Et leporem, quicumque venis, venaberis, hospes,

    et si forte meo tramite quaeris avem :

et me Pana tibi comitem de rupe vocato,

    sive petes calamo praemia, sive cane."

at nunc desertis cessant sacraria lucis :

    aurum omnes victa iam pietate colunt.

auro pulsa fides, auro venalia iura,

    aurum lex sequitur, mox sine lege pudor.   50

torrida sacrilegum testantur limina [4] Brennum,

    dum petit intonsi Pythia regna dei :

at mox [5] laurigero concussus vertice diras

    Gallica Parnasus sparsit in arma nives.

te [6] scelus accepto Thracis Polymestoris auro

    nutrit in hospitio non, Polydore, pio. [7]

tu quoque ut auratos gereres, Eriphyla, lacertos,

    dilapsis nusquam est Amphiaraus equis.

---

[1] hinnulei *Scaliger :* atque hinuli *N :* atque humili *FL.*
[2] letas *F :* lentas *NL.*   [3] nostris *Butler :* vestris *NFL.*
[4] limina *N :* lumina *FL.*   [5] mox *FL :* mons *N.*
[6] te *Itali :* et *NFL.*   [7] pio *N :* tuo *FL.*

proloquar :—atque utinam patriae sim verus
  haruspex !—
frangitur ipsa suis Roma superba bonis.   60
certa loquor, sed nulla fides; neque enim Ilia
  quondam
verax Pergameis Maenas habenda malis :
sola Parim Phrygiae fatum componere, sola
  fallacem patriae serpere dixit equum.
ille furor patriae fuit utilis, ille parenti :
  experta est veros irrita lingua deos.

XIV

Mvlta tuae, Sparte, miramur iura palaestrae,
  sed mage virginei tot bona gymnasii,
quod non infames exercet corpore ludos [1]
  inter luctantes nuda puella viros,
cum pila veloces fallit per bracchia iactus,
  increpat et versi clavis adunca trochi,
pulverulentaque ad extremas stat femina metas,
  et patitur duro vulnera pancratio :
nunc ligat ad caestum gaudentia bracchia loris,
  missile nunc disci pondus in orbe rotat,   10
et modo Taygeti, crines aspersa pruina,   15
  sectatur patrios per iuga longa canes,[2]   16
gyrum pulsat equis, niveum latus ense revincit,   11
  virgineumque cavo protegit aere caput,

[1] ludos *Auratus :* lαudes *NFL.*
[2] *15, 16 transposed after 10 by Housman.*

qualis Amazonidum nudatis bellica mammis
    Thermodontiacis turba lavatur aquis;   14
qualis et Eurotae Pollux et Castor harenis,[1]   17
    hic victor pugnis, ille futurus equis,
inter quos Helene nudis capere arma papillis
    fertur nec fratres erubuisse deos.   20
lex igitur Spartana vetat secedere amantes,
    et licet in triviis ad latus esse suae,
nec timor aut ulla est clausae tutela puellae,
    nec gravis austeri poena cavenda viri.
nullo praemisso de rebus tute loquaris
    ipse tuis: longae nulla repulsa morae.
nec Tyriae vestes errantia lumina fallunt,
    est neque odoratae cura molesta comae.[2]
at nostra ingenti vadit circumdata turba,
    nec digitum angusta est inseruisse via;   30
nec quae sint facies nec quae sint verba rogandi
    invenias: caecum versat amator iter.
quod si iura fores pugnasque imitata Laconum,
    carior hoc esses tu mihi, Roma, bono.

XV

Sic ego non ullos iam norim in amore tumultus,
    nec veniat sine te nox vigilanda mihi!
ut mihi praetexti pudor est velatus amictus[3]
    et data libertas noscere amoris iter,

[1] harenis *Volscus:* habenis *N:* athenis *FL.*
[2] odoratae *FL:* adoratae *N.* comae *Canter:* domi *NFL.*
[3] praetexti *N:* praetexta *FL.* amictus *L:* amicus *NF.*

[383]

illa rudes animos per noctes conscia primas
   imbuit, heu nullis capta Lycinna datis !
tertius (haud multo minus est) cum ducitur annus,
   vix memini nobis verba coisse decem.
cuncta tuus sepelivit amor, nec femina post te
   ulla dedit collo dulcia vincla meo.   10

.   .   .   .   .

[1] testis erit Dirce tam vero crimine saeva,
   Nycteos Antiopen accubuisse Lyco.
a quotiens pulchros ussit regina capillos,
   molliaque immites [2] fixit in ora manus !
a quotiens famulam pensis oneravit iniquis,
   et caput in dura ponere iussit humo !
saepe illam immundis passa est habitare tenebris,
   vilem ieiunae saepe negavit aquam.
Iuppiter, Antiopae nusquam succurris habenti
   tot mala ? corrumpit dura catena manus.   20
si deus es, tibi turpe tuam servire puellam :
   invocet Antiope quem nisi vincta [3] Iovem ?
sola tamen, quaecumque aderant in corpore vires,
   regales manicas rupit utraque manu.
inde Cithaeronis timido pede currit in arces.
   nox erat, et sparso triste cubile gelu.
saepe vago [4] Asopi sonitu permota fluentis
   credebat dominae pone venire pedes.

---

[1] *At this point NFL mark a new elegy. Some verses have
clearly fallen out.*
  [2] immites ſ : immittens *NFL.*
  [3] vincta ſ : victa *NFL.*   [4] vago *F :* vaga *NL.*

et durum Zethum et lacrimis Amphiona mollem
    experta est stabulis[1] mater abacta suis.   30
ac veluti, magnos cum ponunt aequora motus,
    Eurus ubi adverso desinit ire Noto,[2]
litore sic tacito sonitus rarescit harenae,
    sic cadit inflexo lapsa puella genu.
sera, tamen pietas : natis est cognitus error.
    digne Iovis natos qui tueare senex,
tu reddis pueris matrem ; puerique trahendam
    vinxerunt Dircen sub trucis ora bovis.
Antiope, cognosce Iovem : tibi gloria Dirce
    ducitur in multis mortem habitura locis.   40
prata[3] cruentantur Zethi, victorque canebat
    paeana Amphion rupe, Aracynthe, tua.
at tu non meritam parcas vexare Lycinnam :
    nescit vestra ruens ira referre pedem.
fabula nulla tuas de nobis concitet aures :
    te solam et lignis funeris ustus amem.

XVI

Nox media, et dominae mihi venit epistula nostrae :
    Tibure me missa iussit adesse mora,
candida qua geminas ostendunt culmina turres,
    et cadit in patulos nympha Aniena lacus.
quid faciam ? obductis committam mene tenebris,
    ut timeam audaces in mea membra manus ?

[1] stabulis ς : tabulis *NFL*.
[2] ubi adverso . . . Noto *Lachmann :* sub adverso . . . notho
N : in adversos . . . notos *FL*.   [3] prata ς : parta *NFL*.

at si distulero haec nostro mandata timore,
    nocturno fletus saevior hoste mihi.
peccaram semel, et totum sum pulsus[1] in annum :
    in me mansuetas non habet illa manus.   10
nec tamen est quisquam, sacros qui laedat amantes :
    Scironis media sic licet[2] ire via.
quisquis amator erit, Scythicis licet ambulet[3] oris,
    nemo adeo[4] ut noceat barbarus esse volet.
luna ministrat iter, demonstrant astra salebras,
    ipse Amor accensas praecutit[5] ante faces,
saeva canum rabies morsus avertit hiantis :
    huic generi quovis tempore tuta via est.
sanguine tam parvo quis enim spargatur amantis
    improbus, et cuius sit[6] comes ipsa Venus ?   20
quod si certa meos sequerentur funera casus,
    tali[7] mors pretio vel sit emenda mihi.
afferet huc unguenta mihi sertisque sepulcrum
    ornabit custos ad mea busta sedens.
di faciant, mea ne terra locet ossa frequenti,
    qua facit assiduo tramite vulgus iter !
post mortem tumuli sic infamantur amantum.
    me tegat arborea devia terra coma,
aut humer ignotae cumulis vallatus harenae :
    non iuvat in media nomen habere via.   30

[1] pulsus *FL :* portus *N.*
[2] sic licet *ς :* scilicet *N :* si licet *FL.*
[3] Scythiae *inscriptio Pompeiana, C.I.L. 4, 1950.* ambulet *inscr. Pomp. :* ambulat *NFL.*
[4] adeo *inscr. Pomp. :* deo *NFL :* feriat *inscr. Pomp.*
[5] praecutit *Guyetus :* percutit *NFL.*
[6] et cuius sit *Palmer :* exclusis fit *NFL.*
[7] tali *ς :* talis *NFL.*

XVII

Nvnc, o Bacche, tuis humiles advolvimur aris:
    da mihi pacato vela secunda, pater.
tu potes insanae Veneris compescere fastus,
    curarumque tuo fit medicina mero.
per te iunguntur, per te solvuntur amantes:
    tu vitium ex animo dilue, Bacche, meo.
te quoque enim non esse rudem testatur in astris
    lyncibus ad caelum vecta Ariadna tuis.
hoc mihi, quod veteres custodit in ossibus ignes,
    funera sanabunt aut tua vina malum.   10
semper enim vacuos nox sobria torquet amantes,
    spesque timorque animos[1] versat utroque modo.
quod si, Bacche, tuis per fervida tempora donis
    accersitus erit somnus in ossa mea,
ipse seram vitis pangamque ex ordine collis,
    quos carpant nullae me vigilante ferae.
dum modo purpureo cumulem[2] mihi dolia musto,
    et nova pressantis inquinet uva pedes,
quod superest vitae per te et tua cornua vivam,
    virtutisque tuae, Bacche, poeta ferar.   20
dicam ego maternos Aetnaeo fulmine partus,
    Indica Nysaeis arma fugata choris,
vesanumque nova nequiquam in vite Lycurgum,
    Pentheos in triplices funera grata greges,

---

[1] animos *Beroaldus:* animo *NFL.*
[2] cumulem *Postgate:* numen *N:* numerem *L:* nūīe *F.*

curvaque Tyrrhenos delphinum corpora nautas
    in vada pampinea desiluisse rate,
et tibi per mediam bene olentia flumina Diam,[1]
    unde tuum potant Naxia turba merum.
candida laxatis onerato colla corymbis
    cinget Bassaricas Lydia mitra comas,   30
levis odorato cervix manabit olivo,
    et feries nudos veste fluente pedes.
mollia Dircaeae pulsabunt tympana Thebae,
    capripedes calamo Panes hiante canent,
vertice turrigero iuxta dea magna Cybelle
    tundet[2] ad Idaeos cymbala rauca choros.
ante fores templi crater antistitis auro
    libabit[3] fundens in tua sacra merum.
haec ego non humili referam memoranda coturno,
    qualis Pindarico spiritus ore tonat :   40
tu modo servitio vacuum me siste superbo,
    atque hoc sollicitum vince sopore caput.

XVIII

CLAVSVS ab umbroso qua alludit[4] pontus Averno
    umida Baiarum stagna tepentis aquae,
qua iacet et Troiae tubicen Misenus harena,
    et sonat Herculeo structa labore via ;
hic, ubi, mortales dexter cum quaereret urbes,
    cymbala Thebano concrepuere deo :—

1 Dlam *Palmer ;* Naxon *NFL.*
2 tundet *Scaliger :* fundet *NFL.*
3 libabit *Foster :* libatum *NFL.*
4 alludit *Lambinus :* ludit *NFL.*

at nunc invisae magno cum crimine Baiae,
   quis deus in vestra constitit hostis aqua ?—
hic[1] pressus Stygias vultum demisit in undas,
   errat et in vestro spiritus ille lacu.   10
quid genus aut virtus aut optima profuit illi
   mater, et amplexum Caesaris esse focos ?
aut modo tam pleno fluitantia vela theatro,
   et per maternas omnia gesta manus ?
occidit, et misero steterat vicesimus annus :
   tot bona tam parvo clausit in orbe dies.
i nunc, tolle animos et tecum finge triumphos,
   stantiaque in plausum tota theatra iuvent,
Attalicas supera vestes, atque omnia magnis
   gemmea sint ludis : ignibus ista dabis.   20
sed tamen huc omnes, huc[2] primus et ultimus
     ordo :
   est mala, sed cunctis ista terenda via est ;
exoranda canis tria sunt latrantia colla,
   scandenda est torvi[3] publica cumba senis.
ille licet ferro cautus se condat et aere,
   mors tamen inclusum protrahit inde caput.
Nirea non facies, non vis exemit Achillem,
   Croesum aut, Pactoli quas parit umor opes.
[hic olim ignaros luctus populavit Achivos,
   Atridae magno cum stetit alter amor.[4]]   30

---

[1] hic *Guyet :* his *NFL.*
[2] huc . . . huc *f :* hoc . . . huc *NFL.*
[3] torvi *f :* torti *FL :* -troci *N.*
[4] *This couplet is clearly alien to its present context. It is conceivable that it should be transposed to follow* II. VI. 16.

at tibi, nauta, pias hominum qui traicis umbras,
    hoc animae portent corpus inane suae : [1]
qua Siculae victor telluris Claudius et qua
    Caesar, ab humana cessit in astra via.

XIX

OBICITVR totiens a te mihi nostra libido :
    crede mihi, vobis imperat ista magis.
vos, ubi contempti rupistis frena pudoris,
    nescitis captae mentis habere modum.
flamma per incensas citius sedetur aristas,
    fluminaque ad fontis sint reditura caput,
et placidum Syrtes portum et bona litora nautis
    praebeat hospitio saeva Malea suo,
quam possit vestros quisquam reprehendere cursus
    et rapidae stimulos frangere nequitiae.   10
testis, Cretaei fastus quae passa iuvenci
    induit abiegnae cornua falsa bovis ;
testis Thessalico flagrans Salmonis Enipeo,
    quae voluit liquido tota subire deo.
crimen et illa fuit, patria succensa senecta
    arboris in frondes condita Myrrha novae.
nam quid Medeae referam, quo tempore matris
    iram natorum caede piavit amor ?
quidve Clytaemestrae, propter quam tota Mycenis
    infamis stupro stat Pelopea domus ?   20

[1] hoc *Lachmann :* huc *NFL.* suae *Markland :* tuae *NFL.*

tuque, o Minoa venumdata Scylla figura,
  tondes [1] purpurea regna paterna coma.
hanc igitur dotem virgo desponderat hosti!
  Nise, tuas portas fraude reclusit amor.
at vos, innuptae, felicius urite taedas:
  pendet Cretaea tracta puella rate.
non tamen immerito Minos sedet arbiter Orci:
  victor erat quamvis, aequus in hoste fuit.

XX

CREDIS eum iam posse tuae meminisse figurae,
  vidisti a lecto quem dare vela tuo?
durus, qui lucro potuit mutare puellam!
  tantine, his [2] lacrimis, Africa tota fuit?
at tu, stulta, deos, tu fingis inania verba:
  forsitan ille alio pectus amore terat.
est tibi forma potens, sunt castae Palladis artes,
  splendidaque a docto fama refulget avo,
fortunata domus, modo sit tibi fidus amicus.
  fidus ero: in nostros curre, puella, toros!   10
nox mihi prima venit! primae date tempora
  noctis: [3]   13
  longius in primo, Luna, morare toro.   14
tu quoque, qui aestivos spatiosius exigis ignes,   11
  Phoebe, moraturae contrahe lucis iter.   12

---

[1] tondes *Keil:* tondens *NFL.*
[2] tantine his *Paldam:* tantisne in *N:* tantis in *FL.*
[3] *13, 14 transposed before 11, 12 by Scaliger.*

foedera sunt ponenda prius signandaque iura
    et scribenda mihi lex in amore novo.
haec Amor ipse suo constringit pignora signo :
    testis sidereae torta corona deae.
quam multae ante meis cedent sermonibus horae,
    dulcia quam nobis concitet arma Venus !   20
namque ubi non certo vincitur foedere lectus,
    non habet ultores nox vigilata [1] deos,
et quibus imposuit, solvit mox vincla libido :
    contineant nobis omina [2] prima fidem.
ergo, qui pactas in foedera ruperit aras,
    pollueritque novo sacra marita toro,
illi sint quicumque solent in amore dolores,
    et caput argutae praebeat historiae,
nec flenti dominae patefiant nocte fenestrae :
    semper amet, fructu semper amoris egens.   30

XXI

Magnvm iter ad doctas proficisci cogor Athenas,
    ut me longa gravi solvat amore via.
crescit enim assidue spectando [3] cura puellae :
    ipse alimenta sibi maxima praebet amor.
omnia sunt temptata mihi, quacumque fugari
    possit : at ex omni me premit ipse deus.
vix tamen aut semel admittit, cum saepe negarit ;
    seu venit, extremo dormit amicta [4] toro.

----

[1] vigilata *N :* vigilanda *FL.*
[2] omina *S :* omnia *NFL.*
[3] spectando *FL :* spectandi *N.*
[4] amicta *Scaliger :* amica *NFL.*

unum erit auxilium : mutatis Cynthia terris
    quantum oculis, animo tam procul ibit amor.   10
nunc agite, o socii, propellite in aequora [1] navem,
    remorumque pares ducite sorte vices,
iungiteque extremo felicia lintea malo :
    iam liquidum nautis aura secundat iter.
Romanae turres et vos valeatis, amici,
    qualiscumque mihi tuque, puella, vale !
ergo ego nunc rudis Hadriaci vehar aequoris hospes,
    cogar et undisonos nunc prece adire deos.
deinde per Ionium vectus cum fessa Lechaeo
    sedarit placida vela phaselus aqua,   20
quod superest, sufferre pedes properate laborem,
    Isthmos qua terris arcet utrumque mare.
inde ubi Piraei capient me litora portus,
    scandam ego Theseae bracchia longa viae.
illic vel stadiis animum emendare Platonis
    incipiam aut hortis, docte Epicure, tuis;
persequar aut studium linguae, Demosthenis arma,
    librorumque tuos, docte [2] Menandre, sales;
aut certe tabulae capient mea lumina pictae,
    sive ebore exactae, seu magis aere, manus.   30
aut spatia annorum, aut longa intervalla profundi
    lenibunt tacito vulnera nostra sinu :
seu moriar, fato, non turpi fractus amore;
    atque erit illa mihi mortis honesta dies.

---

[1] aequora *F :* aequore *NL.*
[2] docte *NFL ; the repetition of* docte *is scarcely defensible*
scite *L. Müller.*

XXII

FRIGIDA tam multos placuit tibi Cyzicus annos,[1]
Tulle, Propontiaca qua fluit isthmos aqua,
Dindymis et secto fabricata in dente [2] Cybelle,
raptorisque tulit qua via Ditis equos ?
si te forte iuvant Helles Athamantidos urbes,
at [3] desiderio, Tulle, movere meo,—
tu licet aspicias caelum omne Atlanta gerentem,
sectaque Persea Phorcidos ora manu,
Geryonis stabula et luctantum in pulvere signa
Herculis Antaeique, Hesperidumque choros ; 10
tuque tuo Colchum propellas remige Phasim,
Peliacaeque trabis totum iter ipse legas,
qua rudis Argea [4] natat inter saxa columba
in faciem prorae pinus adacta novae ;
aut si qua Ortygie et [5] visenda est ora Caystri,
et qua septenas temperat unda vias ;
omnia Romanae cedent miracula terrae :
natura hic posuit, quidquid ubique fuit.
armis apta magis tellus quam commoda noxae :
Famam, Roma, tuae non pudet historiae. 20
nam quantum ferro tantum pietate potentes
stamus : victrices temperat ira manus.

---

[1] annos *fl :* annus *NFL.*
[2] secto . . . in dente *Barton :* sacra . . . inventa *NFL,*
the passage scarcely admits of certain correction.
[3] at *Phillimore :* et *NFL.*   [4] Argea *F :* Argoa *NL.*
[5] aut *Fonteine :* et *N :* at *FL.* Ortygie et *Haupt :* orige
NFL.

hic Anio Tiburne fluis,[1] Clitumnus ab Vmbro
   tramite, et aeternum Marcius umor opus,
Albanus lacus et foliis Nemorensis abundans,[2]
   potaque Pollucis nympha salubris equo.
at non squamoso labuntur ventre cerastae,
   Itala portentis nec furit[3] unda novis ;
non hic Andromedae resonant pro matre catenae,
   nec tremis Ausonias, Phoebe fugate, dapes,   30
nec cuiquam absentes arserunt in caput ignes
   exitium nato matre movente suo ;
Penthea non saevae venantur in arbore Bacchae,
   nec solvit Danaas subdita cerva rates,
cornua nec valuit curvare in paelice Iuno
   aut faciem turpi dedecorare bove ;

     .   .   .   .   .[4]

arboreasque cruces Sinis, et non hospita Grais
   saxa, et curvatas in sua fata trabes.
haec tibi, Tulle, parens, haec est pulcherrima sedes,
   hic tibi pro digna gente petendus honos,   40
hic tibi ad eloquium cives, hic ampla nepotum
   spes et venturae coniugis aptus amor.

[1] fluis *ς* : flues *NFL*.
[2] foliis *Housman:* sotii *FL:* socii *N.*   abundans *Housman :*
ab unda *NFL*.
[3] furit *ς* : fuit *NFL*.
[4] *At least a couplet seems to have been lost.*

XXIII

ERGO tam doctae nobis periere tabellae,
  scripta quibus pariter tot periere bona !
has quondam nostris manibus detriverat usus,
  qui non signatas iussit habere fidem.
illae iam sine me norant placare puelias,
  et quaedam sine me verba diserta loqui.
non illas fixum caras effecerat aurum :
  vulgari buxo sordida cera fuit.
qualescumque mihi semper mansere fideles,
  semper et effectus promeruere bonos.   10
forsitan haec illis fuerint mandata tabellis :
  " Irascor quoniam es, lente, moratus heri.
an tibi nescio quae visa est formosior ?   an tu
  non bona de nobis crimina ficta iacis ? "
aut dixit : " Venies hodie, cessabimus una :
  hospitium tota nocte paravit Amor,"
et quaecumque volens¹ reperit non stulta puella
  garrula, cum blandis dicitur² hora dolis.
me miserum, his aliquis rationem scribit avarus³
  et ponit diras⁴ inter ephemeridas !   20
quas si quis mihi rettulerit, donabitur auro :
  quis pro divitiis ligna⁵ retenta velit ?
i puer, et citus haec aliqua propone columna,
  et dominum Esquiliis scribe habitare tuum.

---

¹ voiens *Broekhuyzen :* dolens *NFL.*
² dioitur ς : ducitur *NFL.*   ³ avarus ς : avari *NFL.*
⁴ diras *N :* duras *FL.*   ⁵ ligna *Beroaldus :* signa *NFL.*

XXIV

FALSA est ista tuae, mulier, fiducia formae,
    olim oculis nimium facta superba meis.
noster amor tales tribuit tibi, Cynthia, laudes.
    versibus insignem te pudet esse meis.
mixtam te varia laudavi saepe figura,
    ut, quod non esses, esse putaret amor ;
et color est totiens roseo collatus Eoo,
    cum tibi quaesitus candor in ore foret :
quod mihi non patrii poterant avertere amici,
    eluere aut vasto Thessala saga mari.   10
haec ego non ferro, non igne coactus, et ipsa
    naufragus Aegaea vera fatebar[1] aqua :
correptus saevo Veneris torrebar aeno ;
    vinctus eram versas in mea terga manus.
ecce coronatae portum tetigere carinae,
    traiectae Syrtes, ancora iacta mihi est.
nunc demum vasto fessi resipiscimus aestu,
    vulneraque ad sanum nunc coiere mea.
Mens Bona, si qua dea es, tua me in sacraria dono !
    exciderant surdo tot mea vota Iovi.   20

[1] vera *Passerat :* verba *NFL.*   fatebar ς⁻: fatebor *NFL.*

XXV

Risvs eram positis inter convivia mensis,
  et de me poterat quilibet esse loquax.
quinque tibi potui servire fideliter annos :
  ungue meam morso saepe querere fidem.
nil moveor lacrimis : ista sum captus ab arte;
  semper ab insidiis, Cynthia, flere soles.
flebo ego discedens, sed fletum iniuria vincit :
  tu bene conveniens non sinis ire iugum.
limina iam nostris valeant lacrimantia verbis,
  nec tamen irata ianua fracta manu.   10
at te celatis aetas gravis urgeat annis,
  et veniat formae ruga sinistra tuae !
vellere tum cupias albos a stirpe capillos,
  a ! speculo rugas increpitante tibi,
exclusa inque vicem fastus patiare superbos,
  et quae fecisti facta queraris anus !
has tibi fatales cecinit mea pagina diras :
  eventum formae disce timere tuae !

LIBER QVARTVS

I

Hoc quodcumque vides, hospes, qua maxima Roma
  est,
  ante Phrygem Aenean collis et herba fuit;
atque ubi Navali stant sacra Palatia Phoebo,
  Euandri profugae concubuere boves.
fictilibus crevere deis haec aurea templa,
  nec fuit opprobrio facta sine arte casa;
Tarpeiusque pater nuda de rupe tonabat,
  et Tiberis nostris advena bubus erat.
qua gradibus domus ista Remi se sustulit, olim
  unus erat fratrum maxima regna focus.   10
Curia, praetexto quae nunc nitet alta senatu,
  pellitos habuit, rustica corda, Patres.
bucina cogebat priscos ad verba Quirites:
  centum illi in prato saepe senatus erat.
nec sinuosa cavo pendebant vela theatro,
  pulpita sollemnes non oluere crocos.
nulli cura fuit externos quaerere divos;
  cum tremeret patrio pendula turba sacro,

annua at [1] accenso celebrare Parilia faeno,
 qualia nunc curto lustra novantur equo.   20
Vesta coronatis pauper gaudebat asellis,
 ducebant macrae vilia sacra boves.
parva saginati lustrabant compita porci,
 pastor et ad calamos exta litabat ovis.
verbera pellitus saetosa movebat arator,
 unde licens Fabius sacra Lupercus habet.
nec rudis infestis miles radiabat in armis:
 miscebant usta proelia nuda sude.
prima galeritus posuit praetoria Lycmon,
 magnaque pars Tatio rerum erat inter oves.   30
hinc Titiens Ramnesque viri Luceresque Soloni,[2]
 quattuor hinc albos Romulus egit equos.
quippe suburbanae parva minus urbe Bovillae
 et, qui nunc nulli, maxima turba Gabi.
et stetit Alba potens, albae suis omine nata,
 hinc ubi Fidenas longa erat isse via.[3]

[1] annua at *Lachmann*. annuaque *NFL*.
[2] soloni *N :* coloni *FL*.
[3] hinc *Postgate :* hac *NFL*. longa ... via ⲋ : longe ...
vias *NFL*.

nil patrium nisi nomen habet Romanus alumnus :
   sanguinis altricem non putet esse lupam.
huc melius profugos misisti, Troia, Penates.
   huc[1] quali vecta est Dardana puppis ave !   40
iam bene spondebant tunc omina, quod nihil illam
   laeserat abiegni venter apertus equi,
cum pater in nati trepidus cervice pependit,
   et verita est umeros urere flamma pios.
tunc animi venere Deci Brutique secures,
   vexit et ipsa sui Caesaris arma Venus,
arma resurgentis portans victricia Troiae :
   felix terra tuos cepit, Iule, deos,
si modo Avernalis tremulae cortina Sibyllae
   dixit Aventino rura pianda Remo,   50
aut si Pergameae sero rata carmina vatis
   longaevum ad Priami vera fuere caput:
" Vertite equum, Danai ! male vincitis ! Ilia tellus
   vivet, et huic cineri Iuppiter arma dabit ! "
optima nutricum nostris lupa Martia rebus,
   qualia creverunt moenia lacte tuo !
moenia namque pio coner disponere versu :
   ei mihi, quod nostro est parvus in ore sonus !
sed tamen exiguo quodcumque e pectore rivi
   fluxerit, hoc patriae serviet omne meae.   60
Ennius hirsuta cingat sua dicta corona :
   mi folia ex hedera porrige, Bacche, tua,
ut nostris tumefacta superbiat Vmbria libris,
   Vmbria Romani patria Callimachi !

      [1] huc *Baehrens :* heu *NFL.*

scandentis qui Asis[1] cernit de vallibus arces,
  ingenio muros aestimet ille meo!
Roma, fave, tibi surgit opus, date candida cives
  omina, et inceptis dextera cantet avis!   68
dicam: "Troia cades, et Troica Roma resurges"; 87
  et maris et terrae longa pericla[2] canam.[3]   88
sacra diesque canam et cognomina prisca locorum : 69
  has meus ad metas sudet oportet equus.   70

Iᴀ[4]

Qvo ruis imprudens, vage, dicere fata, Properti?
  non sunt a dextro condita fila colo.
accersis lacrimas cantans;[5] aversus Apollo;
  poscis ab invita verba pigenda lyra.
certa feram certis auctoribus, aut ego vates
  nescius aerata signa movere pila.
me creat Archytae suboles Babylonius Orops
  Horon, et a proavo ducta Conone domus.
di mihi sunt testes non degenerasse propinquos,
  inque meis libris nil prius esse fide.   80
nunc pretium fecere deos et (fallitur auro
  Iuppiter) obliquae signa iterata rotae,

1 qui Asis *Butler, following O. L. Richmond, who read* -que
Asis cernit qui vallibus (asis μυf) : quasuis *FL :* quisquis *N.*
2 pericla ⟨ : sepulcra *NFL.*
3 *87, 88 transposed after 68 by Scaliger.*
4 *No break in MSS. The separation is due to early Renaissance
scholars.*
5 cantans *Baehrens :* cantas *NFL.*

felicesque Iovis stellas Martisque rapaces [1]

    et grave Saturni sidus in omne caput;

quid moveant Pisces animosaque signa Leonis,

    lotus et Hesperia quid Capricornus aqua.   86

dixi ego, cum geminos produceret Arria natos   89

    (illa dabat natis arma vetante deo):   90

non posse ad patrios sua pila referre Penates:

    nempe meam firmant nunc duo busta fidem.

quippe Lupercus, eques [2] dum saucia protegit ora,

    heu sibi prolapso non bene cavit equo;

Gallus at, in castris dum credita signa tuetur,

    concidit ante aquilae rostra cruenta suae:

fatales pueri, duo funera matris avarae!

    vera, sed invito, contigit ista fides.

idem ego, cum Cinarae traheret Lucina dolores,

    et facerent uteri pondera lenta moram,   100

" Iunonis facito [3] votum impetrabile " dixi:

    illa parit: libris est data palma meis!

hoc neque harenosum Libyae Iovis explicat antrum,

    aut sibi commissos fibra locuta deos,

aut si quis motas cornicis senserit alas,

    umbrave quae [4] magicis mortua prodit aquis.

aspicienda via est caeli verusque per astra

    trames, et ab zonis quinque petenda fides.

---

[1] rapaces *Livineius:* rapacis *NFL.*
[2] eques *Heinsius:* equi *NFL.*
[3] facito *Lachmann:* facite *NFL.*
[4] umbrave quae *Turnebus:* umbrane quae *N:* umbraque
ne *FL.*

exemplum grave erit Calchas : namque Aulide solvit
    ille bene haerentes ad pia saxa rates ;   110
idem Agamemnoniae ferrum cervice puellae
    tinxit, et Atrides vela cruenta dedit ;
nec rediere tamen Danai : tu, diruta, fletum
    supprime et Euboicos respice, Troia, sinus !
Nauplius ultores sub noctem porrigit ignes,
    et natat exuviis Graecia pressa suis.
victor Oiliade, rape nunc et dilige vatem,
    quam vetat avelli veste Minerva sua !
hactenus historiae : nunc ad tua devehar astra ;
    incipe tu lacrimis aequus adesse novis.   120
Vmbria te notis antiqua Penatibus edit :
    mentior ?   an patriae tangitur ora tuae ?
qua¹ nebulosa cavo rorat Mevania campo,
    et lacus aestivis intepet Vmber aquis,
scandentisque Asis consurgit vertice murus,
    murus ab ingenio notior ille tuo ?
ossaque legisti non illa aetate legenda
    patris et in tenues cogeris ipse lares :
nam tua cum multi versarent rura iuvenci,
    abstulit excultas pertica tristis opes.   130
mox ubi bulla rudi demissa est aurea collo,
    matris et ante deos libera sumpta toga,

¹ qua ⌠ : quam *NFL*.

tum tibi pauca suo de carmine dictat Apollo
et vetat insano verba tonare Foro.
at tu finge elegos, fallax opus :—haec tua castra !—
scribat ut exemplo cetera turba tuo.
militiam Veneris blandis patiere sub armis,
et Veneris pueris utilis hostis eris.
nam tibi victrices quascumque labore parasti,
eludit palmas una puella tuas :   140
et bene confixum mento discusseris[1] uncum,
nil erit hoc : rostro te premet ansa suo.[2]
illius arbitrio noctem lucemque videbis :
gutta quoque ex oculis non nisi iussa cadet.
nec mille excubiae nec te signata iuvabunt
limina : persuasae fallere rima[3] sat est.
nunc tua vel mediis puppis luctetur in undis,
vel licet armatis hostis inermis eas,
vel tremefacta cavum tellus diducat[4] hiatum :
octipedis Cancri terga sinistra time !   150

II

Qvid mirare meas tot in uno corpore formas ?
accipe Vertumni signa paterna dei.
Tuscus ego Tuscis orior, nec paenitet inter
proelia Volsinios deseruisse focos.

[1] discusseris ⟨: discusserit *NFL*.
[2] rostro *Dom. Calderinus:* nostro *NFL*.   ansa *Dom. Calde-
rinus:* ausa *NFL*.   suo *FL:* tuo *N*.
[3] limina ⟨: lumina *NFL*.   rima *Beroaldus:* prima *NFL*.
[4] cavum *f:* cavo *NFL*.   diducat *N:* deducat *FL*.

[405]

haec mea turba iuvat, nec templo laetor eburno :
　　Romanum satis est posse videre Forum.
hac quondam Tiberinus iter faciebat, at aiunt
　　remorum auditos per vada pulsa sonos :
at postquam ille suis tantum concessit alumnis,
　　Vertumnus verso dicor ab amne deus.　　　　　　10
seu, quia vertentis fructum praecepimus anni,
　　Vertumni rursus credis id[1] esse sacrum.
prima mihi variat liventibus uva racemis,
　　et coma lactenti spicea fruge tumet ;
hic dulces cerasos, hic autumnalia pruna
　　cernis et aestivo mora rubere die ;
insitor hic solvit pomosa vota corona,
　　cum pirus invito stipite mala tulit.
mendax fama vaces :[2] alius mihi nominis index :
　　de se narranti tu modo crede deo.　　　　　　20
opportuna mea est cunctis natura figuris :
　　in quamcumque voles verte, decorus ero.
indue me Cois, fiam non dura puella :
　　meque virum sumpta quis neget esse toga ?
da falcem et torto frontem mihi comprime
　　　　faeno :
　　iurabis nostra gramina secta manu.
arma tuli quondam et, memini, laudabar in illis :
　　corbis at[3] imposito pondere messor eram.
sobrius ad lites : at cum est imposta corona,
　　clamabis capiti vina subisse meo.　　　　　　30

[1] credis id *Postgate :* credidit *O.*
[2] vaces *ς :* voces *FL :* noces *N.*
[3] at *Butler :* in *N :* om. *FL.*

[406]

cinge caput mitra, speciem furabor Iacchi ;[1]
  furabor Phoebi, si modo plectra dabis.
cassibus impositis venor : sed harundine sumpta
  fautor[2] plumoso sum deus aucupio.
est etiam aurigae species Vertumnus et eius,
  traicit alterno qui leve pondus equo.
suppetat hoc, pisces calamo praedabor, et ibo
  mundus demissis institor in tunicis.
pastor me ad baculum possum curvare[3] vel idem
  sirpiculis medio pulvere ferre rosam.   40
nam quid ego adiciam, de quo mihi maxima fama est,
  hortorum in manibus dona probata meis ?
caeruleus cucumis tumidoque cucurbita ventre
  me notat et iunco brassica vincta levi ;
nec flos ullus hiat pratis, quin ille decenter
  impositus fronti langueat ante meae.
at mihi, quod formas unus vertebar in omnes,
  nomen ab eventu patria lingua dedit.
et tu, Roma, meis tribuisti praemia Tuscis,
  (unde hodie Vicus nomina Tuscus habet,)   50
tempore quo sociis venit Lycomedius armis
  atque Sabina feri contudit arma Tati.
vidi ego labentes acies et tela caduca,
  atque hostes turpi terga dedisse fugae.
sed facias, divum Sator, ut Romana per aevum
  transeat ante meos turba togata pedes.

---

[1] Iacchi *early Renaissance scholars :* achei *NFL.*
[2] fautor *Rossberg :* fauor *N :* faunor *FL.*
[3] pastor me *Ayrmann :* pastorem *NFL.* curvare ϛ : curare
NFL.

sex superant versus : te, qui ad vadimonia curris,
 non moror : haec spatiis ultima creta meis.
stipes acernus eram, properanti falce dolatus,
 ante Numam grata pauper in urbe deus. 60
at tibi, Mamurri, formae caelator aenae,
 tellus artifices ne terat Osca manus,
qui me tam dociles potuisti fundere in usus.
 unum opus est, operi non datur unus honos.

III

Haec Arethusa suo mittit mandata Lycotae,
 cum totiens absis, si potes esse meus.
si qua tamen tibi lecturo pars oblita derit,
 haec erit e lacrimis facta litura meis :
aut si qua incerto fallet te littera tractu,
 signa meae dextrae iam morientis erunt.
te modo viderunt iteratos Bactra per ortus,
 te modo munito Neuricus [1] hostis equo,
hibernique Getae, pictoque Britannia curru,
 tunsus [2] et Eoa discolor Indus aqua. 10
haecne marita fides et pactae in savia noctes,[3]
 cum rudis urgenti bracchia victa dedi ?
quae mihi deductae fax omen praetulit, illa
 traxit ab everso lumina nigra rogo ;

[1] munito *Beroaldus :* munitus *NFL.* Neuricus *Jacob :*
hericus *NFL.*
[2] tunsus *Housman :* ustus *NFL.*
[3] pactae in savia noctes *Haupt :* et parce avia noctes *N :* et
pacatae mihi noctes *FL.*

et Stygio sum sparsa lacu, nec recta capillis
  vitta data est: nupsi non comitante deo.
omnibus heu portis pendent mea noxia vota:
  texitur haec castris quarta lacerna tuis.
occidat, immerita qui carpsit ab arbore vallum
  et struxit querulas rauca per ossa tubas,   20
dignior obliquo funem qui torqueat Ocno,
  aeternusque tuam pascat, aselle, famem!
dic mihi, num ¹ teneros urit lorica lacertos?
  num gravis imbelles atterit hasta manus?
haec noceant potius, quam dentibus ulla puella
  det mihi plorandas per tua colla notas!
diceris et macie vultum tenuasse: sed opto,
  e desiderio sit color iste meo.
at mihi cum noctes induxit vesper amaras,
  si qua relicta iacent, osculor arma tua;   30
tum queror in toto non sidere pallia lecto,
  lucis et auctores non dare carmen aves.
noctibus hibernis castrensia pensa laboro
  et Tyria in gladios vellera secta suo;
et disco, qua parte fluat vincendus Araxes,
  quot sine aqua Parthus milia currat equus;
cogor et e tabula pictos ediscere mundos,
  qualis et educti sit positura Dai,²
quae tellus sit lenta gelu, quae putris ab aestu,
  ventus in Italiam qui bene vela ferat.   40
assidet una soror curis, et pallida nutrix
  peierat hiberni temporis esse moras.

¹ num 𝒮: dum *NFL*.
² educti . . . Dai *Ellis:* haec docti . . . dei *NFL.*

felix Hippolyte! nuda tulit arma papilla
    et texit galea barbara molle caput.
Romanis utinam patuissent castra puellis!
    essem militiae sarcina fida tuae,
nec me tardarent Scythiae iuga, cum pater altas
    acrius [1] in glaciem frigore nectit aquas.
omnis amor magnus, sed aperto in coniuge maior:
    hanc Venus, ut vivat, ventilat ipsa facem.   50
nam mihi quo Poenis nunc [2] purpura fulgeat ostris
    crystallusque meas ornet aquosa manus?
omnia surda tacent, rarisque assueta kalendis
    vix aperit clausos una puella Lares,
Craugidos et catulae vox est mihi grata querentis:
    illa tui partem vindicat una toro.
flore sacella tego, verbenis compita velo,
    et crepat ad veteres herba Sabina focos.
sive in finitimo gemuit stans noctua tigno,
    seu voluit tangi parca lucerna mero,   60
illa dies hornis caedem denuntiat agnis,
    succinctique calent ad nova lucra popae.
ne, precor, ascensis tanti sit gloria Bactris,
    raptave odorato carbasa lina duci,
plumbea cum tortae sparguntur pondera fundae,
    subdolus et versis increpat arcus equis!
sed (tua sic domitis Parthae telluris alumnis
    pura triumphantis hasta sequatur equos)

    1 acrius *Postgate:* africus *NFL.*
    2 nunc *Housman:* tibi *FL:* te *N.*

incorrupta mei conserva foedera lecti!
hac ego te sola lege redisse velim: 70
armaque cum tulero portae votiva Capenae,
subscribam SALVO GRATA PVELLA VIRO.

IV

TARPEIVM nemus et Tarpeiae turpe sepulcrum
fabor et antiqui limina capta Iovis.
hunc Tatius montem¹ vallo praecingit acerno, 7
fidaque suggesta castra coronat humo.
quid tum Roma fuit, tubicen vicina Curetis
cum quateret lento murmure saxa Iovis, 10
atque ubi nunc terris dicuntur iura subactis,
stabant Romano pila Sabina Foro?²
murus erant montes: ubi nunc est Curia saepta,
bellicus exili³ fonte bibebat equus. 14
lucus erat felix hederoso conditus antro, 3
multaque nativis obstrepit arbor aquis, 4
Silvani ramosa domus, quo dulcis ab aestu 5
fistula poturas ire iubebat oves.⁴ 6
hinc Tarpeia deae fontem libavit: at illi 15
urgebat medium fictilis urna caput.
et satis una malae potuit mors esse puellae,
quae voluit flammas fallere, Vesta, tuas?

¹ montem *Heinsius:* fontem *NFL.*
² foro *f:* foco *NFL.* ³ exili *Postgate:* ex illo *NFL.*
⁴ *3-6 and 7-14 transposed by Baehrens.*

vidit harenosis Tatium proludere campis
    pictaque per flavas arma levare iubas :   20
obstipuit regis facie et regalibus armis,
    interque oblitas excidit urna manus.
saepe illa immeritae causata est omina lunae,
    et sibi tingendas dixit in amne comas :
saepe tulit blandis argentea lilia Nymphis,
    Romula ne faciem laederet hasta Tati :
dumque subit primo Capitolia nubila fumo,
    rettulit hirsutis bracchia secta rubis,
et sua Tarpeia residens ita flevit ab arce
    vulnera, vicino non patienda Iovi :   30
" Ignes castrorum et Tatiae praetoria turmae
    et formosa[1] oculis arma Sabina meis,
o utinam ad vestros sedeam captiva Penates,
    dum captiva mei conspicer ora[2] Tati !
Romani montes, et montibus addita Roma,
    et valeat probro Vesta pudenda meo !
ille equus, ille meos in castra reponet amores,
    cui Tatius dextras collocat ipse iubas !
quid mirum in patrios Scyllam saevisse capillos,
    candidaque in saevos inguina versa canes ?   40
prodita quid mirum fraterni cornua monstri,
    cum patuit lecto stamine torta via ?
quantum ego sum Ausoniis crimen factura puellis,
    improba virgineo lecta ministra foco !
Pallados exstinctos si quis mirabitur ignes,
    ignoscat : lacrimis spargitur ara meis.

---

[1] formosa *ς* : famosa *NFL*.   [2] ora *ς* : esse *NFL*.

cras, ut rumor ait, tota purgabitur[1] urbe :
  tu cape spinosi rorida terga iugi.
lubrica tota via est et perfida : quippe tacentes
  fallaci celat limite semper aquas.   50
o utinam magicae nossem cantamina Musae !
  haec quoque formoso lingua tulisset opem.
te toga picta decet, non quem sine matris honore
  nutrit inhumanae dura papilla lupae.
sic hospes pariamne tua regina sub aula ?
  dos tibi non humilis prodita Roma venit.
si minus, at raptae ne sint impune Sabinae,
  me rape et alterna lege repende vices !
commissas acies ego possum solvere : nuptae,
  vos medium palla foedus inite mea.   60
adde Hymenaee modos, tubicen fera murmura conde :
  credite, vestra meus molliet arma torus.
et iam quarta canit venturam bucina lucem,
  ipsaque in Oceanum sidera lapsa cadunt.
experiar somnum, de te mihi somnia quaeram :
  fac venias oculis umbra benigna meis."
dixit, et incerto permisit bracchia somno,
  nescia vae furiis[2] accubuisse novis.
nam Vesta, Iliacae felix tutela favillae,
  culpam alit et plures condit in ossa faces.   70
illa ruit, qualis celerem prope Thermodonta
  Strymonis abscisso pectus[3] aperta sinu.

---

[1] purgabitur *codd. Cantab.*, *Voss. 81*, *Berolin. Diez. B. 41;*
pugnabitur *NFL.*
[2] vae furiis *Itali :* nefariis *NFL.*
[3] pectus *Hertzberg :* fertur *NFL.*

urbi festus erat (dixere Parilia Patres),
  hic primus coepit moenibus esse dies,
annua pastorum convivia, lusus in urbe,
  cum pagana madent fercula divitiis,
cumque super raros faeni flammantis acervos
  traicit immundos ebria turba pedes.[1]
Romulus excubias decrevit in otia solvi
  atque intermissa castra silere tuba.   80
hoc Tarpeia suum tempus rata convenit hostem :
  pacta ligat, pactis ipsa futura comes.
mons erat ascensu dubius festoque remissus :[2]
  nec mora, vocales occupat ense canes.
omnia praebebant somnos : sed Iuppiter unus
  decrevit poenis invigilare tuis.
prodiderat portaeque fidem patriamque iacentem,
  nubendique petit, quem velit, ipsa diem.
at Tatius (neque enim sceleri dedit hostis
    honorem)
  "Nube" ait "et regni scande cubile mei!"   90
dixit, et ingestis comitum super obruit armis.
  haec, virgo, officiis dos erat apta tuis.
a duce Tarpeia mons est cognomen adeptus :
  o vigil, iniuste[3] praemia sortis habes.

---

[1] immundos . . . pedes *Itali :* immundas . . . dapes *NFL.*
[2] remissus *N :* remissis *FL.*   [3] iniuste *FL :* iniustae *N.*

V

TERRA tuum spinis obducat, lena, sepulcrum,
    et tua, quod non vis, sentiat umbra sitim ;
nec sedeant cineri Manes, et Cerberus ultor
    turpia ieiuno terreat ossa sono !
docta vel Hippolytum Veneri mollire negantem,
    concordique toro pessima semper avis,
Penelopen quoque neglecto rumore mariti
    nubere lascivo cogeret Antinoo.
illa velit, poterit magnes non ducere ferrum,
    et volucris nidis esse noverca suis.   10
quippe et, Collinas ad fossam moverit herbas,
    stantia currenti diluerentur aqua :
audax cantatae leges imponere lunae
    et sua nocturno fallere terga lupo,
posset ut [1] intentos astu caecare maritos,
    cornicum immeritas eruit ungue genas,
consuluitque striges nostro de sanguine, et in me
    hippomanes fetae semina legit equae.
exercebat opus verbis heu blanda perinde
    saxosam atque forat sedula talpa [2] viam :   20
" Si te Eoa †Dorozantum [3] iuvat aurea ripa,
    et quae sub Tyria concha superbit aqua,

---

[1] ut ς : et NFL.
[2] exercebat . . . heu blanda perinde saxosam atque Hous-
man : exorabat . . . ceu blanda perure saxosamque NFL.
forat Rossberg : ferat NFL.   talpa v : culpa NFL.
[3] dorozantum N : derorantum FL ; probably corrupt.

[415]

Eurypylique placet Coae textura Minervae,
  sectaque ab Attalicis putria signa toris,
seu quae palmiferae mittunt venalia Thebae,
  murreaque in Parthis pocula cocta focis;
sperne fidem, provolve deos, mendacia vincant,
  frange et[1] damnosae iura pudicitiae!
et simulare virum pretium facit: utere causis!
  maior dilata nocte recurret amor.   30
si tibi forte comas vexaverit, utilis ira:
  postmodo mercata pace premendus erit.
denique ubi amplexu Venerem promiseris empto,
  fac simules puros Isidis esse dies.
ingerat Apriles Iole tibi, tundat Amycle
  natalem Mais Idibus esse tuum.
supplex ille sedet—posita tu scribe cathedra
  quidlibet: has artes si pavet ille, tenes!
semper habe morsus circa tua colla recentes,
  litibus alternis quos putet esse datos.   40
nec te Medeae delectent probra sequacis
  (nempe tulit fastus ausa rogare prior),
sed potius mundi Thais pretiosa Menandri,
  cum ferit astutos comica moecha Getas.
in mores te verte viri: si cantica iactat,
  i comes et voces ebria iunge tuas.
ianitor ad dantes vigilet: si pulset inanis,
  surdus in obductam somniet usque seram.[2]

---

[1] frange et ⌐ : frangent *NFL*.
[2] *This couplet is found in a Pompeian wall-inscription; see*
C.I.L. 4, 1894. The inscription gives dantis *and* pulsat.

nec tibi displiceat miles non factus amori,
  nauta nec attrita si ferat aera manu,   50
aut quorum titulus per barbara colla pependit,
  cretati[1] medio cum saluere foro.
aurum spectato, non quae manus afferat aurum!
  versibus auditis quid nisi verba feres?
Quid iuvat ornato procedere, vita, capillo
  et tenuis Coa veste movere sinus?'
qui versus, Coae dederit nec munera vestis,
  ipsius tibi sit surda sine aere[2] lyra.
dum vernat sanguis, dum rugis integer annus,
  utere, ne quid cras libet ab ore dies!   60
vidi ego odorati victura rosaria Paesti
  sub matutino cocta iacere Noto."
his animum nostrae dum versat Acanthis amicae,
  per tenuem ossa mihi sunt numerata cutem.[3]
sed cape torquatae, Venus o regina, columbae
  ob meritum ante tuos guttura secta focos.
vidi ego rugoso tussim concrescere collo,
  sputaque per dentes ire cruenta cavos,
atque animam in tegetes putrem exspirare paternas:
  horruit algenti pergula curta[4] foco.   70
exsequiae fuerant rari furtiva capilli
  vincula et immundo pallida mitra situ,
et canis, in nostros nimis experrecta dolores,
  cum fallenda meo pollice clatra forent.

[1] cretati *Passerat:* caelati *NFL.*   [2] aere *N:* arte *FL.*
[3] tenuem ossa mihi . . . cutem *Jacob:* tenues ossa . . .
cutes *NFL.*
[4] pergula *Beroaldus:* percula *NL:* parvula *F.* curta *ς:*
curva *NFL.*

[417]

sit tumulus lenae curto vetus amphora collo :
urgeat hunc supra vis, caprifice, tua.
quisquis amas, scabris hoc bustum caedite saxis,
mixtaque cum saxis addite verba mala !

VI

Sacra facit vates : sint ora faventia sacris,
et cadat ante meos icta iuvenca focos.
serta [1] Philetaeis certet Romana corymbis,
et Cyrenaeas urna ministret aquas.
costum molle date et blandi mihi turis honores,
terque focum circa laneus orbis eat.
spargite me lymphis, carmenque recentibus aris
tibia Mygdoniis libet eburna cadis.
ite procul fraudes, alio sint aere noxae :
pura novum vati laurea mollit iter.   10
Musa, Palatini referemus Apollinis aedem :
res est, Calliope, digna favore tuo.
Caesaris in nomen ducuntur carmina : Caesar
dum canitur, quaeso, Iuppiter ipse vaces.
est Phoebi fugiens Athamana ad litora portus,
qua sinus Ioniae murmura condit aquae,
Actia Iuleae pelagus monumenta carinae,
nautarum votis non operosa via.
huc mundi coiere manus : stetit aequore moles
pinea, nec remis aequa favebat avis.   20

[1] serta *Scaliger :* cera *NFL.*

SEXTI PROPERTI ELEGIARVM LIBER IV

altera classis erat Teucro damnata Quirino,
  pilaque femineae turpiter apta manu :
hinc Augusta ratis plenis Iovis omine velis,
  signaque iam patriae vincere docta suae.
tandem acies geminos Nereus lunarat in arcus,
  armorum et radiis picta tremebat aqua,
cum Phoebus linquens stantem se vindice Delon
  (nam tulit iratos mobilis una [1] Notos)
astitit Augusti puppim super, et nova flamma
  luxit in obliquam ter sinuata facem.   30
non ille attulerat crines in colla solutos
  aut testudineae carmen inerme lyrae,
sed quali aspexit Pelopeum Agamemnona vultu,
  egessitque avidis Dorica castra rogis,
aut qualis flexos solvit Pythona per orbes
  serpentem, imbelles quem timuere deae.[2]
mox ait " O longa mundi servator ab Alba,
  Auguste, Hectoreis cognite maior avis,
vince mari : iam terra tua est : tibi militat arcus
  et favet ex umeris hoc onus omne meis.   40
solve metu patriam, quae nunc te vindice freta
  imposuit prorae publica vota tuae.
quam nisi defendes, murorum Romulus augur
  ire Palatinas non bene vidit aves.
et nimium remis audent prope : turpe Latinos [3]
  principe te fluctus regia vela pati.

---

[1] una ϛ: unda *NFL.*
[2] deae *ed. Etonensis:* lyrae *NFL.*
[3] Latinos *Markland:* latinis *NFL.*

[419]

nec te, quod classis centenis remiget alis,
   terreat : invito labitur illa mari :
quodque vehunt prorae Centaurica saxa minantes,
   tigna cava et pictos experiere metus.   50
frangit et attollit vires in milite causa ;
   quae nisi iusta subest, excutit arma pudor.
tempus adest, committe rates : ego temporis auctor
   ducam laurigera Iulia rostra manu."
dixerat, et pharetrae pondus consumit in arcus :
   proxima post arcus Caesaris hasta fuit.
vincit Roma fide Phoebi : dat femina poenas :
   sceptra per Ionias fracta vehuntur aquas.
at pater Idalio miratur Caesar ab astro :
   " Sum deus ; est nostri sanguinis ista fides."   60
prosequitur cantu Triton, omnesque marinae
   plauserunt circa libera signa deae.
illa petit Nilum cumba male nixa fugaci,
   hoc unum, iusso non moritura die.
di melius ! quantus mulier foret una triumphus,
   ductus erat per quas ante Iugurtha vias !
Actius hinc traxit Phoebus monumenta, quod eius
   una decem vicit missa sagitta rates.
bella satis cecini : citharam iam poscit Apollo
   victor et ad placidos exuit arma choros.   70
candida nunc molli subeant convivia luco ;
   blanditiaeque fluant per mea colla rosae,

vinaque fundantur prelis elisa Falernis,
   terque [1] lavet nostras spica Cilissa comas.
ingenium potis [2] irritet Musa poetis :
   Bacche, soles Phoebo fertilis esse tuo.
ille paludosos memoret servire Sycambros,
   Cepheam hic Meroen fuscaque regna canat,
hic referat sero confessum foedere Parthum :
   " Reddat signa Remi, mox dabit ipse sua :   80
sive aliquid pharetris Augustus parcet Eois,
   differat in pueros ista tropaea suos.
gaude, Crasse, nigras si quid sapis inter harenas :
   ire per Euphraten ad tua busta licet."
sic noctem patera, sic ducam carmine, donec
   iniciat radios in mea vina dies.

VII

Svnt aliquid Manes : letum non omnia finit,
   luridaque evictos [3] effugit umbra rogos.
Cynthia namque meo visa est incumbere fulcro,
   murmur ad extremae nuper humata viae,
cum mihi somnus ab exsequiis penderet amoris,
   et quererer lecti frigida regna mei.
eosdem habuit secum quibus est elata capillis,
   eosdem oculos : lateri vestis adusta fuit,
et solitum digito beryllon adederat ignis,
   summaque Lethaeus triverat ora liquor.   10
spirantisque animos et vocem misit : at illi
   pollicibus fragiles increpuere manus :

[1] terque *ς* : perque *NFL*.   [2] potis *ς* : positis *NFL*.
[3] evictos *ς* : eiunctos *N :* evinctos *FL*.

" Perfide nec cuiquam melior sperande puellae,
 in te iam vires somnus habere potest ?
ıamne tibi exciderant vigilacis furta Suburae
 et mea nocturnis trita fenestra dolis ?
per quam demisso quotiens tibi fune pependi,
 alterna veniens in tua colla manu !
saepe Venus trivio commissa[1] est, pectore mixto
 fecerunt tepidas pallia nostra vias.   20
foederis heu taciti, cuius fallacia verba
 non audituri diripuere Noti !
at mihi non oculos quisquam inclamavit euntis :
 unum impetrassem te revocante diem :
nec crepuit fissa me propter harundine custos,
 laesit et obiectum tegula curta caput.
denique quis nostro curvum te funere vidit,
 atram quis lacrimis incaluisse togam ?
si piguit portas ultra procedere, at illuc
 iussisses lectum lentius ire meum.   30
cur ventos non ipse rogis, ingrate, petisti ?
 cur nardo flammae non oluere meae ?
hoc etiam grave erat, nulla mercede hyacinthos
 inicere et fracto busta piare cado.
Lygdamus uratur, candescat lammina vernae :
 sensi ego, cum insidiis pallida vina bibi.
aut Nomas arcanas tollat versuta salivas :
 dicet damnatas ignea testa manus.

---

[1] commissa ς : commixta NFL

quae modo per viles inspecta est publica noctes,
    haec nunc aurata cyclade signat humum,   40
et graviora rependit iniquis pensa quasillis,
    garrula de facie si qua locuta mea est ;
nostraque quod Petale tulit ad monumenta
        coronas,
    codicis immundi vincula sentit anus ;
caeditur et Lalage tortis suspensa capillis,
    per nomen quoniam est ausa rogare meum ;
te patiente meae conflavit imaginis aurum,
    ardente e nostro dotem habitura rogo.
non tamen insector, quamvis mereare, Properti :
    longa mea in libris regna fuere tuis.   50
iuro ego Fatorum nulli revolubile carmen,
    tergeminusque canis sic mihi molle sonet,
me servasse fidem.   si fallo, vipera nostris
    sibilet in tumulis et super ossa cubet.
nam gemina est sedes turpem sortita per amnem,
    turbaque diversa remigat omnis aqua :
una Clytaemestrae stuprum vehit, altera Cressae
    portat mentitae lignea monstra bovis :
ecce coronato pars altera rapta [1] phaselo,
    mulcet ubi Elysias aura beata rosas,   60
qua numerosa fides, quaque aera rotunda [2] Cybelles
    mitratisque sonant Lydia plectra choris.
Andromedeque et Hypermestre sine fraude
        maritae
    narrant historias, pectora nota, suas : [3]
haec sua maternis [4] queritur livere catenis
    bracchia nec meritas frigida saxa manus ;

[1] rapta *Palmer :* parta *NFL.*
[2] quaque aera rotunda *Turnebus :* qua quaerar ut unda *N,*
and similar corruptions in FL.
[3] historias . . . suas *Markland :* historiae . . . suae *NFL.*
[4] sua maternis *μ :* suma eternis *L :* summa eternis *NF.*

[423]

narrat Hypermestre magnum ausas esse sorores,
    in scelus hoc animum non valuisse suum.
sic mortis lacrimis vitae sanamus amores :
    celo ego perfidiae crimina multa tuae.   70
sed tibi nunc mandata damus, si forte moveris
    si te non totum Chloridos herba tenet :
nutrix in tremulis ne quid desideret annis
    Parthenie : patuit,[1] nec tibi avara fuit :
deliciaeque meae Latris, cui nomen ab usu est,
    ne speculum dominae porrigat illa novae :
et quoscumque meo fecisti nomine versus,
    ure mihi : laudes desine habere meas.
pelle hederam tumulo, mihi quae pugnante
        corymbo
    mollia[2] contortis alligat ossa comis ;   80
ramosis Anio qua pomifer incubat arvis,
    et numquam Herculeo numine pallet ebur ;
hic carmen media dignum me scribe columna,
    sed breve, quod currens vector ab urbe legat :
HIC TIBVRTINA IACET AVREA CYNTHIA TERRA :
    ACCESSIT RIPAE LAVS, ANIENE, TVAE.
nec tu sperne piis venientia somnia portis :
    cum pia venerunt somnia, pondus habent.
nocte vagae ferimur, nox clausas liberat umbras,
    errat et abiecta Cerberus ipse sera.   90
luce iubent leges Lethaea ad stagna reverti :
    nos vehimur, vectum nauta recenset onus.

---

[1] patuit *ς* : potuit *NFL*.
[2] mollia *ς* : molli *NFL*.

nunc [1] te possideant aliae : mox sola tenebo :
mecum eris, et mixtis ossibus ossa teram."
haec postquam querula mecum sub lite peregit,
inter complexus excidit umbra meos.

VIII

DISCE, quid Esquilias hac nocte fugarit aquosas,
   cum vicina Novis turba cucurrit Agris.
Lanuvium annosi vetus est tutela draconis :
   hic tibi [2] tam rarae non perit hora morae ;
qua sacer abripitur caeco descensus hiatu,
   qua penetrat (virgo, tale iter omne cave !)
ieiuni serpentis honos, cum pabula poscit
   annua et ex ima sibila torquet humo.
talia demissae pallent ad sacra puellae,
   cum temere anguino creditur ore manus.   10
ille sibi admotas a virgine corripit escas :
   virginis in palmis ipsa canistra tremunt.
si fuerint castae, redeunt in colla parentum,
   clamantque agricolae " Fertilis annus erit."
huc mea detonsis avecta est Cynthia mannis :[3]
   causa fuit Iuno, sed mage causa Venus.
Appia, dic quaeso, quantum te teste triumphum
   egerit effusis per tua saxa rotis,
[turpis in arcana sonuit cum rixa taberna ;
   si sine me, famae non sine labe meae.[4]]   20

---

[1] nunc *N :* nec *FL.*   [2] hic tibi *S :* hic ubi *NFL.*
[3] mannis *Beroaldus :* ab annis *NFL.*
[4] *This couplet is clearly alien to the context : Lütjohann would
place it after line 2, perhaps rightly.*

spectaclum ipsa sedens primo temone pependit,
  ausa per impuros frena movere locos.
Serica nam taceo vulsi carpenta nepotis [1]
  atque armillatos colla Molossa canes,
qui dabit immundae venalia fata saginae,
  vincet ubi erasas barba pudenda genas.
cum fieret nostro totiens iniuria lecto,
  mutato volui [2] castra movere toro.
Phyllis Aventinae quaedam est vicina Dianae,
  sobria grata parum : cum bibit, omne decet. 30
altera Tarpeios est inter Teia lucos,
  candida, sed potae non satis unus erit.
his ego constitui noctem lenire vocatis,
  et Venere ignota furta novare mea.
unus erat tribus in secreta lectulus herba.
  quaeris concubitus? inter utramque fui.
Lygdamus ad cyathos, vitrique [3] aestiva supellex
  et Methymnaei Graeca saliva meri.
Nile, tuus tibicen erat, crotalistria [4] Phyllis,
  et facilis spargi munda sine arte rosa, 40
Magnus et ipse suos breviter concretus in artus
  iactabat truncas ad cava buxa manus.
sed neque suppletis constabat flamma lucernis,
  reccidit inque suos mensa supina pedes.

[1] Serica nam taceo *Beroaldus :* si riganam tacto *NFL.*
nepotis *ς* : nepoti *NFL.*
[2] mutato *ς*: mulctato *NFL.*   volui *Beroaldus :* voluit
NFL.
[3] vitrique *Scaliger :* utrique *N :* uterque *FL.*
[4] crotalistria *Turnebus :* eboralistria *N :* colistria *F :* coral-
istria *L.*

me quoque per talos Venerem quaerente secundos
semper damnosi subsiluere canes.
cantabant surdo, nudabant pectora caeco :
Lanuvii ad portas, ei mihi, solus eram ;
cum subito rauci sonuerunt cardine postes,
et levia ad primos murmura facta Lares.   50
nec mora, cum totas resupinat Cynthia valvas,
non operosa comis, sed furibunda decens.
pocula mi digitos inter cecidere remissos,
pallueruntque ipso labra soluta mero.
fulminat illa oculis et quantum femina saevit,
spectaclum capta nec minus urbe fuit.
Phyllidos iratos in vultum conicit ungues :
territa vicinas Teia clamat aquas.
lumina sopitos turbant elata Quirites,
omnis et insana semita nocte sonat.   60
illas direptisque comis tunicisque solutis
excipit obscurae prima taberna viae.
Cynthia gaudet in exuviis victrixque recurrit
et mea perversa sauciat ora manu,
imponitque notam collo morsuque cruentat,
praecipueque oculos, qui meruere, ferit.
atque ubi iam nostris lassavit bracchia plagis,
Lygdamus ad plutei fulcra [1] sinistra latens
eruitur, geninmque meum protractus adorat.
Lygdame, nil potui : tecum ego captus eram.   70
supplicibus palmis tum demum ad foedera veni,[2]
cum vix tangendos praebuit illa pedes,

[1] fulcra *Beroaldus :* fusca *NFL.*   [2] veni *ᕝ :* venit *NFL.*

atque ait " Admissae si vis me ignoscere culpae,
  accipe, quae nostrae formula legis erit.
tu neque Pompeia spatiabere cultus in umbra,
  nec cum lascivum sternet harena Forum.
colla cave inflectas ad summum obliqua theatrum,
  aut lectica tuae se det [1] aperta morae.
Lygdamus in primis, omnis mihi causa querelae,
  veneat et pedibus vincula bina trahat."   80
indixit legem : respondi ego " Legibus utar."
  riserat imperio facta superba dato.
dein quemcumque locum externae tetigere puellae,
  suffiit,[2] ac pura limina tergit aqua,
imperat et totas iterum mutare lacernas,
  terque meum tetigit sulpuris igne caput.
atque ita mutato per singula pallia lecto
  respondi, et noto [3] solvimus arma toro.

IX

AMPHITRYONIADES qua tempestate iuvencos
  egerat a stabulis, o Erythea, tuis,
venit ad invictos pecorosa Palatia montes,
  et statuit fessos fessus et ipse boves,
qua Velabra suo stagnabant flumine quaque [4]
  nauta per urbanas velificabat aquas.

[1] se det *Gruter :* sudet *NFL.*
[2] suffiit *Beroaldus*, ac *Baehrens :* sufficat *NFL.*
[3] respondi *NFL, perhaps corrupt :* escendi *Postgate.* noto
Heinsius : toto *NFL.*   [4] quaque ς : quoque *NFL.*

sed non infido manserunt hospite Caco
  incolumes : furto polluit ille Iovem.
incola Cacus erat, metuendo raptor ab antro,
  per tria partitos qui dabat ora sonos.   10
hic, ne certa forent manifestae signa rapinae,
  aversos cauda traxit in antra boves,
nec sine teste deo : furem sonuere iuvenci,
  furis et implacidas diruit ira fores.
Maenalio iacuit pulsus tria tempora ramo
  Cacus, et Alcides sic ait : " Ite boves,
Herculis ite boves, nostrae labor ultime clavae,
  bis mihi quaesitae, bis mea praeda, boves,
arvaque mugitu sancite Bovaria longo :
  nobile erit Romae pascua vestra Forum."   20
dixerat, et sicco torquet sitis ora palato,
  terraque non ullas[1] feta ministrat aquas.
sed procul inclusas audit ridere puellas,
  lucus ubi[2] umbroso fecerat orbe nemus,
femineae loca clausa deae fontesque piandos,
  impune et nullis sacra retecta viris.
devia puniceae velabant limina vittae,
  putris odorato luxerat igne casa,
populus et longis ornabat frondibus aedem,
  multaque cantantes umbra tegebat aves.   30
huc ruit in siccam congesta pulvere barbam,
  et iacit ante fores verba minora deo :
" Vos precor, o luci sacro quae luditis antro,
  pandite defessis hospita fana[3] viris.

[1] ullas 𝔰 : nullas *NFL.*   [2] ubi *Heinsius :* ab *NFL.*
[3] fana *Scaliger :* vana *NFL.*

fontis egens erro circaque sonantia lymphis,
et cava suscepto flumine palma sat est.
audistisne aliquem, tergo qui sustulit orbem ?
ille ego sum : Alciden terra recepta vocat.
quis facta Herculeae non audit fortia clavae
    et numquam ad nocuas [1] irrita tela feras,   40
atque uni Stygias homini luxisse tenebras ?
    accipite : haec [2] fesso vix mihi terra patet.
quodsi Iunoni sacrum faceretis amarae,
    non clausisset aquas ipsa noverca suas.
sin aliquem vultusque meus saetaeque leonis
    terrent et Libyco sole perusta coma,
idem ego Sidonia feci servilia palla
    officia et Lydo pensa diurna colo,
mollis et hirsutum cepit mihi fascia pectus,
    et manibus duris apta puella fui."   50
talibus Alcides ; at talibus alma sacerdos,
    puniceo canas stamine vincta comas :
" Parce oculis, hospes, lucoque abscede verendo
    cede agedum et tuta limina linque fuga.
interdicta viris metuenda lege piatur,
    quae se summota vindicat ara casa.
magno [3] Tiresias aspexit Pallada vates,
    fortia dum posita Gorgone membra lavat.
di tibi dent alios fontes : haec lympha puellis
    avia secreti limitis una fluit."   60

[1] nocuas *Santen :* vatas *N :* natas *FL.*
[2] accipite *ς :* accipit *NFL.* haec *f :* et *N :* hic *FL.* The
whole line is perhaps interpolated : compare l. 66.
[3] magno *Passerat :* magnam *NFL.*

sic anus : ille umeris postes concussit opacos,
    nec tulit iratam ianua clausa sitim.
at postquam exhausto iam flumine vicerat aestum,
    ponit vix siccis tristia iura labris :
" Angulus hic mundi nunc me mea fata trahentem
    accipit : haec fesso vix mihi terra patet.
Maxima quae gregibus devota est Ara repertis,
    ara per has " inquit " maxima facta manus,
haec nullis umquam pateat veneranda puellis,
    Herculis aeternum ne sit [1] inulta sitis."   70
Sancte pater salve, cui iam favet aspera Iuno :
    Sancte, velis libro dexter inesse meo.
hunc, quoniam manibus purgatum sanxerat orbem,
    sic Sanctum Tatiae composuere Cures.

X

Nvnc Iovis incipiam causas aperire Feretri
    armaque de ducibus trina recepta tribus.
magnum iter ascendo, sed dat mihi gloria vires :
    non iuvat e facili lecta corona iugo.
imbuis exemplum primae tu, Romule, palmae
    huius, et exuvio plenus ab hoste redis,
tempore quo portas Caeninum Acronta petentem
    victor in eversum cuspide fundis equum.
Acron Herculeus Caenina ductor ab arce,
    Roma, tuis quondam finibus horror erat.   10

_____

[1] Herculis aeternum *Housman :* Hercule exterminium *NFL.*
ne sit *ς :* nascit *NFL.*

hic spolia ex umeris ausus sperare Quirini
ipse dedit, sed non sanguine sicca suo.
hunc videt ante cavas librantem spicula turres
Romulus et votis occupat ante ratis :
" Iuppiter, haec hodie tibi victima corruet Acron."
voverat, et spolium corruit ille Iovi.
Vrbis virtutumque [1] parens sic vincere suevit,
qui tulit a parco frigida castra lare.
idem eques et frenis, idem fuit aptus aratris,
et galea hirsuta compta lupina iuba ;   20
picta neque inducto fulgebat parma pyropo :
praebebant caesi baltea lenta boves ;
necdum ultra Tiberim belli sonus, ultima praeda   25
Nomentum et captae iugera terna [2] Corae.   26
Cossus at insequitur Veientis caede Tolumni,   23
vincere cum Veios posse laboris erat,[3]   24
heu Vei veteres ! et vos tum regna fuistis,
et vestro posita est aurea sella foro :
nunc intra muros pastoris bucina lenti
cantat, et in vestris ossibus arva metunt.   30
forte super portae dux Veius astitit arcem
colloquiumque sua fretus ab urbe dedit :
dumque aries murum cornu pulsabat aeno,
vinea qua ductum longa tegebat opus,
Cossus ait " Forti melius concurrere campo."
nec mora fit, plano sistit uterque gradum.

---

[1] virtutumque *ς* : virtutemque *FL :* virtutis *N.*
[2] terna *ς* : terra *NFL.*
[3] *25, 26 and 23, 24 transposed by Passerat.*

di Latias iuvere manus, desecta Tolumni
   cervix Romanos sanguine lavit equos.
Claudius a Rhodano [1] traiectos arcuit hostes,
   Belgica cum vasti parma relata ducis   40
Virdomari.   genus hic Rheno iactabat ab ipso,
   mobilis e rectis [2] fundere gaesa rotis.
illi virgatis iaculans it ab [3] agmine bracis
   torquis ab incisa decidit unca gula.
nunc spolia in templo tria condita : causa Feretri,
   omine quod certo dux ferit ense ducem ;
seu quia victa suis umeris haec arma ferebant,
   hinc Feretri dicta est ara superba Iovis.

XI

DESINE, Paulle, meum lacrimis urgere sepulcrum :
   panditur ad nullas ianua nigra preces ;
cum semel infernas intrarunt funera leges,
   non exorato stant adamante viae.
te licet orantem fuscae deus audiat aulae :
   nempe tuas lacrimas litora surda bibent.
vota movent superos : ubi portitor aera recepit,
   obserat umbrosos lurida porta locos. [4]
sic maestae cecinere tubae, cum subdita nostrum
   detraheret lecto fax inimica caput.   10

[1] a Rhodano *Postgate :* a Rheno *NFL.*
[2] e rectis *Passerat :* erecti *N :* effecti *FL.*
[3] ut . . . iaculans it *Postgate :* iaculantis *NFL.*
[4] umbrosos *ς* : herbosos *NL :* erbosos *F.* locos *Markland :*
rogos *NFL.*

SEXTI PROPERTI ELEGIARVM LIBER IV

quid mihi coniugium Paulli, quid currus avorum
  profuit aut famae pignora tanta meae?
non minus immites habuit Cornelia Parcas :
  et sum, quod digitis quinque legatur, onus.
damnatae noctes et vos vada lenta paludes,
  et quaecumque meos implicat unda pedes,
immatura licet, tamen huc non noxia veni :
  det pater hic umbrae mollia iura meae.
aut si quis posita iudex sedet Aeacus urna,
  in mea sortita vindicet ossa pila :   **20**
assideant fratres, iuxta et Minoida sellam [1]
  Eumenidum intento turba severa foro.
Sisyphe, mole vaces ; taceant Ixionis orbes ;
  fallax Tantaleo corripere [2] ore liquor ;
Cerberus et nullas hodie petat improbus
  umbras ;
  et iaceat tacita laxa catena sera.
ipsa loquor pro me : si fallo, poena sororum
  infelix umeros urgeat urna meos.
si cui fama fuit per avita tropaea decori,
  nostra Numantinos signa [3] loquuntur avos :   **30**
altera maternos exaequat turba Libones,
  et domus est titulis utraque fulta suis.
mox, ubi iam facibus cessit praetexta maritis,
  vinxit et acceptas altera vitta comas,

---

[1] iuxta et *Itali :* iuxta *FL.*   Minoida ς : Minoia *FL.*   sellam
ς : sella et μυ : sella *FL.*
[2] corripere ore *Auratus :* corripiare *FL.*
[3] nostra . . . signa *Baehrens :* et . . . regna *L :* aera . . .
regna μυ : *omitted by F.*

[434]

iungor, Paulle, tuo sic discessura cubili :
  in lapide hoc uni nupta fuisse legar.
testor maiorum cineres tibi, Roma, verendos,
  sub quorum titulis, Africa, tunsa iaces,

   .   .   .   .   .[1]

et Persen proavo stimulantem pectus Achille,
  quique tuas proavus fregit, Averne,[2] domos,   40
me neque censurae legem mollisse neque ulla
  labe mea nostros erubuisse focos.
non fuit exuviis tantis Cornelia damnum :
  quin et erat magnae pars imitanda domus.
nec mea mutata est aetas, sine crimine tota
  est :
  viximus insignes inter utramque facem.
mi natura dedit leges a sanguine ductas,
  ne possem melior iudicis esse metu.
quaelibet austeras de me ferat urna tabellas :
  turpior assessu [3] non erit ulla meo,   50
vel tu, quae tardam movisti fune Cybellen,
  Claudia, turritae rara ministra deae,
vel cui, iuratos [4] cum Vesta reposceret ignes,
  exhibuit vivos carbasus alba focos.
nec te, dulce caput, mater Scribonia, laesi :
  in me mutatum quid nisi fata velis ?

[1] *Munro pointed out that at least a couplet must be lost here :*
he suggested, e.g., et qui contuderunt animos pugnacis Hiberi,
Hannibalemque armis Antiochumque suis.
[2] proavus *cod.* Urbin *:* Averne *Munro :* Achille *FL.*
[3] assessu ς *:* assensu *FL.*
[4] cui iuratos *Butler :* cuius rasos *FL.*

maternis laudor lacrimis urbisque querelis,
  defensa et gemitu Caesaris ossa mea.
ille sua nata dignam vixisse sororem
  increpat, et lacrimas vidimus ire deo.   60
et tamen emerui generosos vestis honores,
  nec mea de sterili facta rapina domo.
tu, Lepide, et tu, Paulle, meum post fata levamen ;
  condita sunt vestro lumina nostra sinu.
vidimus et fratrem sellam geminasse curulem ;
  consule quo, festo [1] tempore rapta soror.
filia, tu specimen [2] censurae nata paternae,
  fac teneas unum nos imitata virum.
et serie fulcite genus : mihi cumba volenti
  solvitur aucturis tot mea **facta meis**.[3]   70
haec est feminei merces extrema triumphi,
  laudat ubi emeritum libera fama rogum.
nunc tibi commendo communia pignora natos :
  haec cura et cineri spirat inusta meo.
fungere maternis vicibus, pater : illa meorum
  omnis erit collo turba ferenda tuo.
oscula cum dederis tua flentibus, adice matris :
  tota domus coepit nunc onus esse tuum.
et si quid doliturus eris, sine testibus illis !
  cum venient, siccis oscula falle genis !   80

[1] festo *Koppiers :* facto *FL.*
[2] specimen *ς* : speciem *FL.*
[3] aucturis *ς :* uncturis *L :* nupturis *F.* facta *ς :* fata *FL.*
meis *Paulmier :* malis *FL.*

[436]

sat tibi sint noctes, quas de me, Paulle, fatiges,
   somniaque in faciem credita saepe meam :
atque ubi secreto nostra ad simulacra loqueris,
   ut responsurae singula verba iace.
seu tamen adversum mutarit ianua lectum,
   sederit et nostro cauta noverca toro,
coniugium, pueri, laudate et ferte paternum :
   capta dabit vestris moribus illa manus.
nec matrem laudate nimis : collata priori
   vertet in offensas libera verba suas.   90
seu memor ille mea contentus manserit umbra
   et tanti cineres duxerit esse meos,
discite venturam iam nunc sentire senectam,
   caelibis ad curas nec vacet ulla via.
quod mihi detractum est, vestros accedat ad annos :
   prole mea Paullum sic iuvet esse senem.
et bene habet : numquam mater lugubria sumpsi ; [1]
   venit in exsequias tota caterva meas.
causa perorata est.   flentes me surgite, testes,
   dum pretium vitae grata rependit humus.   100
moribus et caelum patuit : sim digna merendo,
   cuius honoratis ossa vehantur avis.[2]

[1] lugubria sumpsi ς : lubrigia sumptum *N* : lubrica sump-
tum *FL*.
[2] avis *Heinsius :* aquis *NFL*.